Just The

facts101

Textbook Key Facts

Textbook Outlines, Highlights, and Practice Quizzes

Principles of Modern Chemistry

by David W. Oxtoby, 7th Edition

All "Just the Facts101" Material Written or Prepared by Cram101 Textbook Reviews

---

Title Page

facts101
LEARNING SYSTEM

"Just the Facts101" is a Content Technologies publication and tool designed to give you all the facts from your textbooks. Visit JustTheFacts101.com for the full practice test for each of your chapters for virtually any of your textbooks.

Facts101 has built custom study tools specific to your textbook. We provide all of the factual testable information and unlike traditional study guides, we will never send you back to your textbook for more information.

YOU WILL NEVER HAVE TO HIGHLIGHT A BOOK AGAIN!

Facts101 StudyGuides

All of the information in this StudyGuide is written specifically for your textbook. We include the key terms, places, people, and concepts... the information you can expect on your next exam!

Want to take a practice test?

Throughout each chapter of this StudyGuide you will find links to JustTheFacts101.com where you can select specific chapters to take a complete test on, or you can subscribe and get practice tests for up to 12 of your textbooks, along with other exclusive Jtf101.com tools like problem solving labs and reference libraries.

JustTheFacts101.com

Only Jtf101.com gives you the outlines, highlights, and PRACTICE TESTS specific to your textbook. JustTheFacts101.com is an online application where you'll discover study tools designed to make the most of your limited study time.

By purchasing this book, you get 50% off the normal monthly subscription fee!. Just enter the promotional code **'DK73DW20555'** on the Jtf101.com registration screen.

www.JustTheFacts101.com

ISBN(s): 9781497000032. PUBX-1.2014423

Principles of Modern Chemistry
David W. Oxtoby, 7th

CONTENTS

1. The Atom in Modern Chemistry

CHAPTER OUTLINE: KEY TERMS, PEOPLE, PLACES, CONCEPTS

- Atomic mass
- Compressibility
- Compressibility factor
- Efficiency
- Heat capacity
- Ideal solution
- Weak base
- Absolute zero
- Atom
- Coefficient
- Component
- Concentration
- Electron
- Frequency
- Partial pressure
- Quantum state
- Vapor pressure
- Atomic orbital
- Cycloalkane
- Atomic spectroscopy
- Carbon

1. The Atom in Modern Chemistry

CHAPTER OUTLINE: KEY TERMS, PEOPLE, PLACES, CONCEPTS

- Electrolyte
- Hemoglobin
- Quantum number
- Saturation
- -Steady state
- Bohr model
- Bohr radius
- Conservation of energy
- Hydrogen
- Hydrogen atom
- Soda-lime glass
- Photon
- Binary compound
- Quaternary compound
- Ternary compound
- Shielding effect
- Atomic theory
- Acceleration
- Diatomic molecule
- Displacement
- Fullerene

1. The Atom in Modern Chemistry

CHAPTER OUTLINE: KEY TERMS, PEOPLE, PLACES, CONCEPTS

Molecule

Period

Kinetic energy

Volume

Energy level

Electrolysis

Glow discharge

Periodic table

Anode

Cathode

Current

Electrochemical cell

Electrode

Net force

Momentum

Product

Charged particle

Rutherford

Mass spectrometry

Mass-to-charge ratio

Microscopy

1. The Atom in Modern Chemistry

CHAPTER OUTLINE: KEY TERMS, PEOPLE, PLACES, CONCEPTS

______________	Scanning tunneling microscope
______________	Drag
______________	Microscope
______________	Strength
______________	Atomic number
______________	Mass number
______________	Proton
______________	Isotope
______________	Neutron

CHAPTER HIGHLIGHTS & NOTES: KEY TERMS, PEOPLE, PLACES, CONCEPTS

Atomic mass

The atomic mass is the mass of an atomic particle, sub-atomic particle, or molecule. It may be expressed in unified atomic mass units; by international agreement, 1 atomic mass unit is defined as 1/12 of the mass of a single carbon-12 atom (at rest). When expressed in such units, the atomic mass is called the relative isotopic mass .

Compressibility

In thermodynamics and fluid mechanics, compressibility is a measure of the relative volume change of a fluid or solid as a response to a pressure change.

$$\beta = -\frac{1}{V}\frac{\partial V}{\partial p}$$

where V is volume and p is pressure.

Compressibility factor

The compressibility factor, also known as the compression factor, is the ratio of the molar volume of a gas to the molar volume of an ideal gas at the same temperature and pressure. It is a useful thermodynamic property for modifying the ideal gas law to account for the real gas behavior.

Efficiency

Efficiency in general, describes the extent to which time, effort or cost is well used for the intended task or purpose. It is often used with the specific purpose of relaying the capability of a specific application of effort to produce a specific outcome effectively with a minimum amount or quantity of waste, expense, or unnecessary effort. 'Efficiency' has widely varying meanings in different disciplines.

Heat capacity

Heat capacity, or thermal capacity, is the measurable physical quantity of heat energy required to change the temperature of an object or body by a given amount. The SI unit of heat capacity is joule per kelvin, $\frac{\mathrm{J}}{\mathrm{K}}$ and the dimensional form is $M^1L^2T^{-2}T^{-1}$.

Heat capacity is an extensive property of matter, meaning it is proportional to the size of the system.

Ideal solution

In chemistry, an ideal solution or ideal mixture is a solution with thermodynamic properties analogous to those of a mixture of ideal gases. The enthalpy of solution (or 'enthalpy of mixing') is zero as is the volume change on mixing; the closer to zero the enthalpy of solution is, the more 'ideal' the behavior of the solution becomes. The vapour pressure of the solution obeys Raoult's law, and the activity coefficients (which measure deviation from ideality) are equal to one.

Weak base

In chemistry, a weak base is a chemical base that does not ionize fully in an aqueous solution. As Brønsted-Lowry bases are proton acceptors, a weak base may also be defined as a chemical base in which protonation is incomplete. This results in a relatively low pH compared to strong bases.

Absolute zero

Absolute zero is the lowest temperature possible. More formally, it is the temperature at which entropy reaches its minimum value. The laws of thermodynamics state that absolute zero cannot be reached using only thermodynamic means.

Atom

The atom is a basic unit of matter that consists of a dense central nucleus surrounded by a cloud of negatively charged electrons. The atomic nucleus contains a mix of positively charged protons and electrically neutral neutrons, which means 'uncuttable' or 'the smallest indivisible particle of matter'. Although the Indian and Greek concepts of the atom were based purely on philosophy, modern science has retained the name coined by Democritus.

Coefficient

In mathematics, a coefficient is a multiplicative factor in some term of an expression ; it is usually a number, but in any case does not involve any variables of the expression. For instance in $7x^2 - 3xy + 1.5 + y$

the first two terms respectively have the coefficients 7 and -3. The third term 1.5 is a constant. The final term does not have any explicitly written coefficient, but is considered to have coefficient 1, since multiplying by that factor would not change the term.

1. The Atom in Modern Chemistry

CHAPTER HIGHLIGHTS & NOTES: KEY TERMS, PEOPLE, PLACES, CONCEPTS

Component

In thermodynamics, a component is a chemically-independent constituent of a system. The number of components represents the minimum number of independent species necessary to define the composition of all phases of the system.

Calculating the number of components in a system is necessary, for example, when applying Gibbs' phase rule in determination of the number of degrees of freedom of a system.

Concentration

In chemistry, concentration is the abundance of a constituent divided by the total volume of a mixture. Several types of mathematical description can be distinguished: mass concentration, molar concentration, number concentration, and volume concentration. The term concentration can be applied to any kind of chemical mixture, but most frequently it refers to solutes and solvents in solutions.

Electron

The electron is a subatomic particle with a negative elementary electric charge. Electrons belong to the first generation of the lepton particle family, and are generally thought to be elementary particles because they have no known components or substructure. The electron has a mass that is approximately 1/1836 that of the proton.

Frequency

Frequency is the number of occurrences of a repeating event per unit time. It is also referred to as temporal frequency, which emphasizes the contrast to spatial frequency and angular frequency. The period is the duration of one cycle in a repeating event, so the period is the reciprocal of the frequency.

Partial pressure

In a mixture of gases, each gas has a partial pressure which is the hypothetical pressure of that gas if it alone occupied the volume of the mixture at the same temperature. The total pressure of an ideal gas mixture is the sum of the partial pressures of each individual gas in the mixture.

It relies on the following isotherm relation: $V_x \times p_{tot} = V_{tot} \times p_x$ •V_x is the partial volume of any individual gas component (X)•V_{tot} is the total volume in gas mixture•p_x is the partial pressure of gas X•p_{tot} is the total pressure of gas mixture•n_x is the amount of substance of a gas (X)•n_{tot} is the total amount of substance in gas mixture

The partial pressure of a gas is a measure of thermodynamic activity of the gas's molecules.

Quantum state

In quantum physics, quantum state refers to the state of a quantum system. A quantum state is given as a vector in a Hilbert space, called the state vector. The state vector theoretically contains statistical information about the quantum system.

Vapor pressure

Vapor pressure or equilibrium vapor pressure is the pressure exerted by a vapor in thermodynamic equilibrium with its condensed phases at a given temperature in a closed system. The equilibrium vapor pressure is an indication of a liquid's evaporation rate.

Atomic orbital	An atomic orbital is a mathematical function that describes the wave-like behavior of either one electron or a pair of electrons in an atom. This function can be used to calculate the probability of finding any electron of an atom in any specific region around the atom's nucleus. The term may also refer to the physical region or space where the electron can be calculated to be present, as defined by the particular mathematical form of the orbital.
Cycloalkane	Cycloalkanes are types of hydrocarbon compounds that have one or more rings of carbon atoms in the chemical structure of their molecules. Alkanes are types of organic hydrocarbon compounds that have only single chemical bonds in their chemical structure. Cycloalkanes consist of only carbon (C) and hydrogen (H) atoms and are saturated because there are no multiple C-C bonds to hydrogenate (add more hydrogen to).
Atomic spectroscopy	Atomic spectroscopy is the determination of elemental composition by using the Electromagnetic Spectrum or Mass Spectrum, respectively to optical or mass spectroscopy. It can be divided by atomization source or by the type of spectroscopy used. In the latter case, the main division is between optical and mass spectrometry.
Carbon	Carbon fiber, alternatively graphite fiber, carbon graphite or CF, is a material consisting of fibers about 5-10 μm in diameter and composed mostly of carbon atoms. The carbon atoms are bonded together in crystals that are more or less aligned parallel to the long axis of the fiber. The crystal alignment gives the fiber high strength-to-volume ratio (making it strong for its size).
Electrolyte	An electrolyte is a compound that ionizes when dissolved in suitable ionizing solvents such as water. This includes most soluble salts, acids, and bases. Some gases, such as hydrogen chloride, under conditions of high temperature or low pressure can also function as electrolytes.
Hemoglobin	Hemoglobin; also spelled haemoglobin and abbreviated Hb or Hgb, is the iron-containing oxygen-transport metalloprotein in the red blood cells of all vertebrates as well as the tissues of some invertebrates. Hemoglobin in the blood carries oxygen from the respiratory organs (lungs or gills) to the rest of the body (i.e. the tissues) where it releases the oxygen to burn nutrients to provide energy to power the functions of the organism, and collects the resultant carbon dioxide to bring it back to the respiratory organs to be dispensed from the organism. In mammals, the protein makes up about 97% of the red blood cells' dry content (by weight), and around 35% of the total content (including water).
Quantum number	Quantum numbers describe values of conserved quantities in the dynamics of a quantum system. Perhaps the most peculiar aspect of quantum mechanics is the quantization of observable quantities, since quantum numbers are discrete sets of integers or half-integers. This is distinguished from classical mechanics where the values can range continuously.
Saturation	In chemistry, saturation has diverse meanings, all based on reaching a maximum capacity.

•In physical chemistry, saturation is the point at which a solution of a substance can dissolve no more of that substance and additional amounts of it will appear as a separate phase (as a precipitate if solid or as effervescence or inclusion if gaseous). This point of maximum concentration, the saturation point, depends on the temperature and pressure of the solution as well as the chemical nature of the substances involved.

Steady state

In chemistry, a steady state is a situation in which all state variables are constant in spite of ongoing processes that strive to change them. For an entire system to be at steady state, i.e. for all state variables of a system to be constant, there must be a flow through the system (compare mass balance). One of the most simple examples of such a system is the case of a bathtub with the tap open but without the bottom plug: after a certain time the water flows in and out at the same rate, so the water level (the state variable being Volume) stabilizes and the system is at steady state.

Bohr model

In atomic physics, the Bohr model, introduced by Niels Bohr in 1913, depicts the atom as small, positively charged nucleus surrounded by electrons that travel in circular orbits around the nucleus--similar in structure to the solar system, but with attraction provided by electrostatic forces rather than gravity. After the cubic model .•Quantum ruleThe angular momentum L = $m_e vr$ is an integer multiple of h: $m_e vr = n\hbar$ Substituting the expression for the velocity gives an equation for r in terms of n: $\sqrt{Zk_e e^2 m_e r} = n\hbar$ so that the allowed orbit radius at any n is:

$$r_n = \frac{n^2\hbar^2}{Zk_e e^2 m_e}$$

The smallest possible value of r in the hydrogen atom is called the Bohr radius and is equal to:

$$r_1 = \frac{\hbar^2}{k_e e^2 m_e} \approx 5.29 \times 10^{-11}\mathrm{m}$$

The energy of the n-th level for any atom is determined by the radius and quantum number:

$$E = -\frac{Zk_e e^2}{2r_n} = -\frac{Z^2(k_e e^2)^2 m_e}{2\hbar^2 n^2} \approx \frac{-13.6Z^2}{n^2}\mathrm{eV}$$

An electron in the lowest energy level of hydrogen therefore has about 13.6 eV less energy than a motionless electron infinitely far from the nucleus. The next energy level is -3.4 eV. The third (n = 3) is -1.51 eV, and so on.

Bohr radius

The Bohr radius is a physical constant, approximately equal to the most probable distance between the proton and electron in a hydrogen atom in its ground state. It is named after Niels Bohr, due to its role in the Bohr model of an atom. The precise definition of the Bohr radius is:

$$a_0 = \frac{4\pi\varepsilon_0\hbar^2}{m_e e^2} = \frac{\hbar}{m_e\, c\, \alpha}$$

where: ε_0 is the permittivity of free space $\hbar$ is the reduced Planck's constant

m_e is the electron rest mass e is the elementary charge c is the speed of light in vacuum α is the fine structure constant.

Or, in Gaussian units the Bohr radius is simply $a_0 = \frac{\hbar^2}{m_e e^2}$

According to 2010 CODATA the Bohr radius has a value of $5.2917721092(17)\times10^{-11}$ m (i.e., approximately 53 pm or 0.53 angstroms).

Conservation of energy

In physics, the law of conservation of energy states that the total energy of an isolated system cannot change--it is said to be conserved over time. Energy can be neither created nor destroyed, but can change form, for instance chemical energy can be converted to kinetic energy in the explosion of a stick of dynamite.

A consequence of the law of conservation of energy is that a perpetual motion machine of the first kind cannot exist.

Hydrogen

Hydrogen is a chemical element with chemical symbol H and atomic number 1. With an atomic weight of 1.00794 u, hydrogen is the lightest element and its monatomic form (H) is the most abundant chemical substance, constituting roughly 75% of the Universe's baryonic mass. Non-remnant stars are mainly composed of hydrogen in its plasma state.

At standard temperature and pressure, hydrogen is a colorless, odorless, tasteless, non-toxic, nonmetallic, highly combustible diatomic gas with the molecular formula H_2.

Hydrogen atom

A hydrogen atom is an atom of the chemical element hydrogen. The electrically neutral atom contains a single positively charged proton and a single negatively charged electron bound to the nucleus by the Coulomb force. Atomic hydrogen constitutes about 75% of the elemental mass of the universe.

Soda-lime glass

Soda-lime glass, also called soda-lime-silica glass, is the most prevalent type of glass, used for windowpanes, and glass containers for beverages, food, and some commodity items. Glass bakeware is often made of tempered soda-lime glass.

Soda-lime glass is relatively inexpensive, chemically stable, reasonably hard, and extremely workable, because it is capable of being re-softened and re-melted numerous times, is ideal for recycling.

Photon

A photon is an elementary particle, the quantum of light and all other forms of electromagnetic radiation, and the force carrier for the electromagnetic force, even when static via virtual photons.

The effects of this force are easily observable at both the microscopic and macroscopic level, because the photon has zero rest mass; this allows long distance interactions. Like all elementary particles, photons are currently best explained by quantum mechanics and exhibit wave-particle duality, exhibiting properties of both waves and particles.

Binary compound

A binary compound is a chemical compound that contains exactly two different elements. Examples of binary ionic compounds include calcium chloride ($CaCl_2$), sodium fluoride (NaF), and magnesium oxide (MgO), whilst examples of a binary covalent compounds include water (H_2O), carbon monoxide (CO), and sulfur hexafluoride (SF_6).

Quaternary compound

In chemistry, a quaternary compound is a cation consisting of a central positively charged nitrogen group atom with four substituents, especially organic groups, discounting hydrogen atoms.

The best known quaternary compounds are quaternary ammonium cations, having a nitrogen atom at the centre. For example, in the following reaction, the nitrogen atom is said to be quaternized as it has gone from 3 to 4 substituents: $R_3N + RCl \longrightarrow R_4N^+ \ Cl^-$

Other examples include substituted phosphonium salts (R_4P^+), substituted arsonium salts (R_4As^+) like arsenobetaine, as well as some arsenic containing superconductors.

Ternary compound

In chemistry, a ternary compound is a compound containing three different elements. An example of this is sodium phosphate, Na_3PO_4. The sodium ion has a charge of 1+ and the phosphate ion has a charge of 3-.

Shielding effect

The shielding effect describes the decrease in attraction between an electron and the nucleus in any atom with more than one electron shell. It is also referred to as the screening effect or atomic shielding. This could also be explained with the help of a helium atom(isolated).

Atomic theory

In chemistry and physics, atomic theory is a scientific theory of the nature of matter, which states that matter is composed of discrete units called atoms, as opposed to the earlier concept which held that matter could be divided into any arbitrarily small quantity. It began as a philosophical concept in ancient Greece (Democritus) and entered the scientific mainstream in the early 19th century when discoveries in the field of chemistry showed that matter did indeed behave as if it were made up of particles.

The word 'atom' (from the ancient Greek adjective atomos, 'indivisible'.

Acceleration

In physics, acceleration is the rate at which the velocity of a body changes with time. Velocity and acceleration are vector quantities, with magnitude, direction, and add according to the parallelogram law.

Diatomic molecule	Diatomic molecules are molecules composed only of two atoms, of either the same or different chemical elements. The prefix di- is of Greek origin, meaning two.
Displacement	In fluid mechanics, displacement occurs when an object is immersed in a fluid, pushing it out of the way and taking its place. The volume of the fluid displaced can then be measured, and from this the volume of the immersed object can be deduced (the volume of the immersed object will be exactly equal to the volume of the displaced fluid). An object that sinks displaces an amount of fluid equal to the object's volume.
Fullerene	A fullerene is any molecule composed entirely of carbon, in the form of a hollow sphere, ellipsoid, tube, and many other shapes. Spherical fullerenes are also called buckyballs, and they resemble the balls used in football (soccer). Cylindrical ones are called carbon nanotubes or buckytubes.
Molecule	A molecule is an electrically neutral group of two or more atoms held together by chemical bonds. Molecules are distinguished from ions by their lack of electrical charge. However, in quantum physics, organic chemistry, and biochemistry, the term molecule is often used less strictly, also being applied to polyatomic ions.
Period	In the periodic table of the elements, elements are arranged in a series of rows (or periods) so that those with similar properties appear in a column. Elements of the same period have the same number of electron shells; with each group across a period, the elements have one more proton and electron and become less metallic. This arrangement reflects the periodic recurrence of similar properties as the atomic number increases.
Kinetic energy	In physics, the kinetic energy of an object is the energy which it possesses due to its motion. It is defined as the work needed to accelerate a body of a given mass from rest to its stated velocity. Having gained this energy during its acceleration, the body maintains this kinetic energy unless its speed changes.
Volume	In thermodynamics, the volume of a system is an important extensive parameter for describing its thermodynamic state. The specific volume, an intensive property, is the system's volume per unit of mass. Volume is a function of state and is interdependent with other thermodynamic properties such as pressure and temperature.
Energy level	A quantum mechanical system or particle that is bound--that is, confined spatially--can only take on certain discrete values of energy. This contrasts with classical particles, which can have any energy. These discrete values are called energy levels.
Electrolysis	In chemistry and manufacturing, electrolysis is a method of using a direct electric current to drive an otherwise non-spontaneous chemical reaction. Electrolysis is commercially highly important as a stage in the separation of elements from naturally occurring sources such as ores using an electrolytic cell.

1. The Atom in Modern Chemistry

CHAPTER HIGHLIGHTS & NOTES: KEY TERMS, PEOPLE, PLACES, CONCEPTS

Glow discharge

A glow discharge is a plasma formed by the passage of electric current through a low-pressure gas. It is created by applying a voltage between two metal electrodes in a glass tube containing gas. When the voltage exceeds a certain value called the striking voltage, the gas in the tube ionizes, becoming a plasma, and begins conducting electricity, causing it to glow with a colored light.

Periodic table

The periodic table is a tabular arrangement of the chemical elements, organized on the basis of their atomic numbers, electron configurations, and recurring chemical properties. Elements are presented in order of increasing atomic number (the number of protons in the nucleus). The standard form of the table consists of a grid of elements laid out in 18 columns and 7 rows, with a double row of elements below that.

Anode

An anode is an electrode through which electric current flows into a polarized electrical device. The direction of electric current is, by convention, opposite to the direction of electron flow. In other words, the electrons flow from the anode into, for example, an electrical circuit.

Cathode

A cathode is an electrode through which electric current flows out of a polarized electrical device. The direction of electric current is, by convention, opposite to the direction of electron flow--thus, electrons are considered to flow toward the cathode electrode while current flows away from it. This convention is sometimes remembered using the mnemonic CCD for cathode current departs.

Current

A current in a fluid is the magnitude and direction of flow within that fluid. An air current presents the same properties specifically for a gaseous medium.

Types of fluid currents include•Boundary current•Current a current in a river or stream•Ocean current•Rip current•Subsurface currents•Turbidity current.

Electrochemical cell

An electrochemical cell is a device capable of either deriving electrical energy from chemical reactions, or facilitating chemical reactions through the introduction of electrical energy. A common example of an electrochemical cell is a standard 1.5-volt 'battery'. (Actually a single 'Galvanic cell'; a battery properly consists of multiple cells, connected in either parallel or series pattern).

Electrode

An electrode is an electrical conductor used to make contact with a nonmetallic part of a circuit . The word was coined by the scientist Michael Faraday from the Greek words elektron (meaning amber, from which the word electricity is derived) and hodos, a way.

Net force

In physics, net force is the overall force acting on an object. In order to calculate the net force, the body is isolated and interactions with the environment or constraints are introduced as forces and torques forming a free-body diagram.

Momentum	In classical mechanics, linear momentum or translational momentum is the product of the mass and velocity of an object. For example, a heavy truck moving fast has a large momentum--it takes a large and prolonged force to get the truck up to this speed, and it takes a large and prolonged force to bring it to a stop afterwards. If the truck were lighter, or moving more slowly, then it would have less momentum.
Product	Product are formed during chemical reactions as reagents are consumed. Products have lower energy than the reagents and are produced during the reaction according to the second law of thermodynamics. The released energy comes from changes in chemical bonds between atoms in reagent molecules and may be given off in the form of heat or light.
Charged particle	In physics, a charged particle is a particle with an electric charge. It may be either a subatomic particle or an ion. A collection of charged particles, or even a gas containing a proportion of charged particles, is called a plasma, which is called the fourth state of matter because its properties are quite different from solids, liquids and gases (plasma is the most common state of matter in the universe).
Rutherford	The rutherford is an obsolete unit of radioactivity, defined as the activity of a quantity of radioactive material in which one million nuclei decay per second. It is therefore equivalent to one megabecquerel. It was named after Ernest Rutherford.
Mass spectrometry	Mass spectrometry is an analytical technique that produces spectra (singular spectrum) of the masses of the atoms or molecules comprising a sample of material. The spectra are used to determine the elemental or isotopic signature of a sample, the masses of particles and of molecules, and to elucidate the chemical structures of molecules, such as peptides and other chemical compounds. Mass spectrometry works by ionizing chemical compounds to generate charged molecules or molecule fragments and measuring their mass-to-charge ratios.
Mass-to-charge ratio	The mass-to-charge ratio ratio is a physical quantity that is widely used in the electrodynamics of charged particles, e.g. in electron optics and ion optics. It appears in the scientific fields of lithography, electron microscopy, cathode ray tubes, accelerator physics, nuclear physics, Auger spectroscopy, cosmology and mass spectrometry. The importance of the mass-to-charge ratio, according to classical electrodynamics, is that two particles with the same mass-to-charge ratio move in the same path in a vacuum when subjected to the same electric and magnetic fields.
Microscopy	Microscopy is the technical field of using microscopes to view samples and objects that cannot be seen with the unaided eye . There are three well-known branches of microscopy: optical, electron, and scanning probe microscopy.

1. The Atom in Modern Chemistry

CHAPTER HIGHLIGHTS & NOTES: KEY TERMS, PEOPLE, PLACES, CONCEPTS

Scanning tunneling microscope

A scanning tunneling microscope is an instrument for imaging surfaces at the atomic level. Its development in 1981 earned its inventors, Gerd Binnig and Heinrich Rohrer (at IBM Zürich), the Nobel Prize in Physics in 1986. For an Scanning tunneling microscope, good resolution is considered to be 0.1 nm lateral resolution and 0.01 nm depth resolution. With this resolution, individual atoms within materials are routinely imaged and manipulated.

Drag

In fluid dynamics, drag refers to forces which act on a solid object in the direction of the relative fluid flow velocity. Unlike other resistive forces, such as dry friction, which is nearly independent of velocity, drag forces depend on velocity.

Drag forces always decrease fluid velocity relative to the solid object in the fluid's path.

Microscope

A microscope is an instrument used to see objects that are too small for the naked eye. The science of investigating small objects using such an instrument is called microscopy. Microscopic means invisible to the eye unless aided by a microscope.

Strength

In explosive materials, strength is the parameter determining the ability of the explosive to move the surrounding material. It is related to the total gas yield of the reaction, and the amount of heat produced. Cf.

Atomic number

In chemistry and physics, the atomic number is the number of protons found in the nucleus of an atom and therefore identical to the charge number of the nucleus. It is conventionally represented by the symbol Z. The atomic number uniquely identifies a chemical element. In an atom of neutral charge, the atomic number is also equal to the number of electrons.

Mass number

The mass number, also called atomic mass number or nucleon number, is the total number of protons and neutrons (together known as nucleons) in an atomic nucleus. Because protons and neutrons both are baryons, the mass number A is identical with the baryon number B as of the nucleus as of the whole atom or ion. The mass number is different for each different isotope of a chemical element.

Proton

The proton is a subatomic particle with the symbol p or p+ and a positive electric charge of 1 elementary charge. One or more protons are present in the nucleus of each atom. The number of protons in each atom is its atomic number.

Isotope

Isotopes are variants of a particular chemical element such that, while all isotopes of a given element have the same number of protons in each atom, they differ in neutron number. The term isotope is formed from the Greek roots isos (?s?? 'equal') and topos (t?p?? 'place'), meaning 'the same place'. Thus, different isotopes of a single element occupy the same position on the periodic table.

Neutron

The neutron is a subatomic hadron particle that has the symbol n or n0, no net electric charge and a mass slightly larger than that of a proton.

CHAPTER HIGHLIGHTS & NOTES: KEY TERMS, PEOPLE, PLACES, CONCEPTS

With the exception of hydrogen-1, nuclei of atoms consist of protons and neutrons, which are therefore collectively referred to as nucleons. The number of protons in a nucleus is the atomic number and defines the type of element the atom forms.

CHAPTER QUIZ: KEY TERMS, PEOPLE, PLACES, CONCEPTS

1. A _________ is a chemical compound that contains exactly two different elements. Examples of binary ionic compounds include calcium chloride ($CaCl_2$), sodium fluoride (NaF), and magnesium oxide (MgO), whilst examples of a binary covalent compounds include water (H_2O), carbon monoxide (CO), and sulfur hexafluoride (SF_6).

   a. Base
   b. Daylight
   c. Binary compound
   d. Tropospheric scatter

2. In explosive materials, _________ is the parameter determining the ability of the explosive to move the surrounding material. It is related to the total gas yield of the reaction, and the amount of heat produced. Cf.

   a. 2,4-Dinitroanisole
   b. Ballistite
   c. Baratol
   d. Strength

3. In fluid mechanics, _________ occurs when an object is immersed in a fluid, pushing it out of the way and taking its place. The volume of the fluid displaced can then be measured, and from this the volume of the immersed object can be deduced (the volume of the immersed object will be exactly equal to the volume of the displaced fluid).

   An object that sinks displaces an amount of fluid equal to the object's volume.

   a. Block and bleed manifold
   b. Bridge scour
   c. Displacement
   d. Capillary surface

4. . In physics, a _________ is a particle with an electric charge. It may be either a subatomic particle or an ion. A collection of _________s, or even a gas containing a proportion of _________s, is called a plasma, which is called the fourth state of matter because its properties are quite different from solids, liquids and gases (plasma is the most common state of matter in the universe).

a. Ballistic conduction
b. Carrier generation and recombination
c. Carrier lifetime
d. Charged particle

5. In the periodic table of the elements, elements are arranged in a series of rows (or _________s) so that those with similar properties appear in a column. Elements of the same _________ have the same number of electron shells; with each group across a _________, the elements have one more proton and electron and become less metallic. This arrangement reflects the periodic recurrence of similar properties as the atomic number increases.

a. Chemical Galaxy
b. Goldschmidt classification
c. Period
d. Metalloid

ANSWER KEY
1. The Atom in Modern Chemistry

---

1. c
2. d
3. c
4. d
5. c

---

2. Chemical Formulas, Equations, and Reaction Yields

CHAPTER OUTLINE: KEY TERMS, PEOPLE, PLACES, CONCEPTS

- Atom
- Mole
- Elementary particle
- Volume
- Elemental analysis
- Combustion
- Hydrocarbon
- Thermodynamics
- Carbon
- Hydrogen
- Stoichiometry
- Ideal solution
- Chemical reaction
- Product

2. Chemical Formulas, Equations, and Reaction Yields

CHAPTER HIGHLIGHTS & NOTES: KEY TERMS, PEOPLE, PLACES, CONCEPTS

Atom

The atom is a basic unit of matter that consists of a dense central nucleus surrounded by a cloud of negatively charged electrons. The atomic nucleus contains a mix of positively charged protons and electrically neutral neutrons, which means 'uncuttable' or 'the smallest indivisible particle of matter'. Although the Indian and Greek concepts of the atom were based purely on philosophy, modern science has retained the name coined by Democritus.

Mole

Mole is a unit of measurement used in chemistry to express amounts of a chemical substance, defined as the amount of any substance that contains as many elementary entities (e.g., atoms, molecules, ions, electrons) as there are atoms in 12 grams of pure carbon-12, the isotope of carbon with relative atomic mass 12. This corresponds to the Avogadro constant, which has a value of $6.02214129(27)\times10^{23}$ elementary entities of the substance. It is one of the base units in the International System of Units, and has the unit symbol mol and corresponds with the dimension symbol N. In honour of the unit, chemists often celebrate October 23 (a reference to the 10^{23} part of Avogadro's number) as 'Mole Day'.

The mole is widely used in chemistry instead of units of mass or volume as a convenient way to express amounts of reactants or of products of chemical reactions.

Elementary particle

In particle physics, an elementary particle or fundamental particle is a particle whose substructure is unknown, thus it is not known to be composed of other particles. Known elementary particles include the fundamental fermions (quarks, leptons, antiquarks, and antileptons), which generally are 'matter particles' and 'antimatter particles', as well as the fundamental bosons (gauge bosons and Higgs boson), which generally are 'force particles' that mediate interactions among fermions. A particle containing two or more elementary particles is a composite particle.

Volume

In thermodynamics, the volume of a system is an important extensive parameter for describing its thermodynamic state. The specific volume, an intensive property, is the system's volume per unit of mass. Volume is a function of state and is interdependent with other thermodynamic properties such as pressure and temperature.

Elemental analysis

Elemental analysis is a process where a sample of some material is analyzed for its elemental and sometimes isotopic composition. Elemental analysis can be qualitative (determining what elements are present), and it can be quantitative (determining how much of each are present). Elemental analysis falls within the ambit of analytical chemistry, the set of instruments involved in deciphering the chemical nature of our world.

Combustion

Combustion or burning is the sequence of exothermic chemical reactions between a fuel and an oxidant accompanied by the production of heat and conversion of chemical species. The release of heat can produce light in the form of either glowing or a flame.

Hydrocarbon

In organic chemistry, a hydrocarbon is an organic compound consisting entirely of hydrogen and carbon. Hydrocarbons from which one hydrogen atom has been removed are functional groups, called hydrocarbyls. Aromatic hydrocarbons (arenes), alkanes, alkenes, cycloalkanes and alkyne-based compounds are different types of hydrocarbons.

Thermodynamics

Thermodynamics is a branch of natural science concerned with heat and its relation to energy and work. It defines macroscopic variables (such as temperature, internal energy, entropy, and pressure) that characterize materials and radiation, and explains how they are related and by what laws they change with time. Thermodynamics describes the average behavior of very large numbers of microscopic constituents, and its laws can be derived from statistical mechanics.

Carbon

Carbon fiber, alternatively graphite fiber, carbon graphite or CF, is a material consisting of fibers about 5-10 μm in diameter and composed mostly of carbon atoms. The carbon atoms are bonded together in crystals that are more or less aligned parallel to the long axis of the fiber. The crystal alignment gives the fiber high strength-to-volume ratio (making it strong for its size).

Hydrogen

Hydrogen is a chemical element with chemical symbol H and atomic number 1. With an atomic weight of 1.00794 u, hydrogen is the lightest element and its monatomic form (H) is the most abundant chemical substance, constituting roughly 75% of the Universe's baryonic mass. Non-remnant stars are mainly composed of hydrogen in its plasma state.

At standard temperature and pressure, hydrogen is a colorless, odorless, tasteless, non-toxic, nonmetallic, highly combustible diatomic gas with the molecular formula H_2.

Stoichiometry

Stoichiometry is a branch of chemistry that deals with the relative quantities of reactants and products in chemical reactions. In a balanced chemical reaction, the relations among quantities of reactants and products typically form a ratio of positive integers. For example, in a reaction that forms ammonia (NH_3), exactly one molecule of nitrogen gas (N_2) reacts with three molecules of hydrogen gas (H_2) to produce two molecules of NH_3:N2 + 3H2 ? 2NH3

This particular kind of stoichiometry - describing the quantitative relationships among substances as they participate in chemical reactions - is known as reaction stoichiometry.

Ideal solution

In chemistry, an ideal solution or ideal mixture is a solution with thermodynamic properties analogous to those of a mixture of ideal gases. The enthalpy of solution (or 'enthalpy of mixing') is zero as is the volume change on mixing; the closer to zero the enthalpy of solution is, the more 'ideal' the behavior of the solution becomes. The vapour pressure of the solution obeys Raoult's law, and the activity coefficients (which measure deviation from ideality) are equal to one.

Chemical reaction

A chemical reaction is a process that leads to the transformation of one set of chemical substances to another.

2. Chemical Formulas, Equations, and Reaction Yields

CHAPTER HIGHLIGHTS & NOTES: KEY TERMS, PEOPLE, PLACES, CONCEPTS

Classically, chemical reactions encompass changes that only involve the positions of electrons in the forming and breaking of chemical bonds between atoms, with no change to the nuclei (no change to the elements present), and can often be described by a chemical equation. Nuclear chemistry is a sub-discipline of chemistry that involves the chemical reactions of unstable and radioactive elements where both electronic and nuclear changes may both occur.

Product

Product are formed during chemical reactions as reagents are consumed. Products have lower energy than the reagents and are produced during the reaction according to the second law of thermodynamics. The released energy comes from changes in chemical bonds between atoms in reagent molecules and may be given off in the form of heat or light.

CHAPTER QUIZ: KEY TERMS, PEOPLE, PLACES, CONCEPTS

1. _________ is a unit of measurement used in chemistry to express amounts of a chemical substance, defined as the amount of any substance that contains as many elementary entities (e.g., atoms, molecules, ions, electrons) as there are atoms in 12 grams of pure carbon-12, the isotope of carbon with relative atomic mass 12. This corresponds to the Avogadro constant, which has a value of $6.02214129(27)\times10^{23}$ elementary entities of the substance. It is one of the base units in the International System of Units, and has the unit symbol mol and corresponds with the dimension symbol N. In honour of the unit, chemists often celebrate October 23 (a reference to the 10^{23} part of Avogadro's number) as '_________ Day'.

   The _________ is widely used in chemistry instead of units of mass or volume as a convenient way to express amounts of reactants or of products of chemical reactions.

   a. Katal
   b. Mole
   c. Bisulfide
   d. Buffering agent

2. . _________ or burning is the sequence of exothermic chemical reactions between a fuel and an oxidant accompanied by the production of heat and conversion of chemical species. The release of heat can produce light in the form of either glowing or a flame.

   In a complete _________ reaction, a compound reacts with an oxidizing element, such as oxygen or fluorine, and the products are compounds of each element in the fuel with the oxidizing element.

   a. Combustion
   b. SEAgel
   c. Ceration

3. The _________ is a basic unit of matter that consists of a dense central nucleus surrounded by a cloud of negatively charged electrons. The atomic nucleus contains a mix of positively charged protons and electrically neutral neutrons, which means 'uncuttable' or 'the smallest indivisible particle of matter'. Although the Indian and Greek concepts of the _________ were based purely on philosophy, modern science has retained the name coined by Democritus.

   a. 3-Deazaneplanocin A
   b. Atom
   c. Calibration curve
   d. Bulk material analyzer

4. In particle physics, an _________ or fundamental particle is a particle whose substructure is unknown, thus it is not known to be composed of other particles. Known _________s include the fundamental fermions (quarks, leptons, antiquarks, and antileptons), which generally are 'matter particles' and 'antimatter particles', as well as the fundamental bosons (gauge bosons and Higgs boson), which generally are 'force particles' that mediate interactions among fermions. A particle containing two or more _________s is a composite particle.

   a. Elementary particle
   b. Subatomic particle
   c. Daylight
   d. Lidar

5. In thermodynamics, the _________ of a system is an important extensive parameter for describing its thermodynamic state. The specific _________, an intensive property, is the system's _________ per unit of mass. _________ is a function of state and is interdependent with other thermodynamic properties such as pressure and temperature.

   a. Bioaerosol
   b. Bjerrum length
   c. Volume
   d. Bolaamphiphile

ANSWER KEY

2. Chemical Formulas, Equations, and Reaction Yields

1. b
2. a
3. b
4. a
5. c

---

3. Chemical Bonding: The Classical Description

CHAPTER OUTLINE: KEY TERMS, PEOPLE, PLACES, CONCEPTS

- Periodic table
- Quantum
- Quantum mechanics
- Valence electron
- Atomic number
- Atom
- Chemical bond
- Electron
- Subatomic particle
- Molecule
- Period
- Isomer
- Density
- Electron density
- Mass spectrometry
- Mass-to-charge ratio
- Nonmetal
- Semimetal
- Alkali metal
- Inert gas
- Noble gas

3. Chemical Bonding: The Classical Description

CHAPTER OUTLINE: KEY TERMS, PEOPLE, PLACES, CONCEPTS

	Semiconductor
	Halide
	Insulator
	Kinetic energy
	Quantization
	Ionization energy
	Energy level
	Core electron
	Electron affinity
	Exothermic
	Exothermic reaction
	Electron acceptor
	Electron donor
	Acceptor
	Donor
	Diatomic molecule
	Bohr model
	Ionic compound
	Ionic bonding
	Mole
	Polarization

3. Chemical Bonding: The Classical Description

CHAPTER OUTLINE: KEY TERMS, PEOPLE, PLACES, CONCEPTS

Distortion

Atmosphere

Rotational spectroscopy

Electron pair

Molecular orbital

Spectroscopy

Stiffness

Strength

Product

Solvent

Atomic orbital

Component

Steric number

Periodic table	The periodic table is a tabular arrangement of the chemical elements, organized on the basis of their atomic numbers, electron configurations, and recurring chemical properties. Elements are presented in order of increasing atomic number (the number of protons in the nucleus). The standard form of the table consists of a grid of elements laid out in 18 columns and 7 rows, with a double row of elements below that.
Quantum	In physics, a quantum is the minimum amount of any physical entity involved in an interaction. Behind this, one finds the fundamental notion that a physical property may be 'quantized,' referred to as 'the hypothesis of quantization'. This means that the magnitude can take on only certain discrete values.
Quantum mechanics	Quantum mechanics is a branch of physics which deals with physical phenomena at microscopic scales, where the action is on the order of the Planck constant. It departs from classical mechanics primarily at the quantum realm of atomic and subatomic length scales. Quantum mechanics provides a mathematical description of much of the dual particle-like and wave-like behavior and interactions of energy and matter.
Valence electron	In chemistry, a valence electron is an electron that is associated with an atom, and that can participate in the formation of a chemical bond; in a single covalent bond, both atoms in the bond contribute one valence electron in order to form a shared pair. The presence of valence electrons can determine the element's chemical properties and whether it may bond with other elements: For a main group element, a valence electron can only be in the outermost electron shell. In a transition metal, a valence electron can also be in an inner shell.
Atomic number	In chemistry and physics, the atomic number is the number of protons found in the nucleus of an atom and therefore identical to the charge number of the nucleus. It is conventionally represented by the symbol Z. The atomic number uniquely identifies a chemical element. In an atom of neutral charge, the atomic number is also equal to the number of electrons.
Atom	The atom is a basic unit of matter that consists of a dense central nucleus surrounded by a cloud of negatively charged electrons. The atomic nucleus contains a mix of positively charged protons and electrically neutral neutrons, which means 'uncuttable' or 'the smallest indivisible particle of matter'. Although the Indian and Greek concepts of the atom were based purely on philosophy, modern science has retained the name coined by Democritus.
Chemical bond	A chemical bond is an attraction between atoms that allows the formation of chemical substances that contain two or more atoms. The bond is caused by the electrostatic force of attraction between opposite charges, either between electrons and nuclei, or as the result of a dipole attraction. The strength of chemical bonds varies considerably; there are 'strong bonds' such as covalent or ionic bonds and 'weak bonds' such as dipole-dipole interactions, the London dispersion force and hydrogen bonding.

3. Chemical Bonding: The Classical Description

CHAPTER HIGHLIGHTS & NOTES: KEY TERMS, PEOPLE, PLACES, CONCEPTS

Electron

The electron is a subatomic particle with a negative elementary electric charge. Electrons belong to the first generation of the lepton particle family, and are generally thought to be elementary particles because they have no known components or substructure. The electron has a mass that is approximately 1/1836 that of the proton.

Subatomic particle

In the physical sciences, subatomic particles are the particles smaller than an atom. (although some subatomic particles have mass greater than some atoms). There are two types of subatomic particles: elementary particles, which according to current theories are not made of other particles; and composite particles.

Molecule

A molecule is an electrically neutral group of two or more atoms held together by chemical bonds. Molecules are distinguished from ions by their lack of electrical charge. However, in quantum physics, organic chemistry, and biochemistry, the term molecule is often used less strictly, also being applied to polyatomic ions.

Period

In the periodic table of the elements, elements are arranged in a series of rows (or periods) so that those with similar properties appear in a column. Elements of the same period have the same number of electron shells; with each group across a period, the elements have one more proton and electron and become less metallic. This arrangement reflects the periodic recurrence of similar properties as the atomic number increases.

Isomer

In chemistry, isomers (; from Greek ?s?µe???, isomerès; isos = 'equal', méros = 'part') are molecules with the same molecular formula but different chemical structures. That is, isomers contain the same number of atoms of each element, but have different arrangements of their atoms in space. Isomers do not necessarily share similar properties, unless they also have the same functional groups.

Density

The density, or more precisely, the volumetric mass density, of a substance is its mass per unit volume. The symbol most often used for density is ? (the lower case Greek letter rho).

Mathematically, density is defined as mass divided by volume: $$\rho = \frac{m}{V},$$

where ? is the density, m is the mass, and V is the volume.

Electron density

Electron density is the measure of the probability of an electron being present at a specific location.

In molecules, regions of electron density are usually found around the atom, and its bonds. In de-localized or conjugated systems, such as phenol, benzene and compounds such as hemoglobin and chlorophyll, the electron density covers an entire region, i.e., in benzene they are found above and below the planar ring.

Mass spectrometry

Mass spectrometry is an analytical technique that produces spectra (singular spectrum) of the masses of the atoms or molecules comprising a sample of material. The spectra are used to determine the elemental or isotopic signature of a sample, the masses of particles and of molecules, and to elucidate the chemical structures of molecules, such as peptides and other chemical compounds. Mass spectrometry works by ionizing chemical compounds to generate charged molecules or molecule fragments and measuring their mass-to-charge ratios.

Mass-to-charge ratio

The mass-to-charge ratio ratio is a physical quantity that is widely used in the electrodynamics of charged particles, e.g. in electron optics and ion optics. It appears in the scientific fields of lithography, electron microscopy, cathode ray tubes, accelerator physics, nuclear physics, Auger spectroscopy, cosmology and mass spectrometry. The importance of the mass-to-charge ratio, according to classical electrodynamics, is that two particles with the same mass-to-charge ratio move in the same path in a vacuum when subjected to the same electric and magnetic fields.

Nonmetal

In chemistry, a nonmetal or non-metal is a chemical element which mostly lacks metallic attributes. Physically, nonmetals tend to be highly volatile (easily vaporised), have low elasticity, and are good insulators of heat and electricity; chemically, they tend to have high ionisation energy and electronegativity values, and gain or share electrons when they react with other elements or compounds. Seventeen elements are generally classified as nonmetals; most are gases (hydrogen, helium, nitrogen, oxygen, fluorine, neon, chlorine, argon, krypton, xenon and radon); one is a liquid (bromine); and a few are solids (carbon, phosphorus, sulfur, selenium, and iodine).

Semimetal

A Semimetal is a material with a very small overlap between the bottom of the conduction band and the top of the valence band. According to electronic band theory, solids can be classified as insulators, semiconductors, semimetals, or metals. In insulators and semiconductors the filled valence band is separated from an empty conduction band by a band gap.

Alkali metal

The alkali metals are a group in the periodic table consisting of the chemical elements lithium, sodium (Na), potassium (K), rubidium (Rb), caesium (Cs), and francium (Fr). This group lies in the s-block of the periodic table as all alkali metals have their outermost electron in an s-orbital. The alkali metals provide the best example of group trends in properties in the periodic table, with elements exhibiting well-characterized homologous behaviour.

Inert gas

An inert gas is a gas which does not undergo chemical reactions under a set of given conditions. The noble gases and nitrogen often do not react with many substances. Inert gases are used generally to avoid unwanted chemical reactions degrading a sample.

Noble gas

The noble gases make a group of chemical elements with similar properties: under standard conditions, they are all odorless, colorless, monatomic gases with very low chemical reactivity. The six noble gases that occur naturally are helium (He), neon (Ne), argon (Ar), krypton (Kr), xenon (Xe), and the radioactive radon (Rn).

3. Chemical Bonding: The Classical Description

CHAPTER HIGHLIGHTS & NOTES: KEY TERMS, PEOPLE, PLACES, CONCEPTS

Semiconductor

A semiconductor is a material which has electrical conductivity to a degree between that of a metal and that of an insulator (such as glass). Semiconductors are the foundation of modern electronics, including transistors, solar cells, light-emitting diodes (LEDs), quantum dots and digital and analog integrated circuits.

A semiconductor may have a number of unique properties, one of which is the ability to change conductivity by the addition of impurities ('doping') or by interaction with another phenomenon, such as an electric field or light; this ability makes a semiconductor very useful for constructing a device that can amplify, switch, or convert an energy input.

Halide

A halide is a binary compound, of which one part is a halogen atom and the other part is an element or radical that is less electronegative than the halogen, to make a fluoride, chloride, bromide, iodide, or astatide compound. Many salts are halides. All Group 1 metals form halides which are white solids at room temperature.

Insulator

An electrical insulator is a material whose internal electric charges do not flow freely, and therefore does not conduct an electric current under the influence of an electric field. A perfect insulator does not exist, but some materials such as glass, paper and Teflon, which have high resistivity, are very good electrical insulators. A much larger class of materials, even though they may have lower bulk resistivity, are still good enough to insulate electrical wiring and cables.

Kinetic energy

In physics, the kinetic energy of an object is the energy which it possesses due to its motion. It is defined as the work needed to accelerate a body of a given mass from rest to its stated velocity. Having gained this energy during its acceleration, the body maintains this kinetic energy unless its speed changes.

Quantization

In physics, quantization is the process of transition from a classical understanding of physical phenomena to a newer understanding known as 'quantum mechanics'. It is a procedure for constructing a quantum field theory starting from a classical field theory. This is a generalization of the procedure for building quantum mechanics from classical mechanics.

Ionization energy

The ionization energy of an atom or molecule describes the amount of energy required to remove an electron from the atom or molecule in the gaseous state. X + energy ? X^+ + e^-

The term ionization potential has been used in the past but is not recommended.

The units for ionization energy vary from discipline to discipline.

Energy level

A quantum mechanical system or particle that is bound--that is, confined spatially--can only take on certain discrete values of energy. This contrasts with classical particles, which can have any energy. These discrete values are called energy levels.

Core electron	Core electrons are the electrons in an atom that are not valence electrons and therefore do not participate in bonding. An example: the carbon atom has a total of 6 electrons, 4 of them being valence electrons. So the remaining 2 electrons must be core electrons.
Electron affinity	In chemistry and atomic physics, the electron affinity of an atom or molecule is defined as the energy change when an electron is added to a neutral atom or molecule to form a negative ion. X + e^- ? X^- + energy In solid state physics, the electron affinity for a surface is defined somewhat differently .
Exothermic	In thermodynamics, the term exothermic describes a process or reaction that releases energy from the system, usually in the form of heat, but also in a form of light (e.g. a spark, flame, or flash), electricity (e.g. a battery), or sound (e.g. explosion heard when burning hydrogen). Its etymology stems from the prefix exo (derived from the Greek word ???, exo, 'outside') and the Greek word thermasi (meaning 'to heat'). The term exothermic was first coined by Marcellin Berthelot.
Exothermic reaction	An exothermic reaction is a chemical reaction that releases energy in the form of light or heat. It is the opposite of an endothermic reaction. Expressed in a chemical equation: reactants ? products + energy
Electron acceptor	An electron acceptor is a chemical entity that accepts electrons transferred to it from another compound. It is an oxidizing agent that, by virtue of its accepting electrons, is itself reduced in the process. Typical oxidizing agents undergo permanent chemical alteration through covalent or ionic reaction chemistry, resulting in the complete and irreversible transfer of one or more electrons.
Electron donor	An electron donor is a chemical entity that donates electrons to another compound. It is a reducing agent that, by virtue of its donating electrons, is itself oxidized in the process. Typical reducing agents undergo permanent chemical alteration through covalent or ionic reaction chemistry.
Acceptor	In semiconductor physics, an acceptor is a dopant atom that when added to a semiconductor can form a p-type region. For example, when silicon, having four valence electrons, needs to be doped as a p-type semiconductor, elements from group III like boron (B) or aluminium (Al), having three valence electrons, can be used. The latter elements are also called trivalent impurities.

3. Chemical Bonding: The Classical Description

Donor

In semiconductor physics, a donor is a dopant atom that, when added to a semiconductor, can form a n-type region.

For example, when silicon, having four valence electrons, needs to be doped as an n-type semiconductor, elements from group V like phosphorus (P) or arsenic (As) can be used because they have five valence electrons. A dopant with five valence electrons is also called a pentavalent impurity.

Diatomic molecule

Diatomic molecules are molecules composed only of two atoms, of either the same or different chemical elements. The prefix di- is of Greek origin, meaning two.

Bohr model

In atomic physics, the Bohr model, introduced by Niels Bohr in 1913, depicts the atom as small, positively charged nucleus surrounded by electrons that travel in circular orbits around the nucleus--similar in structure to the solar system, but with attraction provided by electrostatic forces rather than gravity. After the cubic model .•Quantum ruleThe angular momentum L = $m_e vr$ is an integer multiple of h: $m_e vr = n\hbar$ Substituting the expression for the velocity gives an equation for r in terms of n: $\sqrt{Zk_e e^2 m_e r} = n\hbar$ so that the allowed orbit radius at any n is: $r_n = \frac{n^2\hbar^2}{Zk_e e^2 m_e}$ The smallest possible value of r in the hydrogen atom is called the Bohr radius and is equal to: $r_1 = \frac{\hbar^2}{k_e e^2 m_e} \approx 5.29 \times 10^{-11}\text{m}$ The energy of the n-th level for any atom is determined by the radius and quantum number:

$$E = -\frac{Zk_e e^2}{2r_n} = -\frac{Z^2(k_e e^2)^2 m_e}{2\hbar^2 n^2} \approx \frac{-13.6Z^2}{n^2}\text{eV}$$

An electron in the lowest energy level of hydrogen therefore has about 13.6 eV less energy than a motionless electron infinitely far from the nucleus. The next energy level is -3.4 eV. The third (n = 3) is -1.51 eV, and so on.

Ionic compound

In chemistry, an ionic compound is a chemical compound in which ions are held together in a lattice structure by ionic bonds. Usually, the positively charged portion consists of metal cations and the negatively charged portion is an anion or polyatomic ion. Ions in ionic compounds are held together by the electrostatic forces between oppositely charged bodies.

Ionic bonding

Ionic bonding is a type of chemical bonding that involves the electrostatic attraction between oppositely charged ions. These ions represent atoms that have lost one or more electron (known as cations) and atoms that have gained one or more electrons (known as an anions). In the simplest case, the cation is a metal atom and the anion is a nonmetal atom, but these ions can be of a more complex nature, e.g.

molecular ions like NH_4^+ or SO_4^{2-}

It is important to recognize that pure ionic bonding - in which one atom 'steals' an electron from another - cannot exist: all ionic compounds have some degree of covalent bonding, or electron sharing.

Mole

Mole is a unit of measurement used in chemistry to express amounts of a chemical substance, defined as the amount of any substance that contains as many elementary entities (e.g., atoms, molecules, ions, electrons) as there are atoms in 12 grams of pure carbon-12, the isotope of carbon with relative atomic mass 12. This corresponds to the Avogadro constant, which has a value of $6.02214129(27)\times10^{23}$ elementary entities of the substance. It is one of the base units in the International System of Units, and has the unit symbol mol and corresponds with the dimension symbol N. In honour of the unit, chemists often celebrate October 23 (a reference to the 10^{23} part of Avogadro's number) as 'Mole Day'.

The mole is widely used in chemistry instead of units of mass or volume as a convenient way to express amounts of reactants or of products of chemical reactions.

Polarization

Polarization is a property of waves that can oscillate with more than one orientation. Electromagnetic waves, such as light, and gravitational waves exhibit polarization; sound waves in a gas or liquid do not have polarization because the medium vibrates only along the direction in which the waves are travelling.

By convention, the polarization of light is described by specifying the orientation of the wave's electric field at a point in space over one period of the oscillation.

Distortion

Distortion is the alteration of the original shape (or other characteristic) of something, such as an object, image, sound or waveform. Distortion is usually unwanted, and so engineers strive to eliminate distortion, or minimize it. In some situations, however, distortion may be desirable.

Atmosphere

The standard atmosphere is an international reference pressure defined as 101325 Pa and used as a unit of pressure.

Rotational spectroscopy

Rotational spectroscopy is concerned with the measurement of the energies of transitions between quantized rotational states of molecules in the gas phase. The spectra of polar molecules can be measured in absorption or emission by microwave spectroscopy or by far infrared spectroscopy. The rotational spectra of non-polar molecules cannot be observed by those methods, but can be observed and measured by Raman spectroscopy.

Electron pair

In chemistry, an electron pair consists of two electrons that occupy the same orbital but have opposite spins. The electron pair concept was introduced in a 1916 paper of Gilbert N. Lewis.

3. Chemical Bonding: The Classical Description

Molecular orbital

In chemistry, a molecular orbital is a mathematical function describing the wave-like behavior of an electron in a molecule. This function can be used to calculate chemical and physical properties such as the probability of finding an electron in any specific region. The term orbital was introduced by Robert S. Mulliken in 1932 as an abbreviation for one-electron orbital wave function.

Spectroscopy

Spectroscopy is the study of the interaction between matter and radiated energy. Historically, spectroscopy originated through the study of visible light dispersed according to its wavelength, e.g., by a prism. Later the concept was expanded greatly to comprise any interaction with radiative energy as a function of its wavelength or frequency.

Stiffness

Stiffness is the rigidity of an object -- the extent to which it resists deformation in response to an applied force. The complementary concept is flexibility or pliability: the more flexible an object is, the less stiff it is.

Strength

In explosive materials, strength is the parameter determining the ability of the explosive to move the surrounding material. It is related to the total gas yield of the reaction, and the amount of heat produced. Cf.

Product

Product are formed during chemical reactions as reagents are consumed. Products have lower energy than the reagents and are produced during the reaction according to the second law of thermodynamics. The released energy comes from changes in chemical bonds between atoms in reagent molecules and may be given off in the form of heat or light.

Solvent

A solvent is a substance that dissolves a solute (a chemically different liquid, solid or gas), resulting in a solution. A solvent is usually a liquid but can also be a solid or a gas. The maximum quantity of solute that can dissolve in a specific volume of solvent varies with temperature.

Atomic orbital

An atomic orbital is a mathematical function that describes the wave-like behavior of either one electron or a pair of electrons in an atom. This function can be used to calculate the probability of finding any electron of an atom in any specific region around the atom's nucleus. The term may also refer to the physical region or space where the electron can be calculated to be present, as defined by the particular mathematical form of the orbital.

Component

In thermodynamics, a component is a chemically-independent constituent of a system. The number of components represents the minimum number of independent species necessary to define the composition of all phases of the system.

Calculating the number of components in a system is necessary, for example, when applying Gibbs' phase rule in determination of the number of degrees of freedom of a system.

Steric number

The steric number of a molecule is the number of atoms bonded to the central atom of a molecule plus the number of lone pairs on the central atom.

1. _________ is the alteration of the original shape (or other characteristic) of something, such as an object, image, sound or waveform. _________ is usually unwanted, and so engineers strive to eliminate _________, or minimize it. In some situations, however, _________ may be desirable.

a. Distortion
b. Bandwidth-limited pulse
c. Beam diameter
d. Beam divergence

2. The _________ is a tabular arrangement of the chemical elements, organized on the basis of their atomic numbers, electron configurations, and recurring chemical properties. Elements are presented in order of increasing atomic number (the number of protons in the nucleus). The standard form of the table consists of a grid of elements laid out in 18 columns and 7 rows, with a double row of elements below that.

a. Binary acid
b. Carbonic acid
c. Periodic table
d. Chloroauric acid

3. An _________ is a gas which does not undergo chemical reactions under a set of given conditions. The noble gases and nitrogen often do not react with many substances. _________es are used generally to avoid unwanted chemical reactions degrading a sample.

a. Inert gas
b. Carbogen
c. Cryogenic nitrogen plant
d. Cryogenic oxygen plant

4. A _________ is a binary compound, of which one part is a halogen atom and the other part is an element or radical that is less electronegative than the halogen, to make a fluoride, chloride, bromide, iodide, or astatide compound. Many salts are _________s. All Group 1 metals form _________s which are white solids at room temperature.

a. Bicarbonate
b. Halide
c. Caliche
d. Coral calcium

5. . In chemistry, a _________ is an electron that is associated with an atom, and that can participate in the formation of a chemical bond; in a single covalent bond, both atoms in the bond contribute one _________ in order to form a shared pair. The presence of _________s can determine the element's chemical properties and whether it may bond with other elements: For a main group element, a _________ can only be in the outermost electron shell. In a transition metal, a _________ can also be in an inner shell.

a. Band gap

b. Delocalized electron

c. Valence electron

d. Daylight

ANSWER KEY
3. Chemical Bonding: The Classical Description

1. a
2. c
3. a
4. b
5. c

4. Introduction to Quantum Mechanics

CHAPTER OUTLINE: KEY TERMS, PEOPLE, PLACES, CONCEPTS

_____ Quantum

_____ Quantum mechanics

_____ Subatomic particle

_____ Frequency

_____ Energy level

_____ Electromagnetic radiation

_____ Ionizing radiation

_____ Interference

_____ Quantization

_____ Atom

_____ Thermal equilibrium

_____ Photon

_____ Spectrograph

_____ Spectrum

_____ Ground state

_____ Excited state

_____ Molecule

_____ Bohr model

_____ Bohr radius

_____ Hydrogen

_____ Hydrogen atom

4. Introduction to Quantum Mechanics

CHAPTER OUTLINE: KEY TERMS, PEOPLE, PLACES, CONCEPTS

- Momentum
- Product
- Ionization energy
- Atomic spectroscopy
- Photoelectric effect
- Electron
- Intensity
- Photocathode
- Radiation
- Work function
- Ionization
- D-block
- Electron configuration
- Scandium
- Zinc
- Electron diffraction
- Observable
- Uncertainty principle
- Wave function
- Quantum electrodynamics
- Stationary state

4. Introduction to Quantum Mechanics

CHAPTER OUTLINE: KEY TERMS, PEOPLE, PLACES, CONCEPTS

- Kinetic energy
- Correspondence principle
- Zero-point energy
- Solvent
- Atomic orbital
- Component
- Probability amplitude

CHAPTER HIGHLIGHTS & NOTES: KEY TERMS, PEOPLE, PLACES, CONCEPTS

Quantum

In physics, a quantum is the minimum amount of any physical entity involved in an interaction. Behind this, one finds the fundamental notion that a physical property may be 'quantized,' referred to as 'the hypothesis of quantization'. This means that the magnitude can take on only certain discrete values.

Quantum mechanics

Quantum mechanics is a branch of physics which deals with physical phenomena at microscopic scales, where the action is on the order of the Planck constant. It departs from classical mechanics primarily at the quantum realm of atomic and subatomic length scales. Quantum mechanics provides a mathematical description of much of the dual particle-like and wave-like behavior and interactions of energy and matter.

Subatomic particle

In the physical sciences, subatomic particles are the particles smaller than an atom. (although some subatomic particles have mass greater than some atoms). There are two types of subatomic particles: elementary particles, which according to current theories are not made of other particles; and composite particles.

Frequency

Frequency is the number of occurrences of a repeating event per unit time. It is also referred to as temporal frequency, which emphasizes the contrast to spatial frequency and angular frequency. The period is the duration of one cycle in a repeating event, so the period is the reciprocal of the frequency.

4. Introduction to Quantum Mechanics

CHAPTER HIGHLIGHTS & NOTES: KEY TERMS, PEOPLE, PLACES, CONCEPTS

Energy level	A quantum mechanical system or particle that is bound--that is, confined spatially--can only take on certain discrete values of energy. This contrasts with classical particles, which can have any energy. These discrete values are called energy levels.
Electromagnetic radiation	Electromagnetic radiation is one of the fundamental phenomena of electromagnetism, behaving as waves propagating through space, and also as photon particles traveling through space, carrying radiant energy. In a vacuum, it propagates at a characteristic speed, the speed of light, normally in straight lines. EMR is emitted and absorbed by charged particles.
Ionizing radiation	Ionizing radiation is radiation composed of particles that individually carry enough kinetic energy to liberate an electron from an atom or molecule, ionizing it. Ionizing radiation is generated through nuclear reactions, either artificial or natural, by very high temperature (e.g. plasma discharge or the corona of the Sun), via production of high energy particles in particle accelerators, or due to acceleration of charged particles by the electromagnetic fields produced by natural processes, from lightning to supernova explosions. When ionizing radiation is emitted by or absorbed by an atom, it can liberate an atomic particle (typically an electron, proton, or neutron, but sometimes an entire nucleus) from the atom.
Interference	In physics, interference is a phenomenon in which two waves superimpose to form a resultant wave of greater or lower amplitude. Interference usually refers to the interaction of waves that are correlated or coherent with each other, either because they come from the same source or because they have the same or nearly the same frequency. Interference effects can be observed with all types of waves, for example, light, radio, acoustic, and surface water waves.
Quantization	In physics, quantization is the process of transition from a classical understanding of physical phenomena to a newer understanding known as 'quantum mechanics'. It is a procedure for constructing a quantum field theory starting from a classical field theory. This is a generalization of the procedure for building quantum mechanics from classical mechanics.
Atom	The atom is a basic unit of matter that consists of a dense central nucleus surrounded by a cloud of negatively charged electrons. The atomic nucleus contains a mix of positively charged protons and electrically neutral neutrons, which means 'uncuttable' or 'the smallest indivisible particle of matter'. Although the Indian and Greek concepts of the atom were based purely on philosophy, modern science has retained the name coined by Democritus.
Thermal equilibrium	In physics, the phrase thermal equilibrium is used sometimes in the common parlance of the ordinary language of physical discourse, and sometimes as a specialized technical term in thermodynamics. As common parlance, the phrase refers to steady states of temperature, which may be spatial or temporal.

Photon

A photon is an elementary particle, the quantum of light and all other forms of electromagnetic radiation, and the force carrier for the electromagnetic force, even when static via virtual photons. The effects of this force are easily observable at both the microscopic and macroscopic level, because the photon has zero rest mass; this allows long distance interactions. Like all elementary particles, photons are currently best explained by quantum mechanics and exhibit wave-particle duality, exhibiting properties of both waves and particles.

Spectrograph

A spectrograph is an instrument that separates an incoming wave into a frequency spectrum. There are several kinds of machines referred to as spectrographs, depending on the precise nature of the waves. The term was first used in 1884.

Spectrum

A spectrum is a condition that is not limited to a specific set of values but can vary infinitely within a continuum. The word was first used scientifically within the field of optics to describe the rainbow of colors in visible light when separated using a prism; it has since been applied by analogy to many fields other than optics. Thus, one might talk about the spectrum of political opinion, or the spectrum of activity of a drug, or the autism spectrum.

Ground state

The ground state of a quantum mechanical system is its lowest-energy state; the energy of the ground state is known as the zero-point energy of the system. An excited state is any state with energy greater than the ground state. The ground state of a quantum field theory is usually called the vacuum state or the vacuum.

Excited state

Excitation is an elevation in energy level above an arbitrary baseline energy state. In physics there is a specific technical definition for energy level which is often associated with an atom being excited to an excited state.

In quantum mechanics an excited state of a system (such as an atom, molecule or nucleus) is any quantum state of the system that has a higher energy than the ground state (that is, more energy than the absolute minimum).

Molecule

A molecule is an electrically neutral group of two or more atoms held together by chemical bonds. Molecules are distinguished from ions by their lack of electrical charge. However, in quantum physics, organic chemistry, and biochemistry, the term molecule is often used less strictly, also being applied to polyatomic ions.

Bohr model

In atomic physics, the Bohr model, introduced by Niels Bohr in 1913, depicts the atom as small, positively charged nucleus surrounded by electrons that travel in circular orbits around the nucleus--similar in structure to the solar system, but with attraction provided by electrostatic forces rather than gravity. After the cubic model .•Quantum ruleThe angular momentum L = $m_e vr$ is an integer multiple of h: $m_e vr = n\hbar$ Substituting the expression for the velocity gives an equation for r in terms of n: $\sqrt{Zk_e e^2 m_e r} = n\hbar$ so that the allowed orbit radius at any n is:

$$r_n = \frac{n^2\hbar^2}{Zk_e e^2 m_e}$$ The smallest possible value of r in the hydrogen atom is called the Bohr radius and is equal to: $$r_1 = \frac{\hbar^2}{k_e e^2 m_e} \approx 5.29 \times 10^{-11}\text{m}$$ The energy of the n-th level for any atom is determined by the radius and quantum number: $$E = -\frac{Zk_e e^2}{2r_n} = -\frac{Z^2(k_e e^2)^2 m_e}{2\hbar^2 n^2} \approx \frac{-13.6Z^2}{n^2}\text{eV}$$

An electron in the lowest energy level of hydrogen therefore has about 13.6 eV less energy than a motionless electron infinitely far from the nucleus. The next energy level is -3.4 eV. The third (n = 3) is -1.51 eV, and so on.

Bohr radius

The Bohr radius is a physical constant, approximately equal to the most probable distance between the proton and electron in a hydrogen atom in its ground state. It is named after Niels Bohr, due to its role in the Bohr model of an atom. The precise definition of the Bohr radius is: $$a_0 = \frac{4\pi\varepsilon_0\hbar^2}{m_e e^2} = \frac{\hbar}{m_e\, c\, \alpha}$$

where: ε_0 is the permittivity of free space $\hbar$ is the reduced Planck's constant m_e is the electron rest mass e is the elementary charge c is the speed of light in vacuum α is the fine structure constant.

Or, in Gaussian units the Bohr radius is simply $$a_0 = \frac{\hbar^2}{m_e e^2}$$

According to 2010 CODATA the Bohr radius has a value of $5.2917721092(17)\times10^{-11}$ m (i.e., approximately 53 pm or 0.53 angstroms).

Hydrogen

Hydrogen is a chemical element with chemical symbol H and atomic number 1. With an atomic weight of 1.00794 u, hydrogen is the lightest element and its monatomic form (H) is the most abundant chemical substance, constituting roughly 75% of the Universe's baryonic mass. Non-remnant stars are mainly composed of hydrogen in its plasma state.

At standard temperature and pressure, hydrogen is a colorless, odorless, tasteless, non-toxic, nonmetallic, highly combustible diatomic gas with the molecular formula H_2.

Hydrogen atom

A hydrogen atom is an atom of the chemical element hydrogen.

The electrically neutral atom contains a single positively charged proton and a single negatively charged electron bound to the nucleus by the Coulomb force. Atomic hydrogen constitutes about 75% of the elemental mass of the universe.

Momentum

In classical mechanics, linear momentum or translational momentum is the product of the mass and velocity of an object. For example, a heavy truck moving fast has a large momentum--it takes a large and prolonged force to get the truck up to this speed, and it takes a large and prolonged force to bring it to a stop afterwards. If the truck were lighter, or moving more slowly, then it would have less momentum.

Product

Product are formed during chemical reactions as reagents are consumed. Products have lower energy than the reagents and are produced during the reaction according to the second law of thermodynamics. The released energy comes from changes in chemical bonds between atoms in reagent molecules and may be given off in the form of heat or light.

Ionization energy

The ionization energy of an atom or molecule describes the amount of energy required to remove an electron from the atom or molecule in the gaseous state. X + energy ? X^+ + e^-

The term ionization potential has been used in the past but is not recommended.

The units for ionization energy vary from discipline to discipline.

Atomic spectroscopy

Atomic spectroscopy is the determination of elemental composition by using the Electromagnetic Spectrum or Mass Spectrum, respectively to optical or mass spectroscopy. It can be divided by atomization source or by the type of spectroscopy used. In the latter case, the main division is between optical and mass spectrometry.

Photoelectric effect

In the photoelectric effect, electrons are emitted from solids, liquids or gases when they absorb energy from light. Electrons emitted in this manner may be called photoelectrons.

In 1887, Heinrich Hertz discovered that electrodes illuminated with ultraviolet light create electric sparks more easily.

Electron

The electron is a subatomic particle with a negative elementary electric charge. Electrons belong to the first generation of the lepton particle family, and are generally thought to be elementary particles because they have no known components or substructure. The electron has a mass that is approximately 1/1836 that of the proton.

Intensity

In physics, intensity is the power transferred per unit area. In the SI system, it has units watts per metre squared (W/m^2). It is used most frequently with waves (e.g. sound or light), in which case the average power transfer over one period of the wave is used.

4. Introduction to Quantum Mechanics

CHAPTER HIGHLIGHTS & NOTES: KEY TERMS, PEOPLE, PLACES, CONCEPTS

Photocathode

A photocathode is a negatively charged electrode in a light detection device such as a photomultiplier or phototube that is coated with a photosensitive compound. When this is struck by a quantum of light (photon), the absorbed energy causes electron emission due to the photoelectric effect.

Radiation

In physics, radiation is a process in which energetic particles or energetic waves travel through a vacuum, or through matter-containing media that are not required for their propagation. Waves of a mass filled medium itself, such as water waves or sound waves, are usually not considered to be forms of 'radiation' in this sense.

Radiation can be classified as either ionizing or non-ionizing according to whether it ionizes or does not ionize ordinary chemical matter.

Work function

In solid-state physics, the work function is the minimum thermodynamic work (i.e. energy) needed to remove an electron from a solid to a point in the vacuum immediately outside the solid surface. Here 'immediately' means that the final electron position is far from the surface on the atomic scale, but still too close to the solid to be influenced by ambient electric fields in the vacuum. The work function is not a characteristic of a bulk material, but rather a property of the surface of the material (depending on crystal face and contamination).

Ionization

Ionization is the process by which an atom or a molecule acquires a negative or positive charge by gaining or losing electrons.

D-block

The d-block is the block or portion of the periodic table that contains the element groups 3-12. These groups correspond to the filling of the atomic d-orbital subshell of the second outermost shell (inside an outermost shell only containing 1 or 2 s-orbital electrons) with electron configurations ranging from s^2d^1 (Group 3) to s^2d^{10} (Group 12). There are some irregularities in the sequence; for example Cr is s^1d^5 (not s^2d^4) and the Group 11 metals are s^1d^{10} (not s^2d^9), so that the d-subshell is actually complete at Group 11.

The d-block elements are often also known as transition metals or transition elements.

Electron configuration

In atomic physics and quantum chemistry, the electron configuration is the distribution of electrons of an atom or molecule in atomic or molecular orbitals. For example, the electron configuration of the neon atom is $1s^2\ 2s^2\ 2p^6$.

Electronic configurations describe electrons as each moving independently in an orbital, in an average field created by all other orbitals.

Scandium

Scandium is a chemical element with symbol Sc and atomic number 21. A silvery-white metallic transition metal, it has historically been sometimes classified as a rare earth element, together with yttrium and the lanthanoids.

It was discovered in 1879 by spectral analysis of the minerals euxenite and gadolinite from Scandinavia.

Scandium is present in most of the deposits of rare earth and uranium compounds, but it is extracted from these ores in only a few mines worldwide.

Zinc

Zinc, in commerce also spelter, is a metallic chemical element; it has the symbol Zn and atomic number 30. It is the first element of group 12 of the periodic table. Zinc is, in some respects, chemically similar to magnesium, because its ion is of similar size and its only common oxidation state is +2. Zinc is the 24th most abundant element in the Earth's crust and has five stable isotopes. The most common zinc ore is sphalerite (zinc blende), a zinc sulfide mineral.

Electron diffraction

Electron diffraction refers to the wave nature of electrons. However, from a technical or practical point of view, it may be regarded as a technique used to study matter by firing electrons at a sample and observing the resulting interference pattern. This phenomenon is commonly known as the wave-particle duality, which states that the behavior of a particle of matter (in this case the incident electron) can be described by a wave.

Observable

In physics, particularly in quantum physics, a system observable is a measurable operator, or gauge, where the property of the system state can be determined by some sequence of physical operations. For example, these operations might involve submitting the system to various electromagnetic fields and eventually reading a value off some gauge. In systems governed by classical mechanics, any experimentally observable value can be shown to be given by a real-valued function on the set of all possible system states.

Uncertainty principle

In quantum mechanics, the uncertainty principle is any of a variety of mathematical inequalities asserting a fundamental limit to the precision with which certain pairs of physical properties of a particle known as complementary variables, such as position x and momentum p, can be known simultaneously. For instance, the more precisely the position of some particle is determined, the less precisely its momentum can be known, and vice versa. The original heuristic argument that such a limit should exist was given by Werner Heisenberg in 1927, after whom it is sometimes named the Heisenberg principle.

Wave function

A wave function or wavefunction in quantum mechanics describes the quantum state of a particle and how it behaves. Typically, its values are complex numbers and, for a single particle, it is a function of space and time. The Schrödinger equation describes how the wave function evolves over time.

Quantum electrodynamics

In particle physics, quantum electrodynamics is the relativistic quantum field theory of electrodynamics. In essence, it describes how light and matter interact and is the first theory where full agreement between quantum mechanics and special relativity is achieved.

4. Introduction to Quantum Mechanics

CHAPTER HIGHLIGHTS & NOTES: KEY TERMS, PEOPLE, PLACES, CONCEPTS

Stationary state	In quantum mechanics, a stationary state is an eigenvector of the Hamiltonian, implying the probability density associated with the wavefunction is independent of time. This corresponds to a quantum state with a single definite energy (instead of a quantum superposition of different energies). It is also called energy eigenvector, energy eigenstate, energy eigenfunction, or energy eigenket.
Kinetic energy	In physics, the kinetic energy of an object is the energy which it possesses due to its motion. It is defined as the work needed to accelerate a body of a given mass from rest to its stated velocity. Having gained this energy during its acceleration, the body maintains this kinetic energy unless its speed changes.
Correspondence principle	In physics, the correspondence principle states that the behavior of systems described by the theory of quantum mechanics reproduces classical physics in the limit of large quantum numbers. In other words, it says that for large orbits and for large energies, quantum calculations must agree with classical calculations. The principle was formulated by Niels Bohr in 1920, though he had previously made use of it as early as 1913 in developing his model of the atom.
Zero-point energy	Zero-point energy, also called quantum vacuum zero-point energy, is the lowest possible energy that a quantum mechanical physical system may have; it is the energy of its ground state. All quantum mechanical systems undergo fluctuations even in their ground state and have an associated zero-point energy, a consequence of their wave-like nature. The uncertainty principle requires every physical system to have a zero-point energy greater than the minimum of its classical potential well.
Solvent	A solvent is a substance that dissolves a solute (a chemically different liquid, solid or gas), resulting in a solution. A solvent is usually a liquid but can also be a solid or a gas. The maximum quantity of solute that can dissolve in a specific volume of solvent varies with temperature.
Atomic orbital	An atomic orbital is a mathematical function that describes the wave-like behavior of either one electron or a pair of electrons in an atom. This function can be used to calculate the probability of finding any electron of an atom in any specific region around the atom's nucleus. The term may also refer to the physical region or space where the electron can be calculated to be present, as defined by the particular mathematical form of the orbital.
Component	In thermodynamics, a component is a chemically-independent constituent of a system. The number of components represents the minimum number of independent species necessary to define the composition of all phases of the system.

4. Introduction to Quantum Mechanics

CHAPTER HIGHLIGHTS & NOTES: KEY TERMS, PEOPLE, PLACES, CONCEPTS

Probability amplitude | In quantum mechanics, a probability amplitude is a complex number used in describing the behaviour of systems. The modulus squared of this quantity represents a probability or probability density.

Probability amplitudes provide a physical meaning of the wave function, a link first proposed by Max Born, and this is a pillar of the Copenhagen interpretation of quantum mechanics.

CHAPTER QUIZ: KEY TERMS, PEOPLE, PLACES, CONCEPTS

1. In physics, the _________ of an object is the energy which it possesses due to its motion. It is defined as the work needed to accelerate a body of a given mass from rest to its stated velocity. Having gained this energy during its acceleration, the body maintains this _________ unless its speed changes.

    a. Fermi acceleration
    b. Fundamental equation of constrained motion
    c. Kinetic energy
    d. Bass trap

2. The _________ is a subatomic particle with a negative elementary electric charge. _________s belong to the first generation of the lepton particle family, and are generally thought to be elementary particles because they have no known components or substructure. The _________ has a mass that is approximately 1/1836 that of the proton.

    a. Compton wavelength
    b. Compton scattering
    c. Bohr model
    d. Electron

3. In physics, a _________ is the minimum amount of any physical entity involved in an interaction. Behind this, one finds the fundamental notion that a physical property may be 'quantized,' referred to as 'the hypothesis of quantization'. This means that the magnitude can take on only certain discrete values.

    a. 6-j symbol
    b. 9-j symbol
    c. Quantum
    d. Bloch sphere

4. . The _________ of a quantum mechanical system is its lowest-energy state; the energy of the _________ is known as the zero-point energy of the system. An excited state is any state with energy greater than the _________. The _________ of a quantum field theory is usually called the vacuum state or the vacuum.

a. 6-j symbol
b. 9-j symbol
c. Ground state
d. Bloch sphere

5. In classical mechanics, linear _________ or translational _________ is the product of the mass and velocity of an object. For example, a heavy truck moving fast has a large _________--it takes a large and prolonged force to get the truck up to this speed, and it takes a large and prolonged force to bring it to a stop afterwards. If the truck were lighter, or moving more slowly, then it would have less _________.

a. Bending moment
b. Momentum
c. Cauchy elastic material
d. Cauchy momentum equation

ANSWER KEY
4. Introduction to Quantum Mechanics

1. c
2. d
3. c
4. c
5. b

---

5. Quantum Mechanics and Atomic Structure

CHAPTER OUTLINE: KEY TERMS, PEOPLE, PLACES, CONCEPTS

- Atom
- Hydrogen
- Wave function
- Atomic orbital
- Electron
- Hydrogen atom
- Probability amplitude
- Quantum number
- Energy level
- Quantum state
- Quantum
- Spherical harmonics
- Harmonic
- Atomic spectroscopy
- Isosurface
- Density
- Volume
- Electron density
- Cycloalkane
- Carbon
- Molecule

5. Quantum Mechanics and Atomic Structure

CHAPTER OUTLINE: KEY TERMS, PEOPLE, PLACES, CONCEPTS

- Shielding effect
- Electron configuration
- Aufbau principle
- Argon
- Helium
- Periodic table
- D-block
- Electrochemical cell
- Electrode
- F-block
- Oxidation
- Product
- Scandium
- Zinc
- Atomic number
- Kinetic energy
- Period
- Photon
- Spectroscopy
- Ionization
- Ionization energy

5. Quantum Mechanics and Atomic Structure

CHAPTER OUTLINE: KEY TERMS, PEOPLE, PLACES, CONCEPTS

	Lanthanide contraction
	Periodic trends
	Electron affinity

CHAPTER HIGHLIGHTS & NOTES: KEY TERMS, PEOPLE, PLACES, CONCEPTS

Atom

The atom is a basic unit of matter that consists of a dense central nucleus surrounded by a cloud of negatively charged electrons. The atomic nucleus contains a mix of positively charged protons and electrically neutral neutrons, which means 'uncuttable' or 'the smallest indivisible particle of matter'. Although the Indian and Greek concepts of the atom were based purely on philosophy, modern science has retained the name coined by Democritus.

Hydrogen

Hydrogen is a chemical element with chemical symbol H and atomic number 1. With an atomic weight of 1.00794 u, hydrogen is the lightest element and its monatomic form (H) is the most abundant chemical substance, constituting roughly 75% of the Universe's baryonic mass. Non-remnant stars are mainly composed of hydrogen in its plasma state.

At standard temperature and pressure, hydrogen is a colorless, odorless, tasteless, non-toxic, nonmetallic, highly combustible diatomic gas with the molecular formula H_2.

Wave function

A wave function or wavefunction in quantum mechanics describes the quantum state of a particle and how it behaves. Typically, its values are complex numbers and, for a single particle, it is a function of space and time. The Schrödinger equation describes how the wave function evolves over time.

Atomic orbital

An atomic orbital is a mathematical function that describes the wave-like behavior of either one electron or a pair of electrons in an atom. This function can be used to calculate the probability of finding any electron of an atom in any specific region around the atom's nucleus. The term may also refer to the physical region or space where the electron can be calculated to be present, as defined by the particular mathematical form of the orbital.

Electron

The electron is a subatomic particle with a negative elementary electric charge. Electrons belong to the first generation of the lepton particle family, and are generally thought to be elementary particles because they have no known components or substructure.

5. Quantum Mechanics and Atomic Structure

Hydrogen atom	A hydrogen atom is an atom of the chemical element hydrogen. The electrically neutral atom contains a single positively charged proton and a single negatively charged electron bound to the nucleus by the Coulomb force. Atomic hydrogen constitutes about 75% of the elemental mass of the universe.
Probability amplitude	In quantum mechanics, a probability amplitude is a complex number used in describing the behaviour of systems. The modulus squared of this quantity represents a probability or probability density. Probability amplitudes provide a physical meaning of the wave function, a link first proposed by Max Born, and this is a pillar of the Copenhagen interpretation of quantum mechanics.
Quantum number	Quantum numbers describe values of conserved quantities in the dynamics of a quantum system. Perhaps the most peculiar aspect of quantum mechanics is the quantization of observable quantities, since quantum numbers are discrete sets of integers or half-integers. This is distinguished from classical mechanics where the values can range continuously.
Energy level	A quantum mechanical system or particle that is bound--that is, confined spatially--can only take on certain discrete values of energy. This contrasts with classical particles, which can have any energy. These discrete values are called energy levels.
Quantum state	In quantum physics, quantum state refers to the state of a quantum system. A quantum state is given as a vector in a Hilbert space, called the state vector. The state vector theoretically contains statistical information about the quantum system.
Quantum	In physics, a quantum is the minimum amount of any physical entity involved in an interaction. Behind this, one finds the fundamental notion that a physical property may be 'quantized,' referred to as 'the hypothesis of quantization'. This means that the magnitude can take on only certain discrete values.
Spherical harmonics	In mathematics, spherical harmonics are the angular portion of a set of solutions to Laplace's equation. Represented in a system of spherical coordinates, Laplace's spherical harmonics Y_ℓ^m are a specific set of spherical harmonics that forms an orthogonal system, first introduced by Pierre Simon de Laplace in 1782. Spherical harmonics are important in many theoretical and practical applications, particularly in the computation of atomic orbital electron configurations, representation of gravitational fields, geoids, and the magnetic fields of planetary bodies and stars, and characterization of the cosmic microwave background radiation. In 3D computer graphics, spherical harmonics play a special role in a wide variety of topics including indirect lighting (ambient occlusion, global illumination, precomputed radiance transfer, etc).
Harmonic	A harmonic of a wave is a component frequency of the signal that is an integer multiple of the fundamental frequency, i.e.

Atomic spectroscopy	Atomic spectroscopy is the determination of elemental composition by using the Electromagnetic Spectrum or Mass Spectrum, respectively to optical or mass spectroscopy. It can be divided by atomization source or by the type of spectroscopy used. In the latter case, the main division is between optical and mass spectrometry.
Isosurface	An isosurface is a three-dimensional analog of an isoline. It is a surface that represents points of a constant value (e.g. pressure, temperature, velocity, density) within a volume of space; in other words, it is a level set of a continuous function whose domain is 3D-space. Isosurfaces are normally displayed using computer graphics, and are used as data visualization methods in computational fluid dynamics (CFD), allowing engineers to study features of a fluid flow (gas or liquid) around objects, such as aircraft wings.
Density	The density, or more precisely, the volumetric mass density, of a substance is its mass per unit volume. The symbol most often used for density is ? (the lower case Greek letter rho). Mathematically, density is defined as mass divided by volume: $\rho = \frac{m}{V},$ where ? is the density, m is the mass, and V is the volume.
Volume	In thermodynamics, the volume of a system is an important extensive parameter for describing its thermodynamic state. The specific volume, an intensive property, is the system's volume per unit of mass. Volume is a function of state and is interdependent with other thermodynamic properties such as pressure and temperature.
Electron density	Electron density is the measure of the probability of an electron being present at a specific location. In molecules, regions of electron density are usually found around the atom, and its bonds. In de-localized or conjugated systems, such as phenol, benzene and compounds such as hemoglobin and chlorophyll, the electron density covers an entire region, i.e., in benzene they are found above and below the planar ring.
Cycloalkane	Cycloalkanes are types of hydrocarbon compounds that have one or more rings of carbon atoms in the chemical structure of their molecules. Alkanes are types of organic hydrocarbon compounds that have only single chemical bonds in their chemical structure. Cycloalkanes consist of only carbon (C) and hydrogen (H) atoms and are saturated because there are no multiple C-C bonds to hydrogenate (add more hydrogen to).
Carbon	Carbon fiber, alternatively graphite fiber, carbon graphite or CF, is a material consisting of fibers about 5-10 μm in diameter and composed mostly of carbon atoms. The carbon atoms are bonded together in crystals that are more or less aligned parallel to the long axis of the fiber.

5. Quantum Mechanics and Atomic Structure

Molecule	A molecule is an electrically neutral group of two or more atoms held together by chemical bonds. Molecules are distinguished from ions by their lack of electrical charge. However, in quantum physics, organic chemistry, and biochemistry, the term molecule is often used less strictly, also being applied to polyatomic ions.
Shielding effect	The shielding effect describes the decrease in attraction between an electron and the nucleus in any atom with more than one electron shell. It is also referred to as the screening effect or atomic shielding. This could also be explained with the help of a helium atom(isolated).
Electron configuration	In atomic physics and quantum chemistry, the electron configuration is the distribution of electrons of an atom or molecule in atomic or molecular orbitals. For example, the electron configuration of the neon atom is $1s^2\ 2s^2\ 2p^6$. Electronic configurations describe electrons as each moving independently in an orbital, in an average field created by all other orbitals.
Aufbau principle	The Aufbau principle is used to determine the electron configuration of an atom, molecule or ion. The principle postulates a hypothetical process in which an atom is 'built up' by progressively adding electrons. As they are added, they assume their most stable conditions (electron orbitals) with respect to the nucleus and those electrons already there.
Argon	Argon is a chemical element with symbol Ar and atomic number 18. It is in group 18 of the periodic table and is a noble gas. Argon is the third most common gas in the Earth's atmosphere, at 0.93% (9,300 ppm), making it approximately 23.8 times as abundant as the next most common atmospheric gas, carbon dioxide (390 ppm), and more than 500 times as abundant as the next most common noble gas, neon (18 ppm). Nearly all of this argon is radiogenic argon-40 derived from the decay of potassium-40 in the Earth's crust.
Helium	Helium is a chemical element with symbol He and atomic number 2. It is a colorless, odorless, tasteless, non-toxic, inert, monatomic gas that heads the noble gas group in the periodic table. Its boiling and melting points are the lowest among the elements and it exists only as a gas except in extreme conditions. Helium is the second lightest element and is the second most abundant element in the observable universe, being present at about 24% of the total elemental mass, which is more than 12 times the mass of all the heavier elements combined.
Periodic table	The periodic table is a tabular arrangement of the chemical elements, organized on the basis of their atomic numbers, electron configurations, and recurring chemical properties. Elements are presented in order of increasing atomic number (the number of protons in the nucleus).

D-block

The d-block is the block or portion of the periodic table that contains the element groups 3-12. These groups correspond to the filling of the atomic d-orbital subshell of the second outermost shell (inside an outermost shell only containing 1 or 2 s-orbital electrons) with electron configurations ranging from s^2d^1 (Group 3) to s^2d^{10} (Group 12). There are some irregularities in the sequence; for example Cr is s^1d^5 (not s^2d^4) and the Group 11 metals are s^1d^{10} (not s^2d^9), so that the d-subshell is actually complete at Group 11.

The d-block elements are often also known as transition metals or transition elements.

Electrochemical cell

An electrochemical cell is a device capable of either deriving electrical energy from chemical reactions, or facilitating chemical reactions through the introduction of electrical energy. A common example of an electrochemical cell is a standard 1.5-volt 'battery'. (Actually a single 'Galvanic cell'; a battery properly consists of multiple cells, connected in either parallel or series pattern).

Electrode

An electrode is an electrical conductor used to make contact with a nonmetallic part of a circuit . The word was coined by the scientist Michael Faraday from the Greek words elektron (meaning amber, from which the word electricity is derived) and hodos, a way.

F-block

The f-block of the periodic table of the elements consists of those elements whose atoms or ions have valence electrons in f-orbitals. Actual electronic configurations may be slightly different from what is predicted by the Aufbau principle. The elements are also known as inner transition elements, although that term is normally taken to include lutetium and lawrencium as well, which are part of the d-block.

Oxidation

Redox (reduction-oxidation) reactions include all chemical reactions in which atoms have their oxidation state changed; in general, redox reactions involve the transfer of electrons between species.

This can be either a simple redox process, such as the oxidation of carbon to yield carbon dioxide or the reduction of carbon by hydrogen to yield methane (CH_4), or a complex process such as the oxidation of glucose ($C_6H_{12}O_6$) in the human body through a series of complex electron transfer processes.

The term 'redox' comes from two concepts involved with electron transfer: reduction and oxidation.

Product

Product are formed during chemical reactions as reagents are consumed. Products have lower energy than the reagents and are produced during the reaction according to the second law of thermodynamics. The released energy comes from changes in chemical bonds between atoms in reagent molecules and may be given off in the form of heat or light.

Scandium

Scandium is a chemical element with symbol Sc and atomic number 21.

	A silvery-white metallic transition metal, it has historically been sometimes classified as a rare earth element, together with yttrium and the lanthanoids. It was discovered in 1879 by spectral analysis of the minerals euxenite and gadolinite from Scandinavia. Scandium is present in most of the deposits of rare earth and uranium compounds, but it is extracted from these ores in only a few mines worldwide.
Zinc	Zinc, in commerce also spelter, is a metallic chemical element; it has the symbol Zn and atomic number 30. It is the first element of group 12 of the periodic table. Zinc is, in some respects, chemically similar to magnesium, because its ion is of similar size and its only common oxidation state is +2. Zinc is the 24th most abundant element in the Earth's crust and has five stable isotopes. The most common zinc ore is sphalerite (zinc blende), a zinc sulfide mineral.
Atomic number	In chemistry and physics, the atomic number is the number of protons found in the nucleus of an atom and therefore identical to the charge number of the nucleus. It is conventionally represented by the symbol Z. The atomic number uniquely identifies a chemical element. In an atom of neutral charge, the atomic number is also equal to the number of electrons.
Kinetic energy	In physics, the kinetic energy of an object is the energy which it possesses due to its motion. It is defined as the work needed to accelerate a body of a given mass from rest to its stated velocity. Having gained this energy during its acceleration, the body maintains this kinetic energy unless its speed changes.
Period	In the periodic table of the elements, elements are arranged in a series of rows (or periods) so that those with similar properties appear in a column. Elements of the same period have the same number of electron shells; with each group across a period, the elements have one more proton and electron and become less metallic. This arrangement reflects the periodic recurrence of similar properties as the atomic number increases.
Photon	A photon is an elementary particle, the quantum of light and all other forms of electromagnetic radiation, and the force carrier for the electromagnetic force, even when static via virtual photons. The effects of this force are easily observable at both the microscopic and macroscopic level, because the photon has zero rest mass; this allows long distance interactions. Like all elementary particles, photons are currently best explained by quantum mechanics and exhibit wave-particle duality, exhibiting properties of both waves and particles.
Spectroscopy	Spectroscopy is the study of the interaction between matter and radiated energy. Historically, spectroscopy originated through the study of visible light dispersed according to its wavelength, e.g., by a prism. Later the concept was expanded greatly to comprise any interaction with radiative energy as a function of its wavelength or frequency.

Ionization	Ionization is the process by which an atom or a molecule acquires a negative or positive charge by gaining or losing electrons.
Ionization energy	The ionization energy of an atom or molecule describes the amount of energy required to remove an electron from the atom or molecule in the gaseous state. X + energy ? X^+ + e^- The term ionization potential has been used in the past but is not recommended. The units for ionization energy vary from discipline to discipline.
Lanthanide contraction	Lanthanide contraction is a term used in chemistry to describe the greater than expected decrease in ionic radii of the elements in the lanthanide series from atomic number 57, lanthanum, to 71, lutetium, which results in smaller than otherwise expected ionic radii for the subsequent elements starting with 72, hafnium. The term was coined by the Norwegian geochemist Victor Goldschmidt in his series 'Geochemische Verteilungsgesetze Der Elemente'.
Periodic trends	In chemistry, periodic trends are the tendencies of certain elemental characteristics to increase or decrease as one progresses along a row or column of the periodic table of elements. All periodic trends of the chemicals are based on Coulomb's law $F_C = \frac{kq_1q_2}{d^2}$. As distance from the protons in the nucleus to the valence electrons increases values associated with attributes such as electron affinity, ionization energy, and electronegativity decrease.
Electron affinity	In chemistry and atomic physics, the electron affinity of an atom or molecule is defined as the energy change when an electron is added to a neutral atom or molecule to form a negative ion. X + e^- ? X^- + energy In solid state physics, the electron affinity for a surface is defined somewhat differently .

5. Quantum Mechanics and Atomic Structure

CHAPTER QUIZ: KEY TERMS, PEOPLE, PLACES, CONCEPTS

1. An _________ is a three-dimensional analog of an isoline. It is a surface that represents points of a constant value (e.g. pressure, temperature, velocity, density) within a volume of space; in other words, it is a level set of a continuous function whose domain is 3D-space.

   _________s are normally displayed using computer graphics, and are used as data visualization methods in computational fluid dynamics (CFD), allowing engineers to study features of a fluid flow (gas or liquid) around objects, such as aircraft wings.

   a. Isosurface
   b. Bone scintigraphy
   c. CapeRay
   d. Cardiovascular and Interventional Radiological Society of Europe

2. _________ is a chemical element with symbol Ar and atomic number 18. It is in group 18 of the periodic table and is a noble gas. _________ is the third most common gas in the Earth's atmosphere, at 0.93% (9,300 ppm), making it approximately 23.8 times as abundant as the next most common atmospheric gas, carbon dioxide (390 ppm), and more than 500 times as abundant as the next most common noble gas, neon (18 ppm). Nearly all of this _________ is radiogenic _________-40 derived from the decay of potassium-40 in the Earth's crust.

   a. Chemical element
   b. Systematic element name
   c. Daylight
   d. Argon

3. _________ is the measure of the probability of an electron being present at a specific location.

   In molecules, regions of _________ are usually found around the atom, and its bonds. In de-localized or conjugated systems, such as phenol, benzene and compounds such as hemoglobin and chlorophyll, the _________ covers an entire region, i.e., in benzene they are found above and below the planar ring.

   a. Compton wavelength
   b. Compton scattering
   c. Bohr model
   d. Electron density

4. . _________ is a chemical element with symbol He and atomic number 2. It is a colorless, odorless, tasteless, non-toxic, inert, monatomic gas that heads the noble gas group in the periodic table. Its boiling and melting points are the lowest among the elements and it exists only as a gas except in extreme conditions.

   _________ is the second lightest element and is the second most abundant element in the observable universe, being present at about 24% of the total elemental mass, which is more than 12 times the mass of all the heavier elements combined.

   a. Barium

b. Berkelium
c. Beryllium
d. Helium

5. An _________ is an electrical conductor used to make contact with a nonmetallic part of a circuit . The word was coined by the scientist Michael Faraday from the Greek words elektron (meaning amber, from which the word electricity is derived) and hodos, a way.

a. Binder
b. Electrode
c. Blu-Tack
d. Canada balsam

ANSWER KEY
5. Quantum Mechanics and Atomic Structure

---

1. a
2. d
3. d
4. d
5. b

---

6. Quantum Mechanics and Molecular Structure

CHAPTER OUTLINE: KEY TERMS, PEOPLE, PLACES, CONCEPTS

______	Energy level
______	Quantum mechanics
______	Atomic orbital
______	Molecular orbital
______	Atom
______	Electron
______	Molecule
______	Probability amplitude
______	Wave function
______	Zero-point energy
______	Chemical bond
______	Hydrogen
______	Electron density
______	Strength
______	Hydrogen atom
______	Diatomic molecule
______	Electron pair
______	Ionization
______	Ionization energy
______	Kinetic energy
______	Photon

6. Quantum Mechanics and Molecular Structure

CHAPTER OUTLINE: KEY TERMS, PEOPLE, PLACES, CONCEPTS

______	Spectroscopy
______	Period
______	Scanning tunneling microscope
______	Solvent
______	Component
______	Mixing
______	Carbon
______	Quantum

CHAPTER HIGHLIGHTS & NOTES: KEY TERMS, PEOPLE, PLACES, CONCEPTS

Energy level	A quantum mechanical system or particle that is bound--that is, confined spatially--can only take on certain discrete values of energy. This contrasts with classical particles, which can have any energy. These discrete values are called energy levels.
Quantum mechanics	Quantum mechanics is a branch of physics which deals with physical phenomena at microscopic scales, where the action is on the order of the Planck constant. It departs from classical mechanics primarily at the quantum realm of atomic and subatomic length scales. Quantum mechanics provides a mathematical description of much of the dual particle-like and wave-like behavior and interactions of energy and matter.
Atomic orbital	An atomic orbital is a mathematical function that describes the wave-like behavior of either one electron or a pair of electrons in an atom. This function can be used to calculate the probability of finding any electron of an atom in any specific region around the atom's nucleus. The term may also refer to the physical region or space where the electron can be calculated to be present, as defined by the particular mathematical form of the orbital.
Molecular orbital	In chemistry, a molecular orbital is a mathematical function describing the wave-like behavior of an electron in a molecule. This function can be used to calculate chemical and physical properties such as the probability of finding an electron in any specific region.

The term orbital was introduced by Robert S. Mulliken in 1932 as an abbreviation for one-electron orbital wave function.

Atom

The atom is a basic unit of matter that consists of a dense central nucleus surrounded by a cloud of negatively charged electrons. The atomic nucleus contains a mix of positively charged protons and electrically neutral neutrons, which means 'uncuttable' or 'the smallest indivisible particle of matter'. Although the Indian and Greek concepts of the atom were based purely on philosophy, modern science has retained the name coined by Democritus.

Electron

The electron is a subatomic particle with a negative elementary electric charge. Electrons belong to the first generation of the lepton particle family, and are generally thought to be elementary particles because they have no known components or substructure. The electron has a mass that is approximately 1/1836 that of the proton.

Molecule

A molecule is an electrically neutral group of two or more atoms held together by chemical bonds. Molecules are distinguished from ions by their lack of electrical charge. However, in quantum physics, organic chemistry, and biochemistry, the term molecule is often used less strictly, also being applied to polyatomic ions.

Probability amplitude

In quantum mechanics, a probability amplitude is a complex number used in describing the behaviour of systems. The modulus squared of this quantity represents a probability or probability density.

Probability amplitudes provide a physical meaning of the wave function, a link first proposed by Max Born, and this is a pillar of the Copenhagen interpretation of quantum mechanics.

Wave function

A wave function or wavefunction in quantum mechanics describes the quantum state of a particle and how it behaves. Typically, its values are complex numbers and, for a single particle, it is a function of space and time. The Schrödinger equation describes how the wave function evolves over time.

Zero-point energy

Zero-point energy, also called quantum vacuum zero-point energy, is the lowest possible energy that a quantum mechanical physical system may have; it is the energy of its ground state. All quantum mechanical systems undergo fluctuations even in their ground state and have an associated zero-point energy, a consequence of their wave-like nature. The uncertainty principle requires every physical system to have a zero-point energy greater than the minimum of its classical potential well.

Chemical bond

A chemical bond is an attraction between atoms that allows the formation of chemical substances that contain two or more atoms. The bond is caused by the electrostatic force of attraction between opposite charges, either between electrons and nuclei, or as the result of a dipole attraction.

6. Quantum Mechanics and Molecular Structure

CHAPTER HIGHLIGHTS & NOTES: KEY TERMS, PEOPLE, PLACES, CONCEPTS

Hydrogen

Hydrogen is a chemical element with chemical symbol H and atomic number 1. With an atomic weight of 1.00794 u, hydrogen is the lightest element and its monatomic form (H) is the most abundant chemical substance, constituting roughly 75% of the Universe's baryonic mass. Non-remnant stars are mainly composed of hydrogen in its plasma state.

At standard temperature and pressure, hydrogen is a colorless, odorless, tasteless, non-toxic, nonmetallic, highly combustible diatomic gas with the molecular formula H_2.

Electron density

Electron density is the measure of the probability of an electron being present at a specific location.

In molecules, regions of electron density are usually found around the atom, and its bonds. In de-localized or conjugated systems, such as phenol, benzene and compounds such as hemoglobin and chlorophyll, the electron density covers an entire region, i.e., in benzene they are found above and below the planar ring.

Strength

In explosive materials, strength is the parameter determining the ability of the explosive to move the surrounding material. It is related to the total gas yield of the reaction, and the amount of heat produced. Cf.

Hydrogen atom

A hydrogen atom is an atom of the chemical element hydrogen. The electrically neutral atom contains a single positively charged proton and a single negatively charged electron bound to the nucleus by the Coulomb force. Atomic hydrogen constitutes about 75% of the elemental mass of the universe.

Diatomic molecule

Diatomic molecules are molecules composed only of two atoms, of either the same or different chemical elements. The prefix di- is of Greek origin, meaning two.

Electron pair

In chemistry, an electron pair consists of two electrons that occupy the same orbital but have opposite spins. The electron pair concept was introduced in a 1916 paper of Gilbert N. Lewis.

Because electrons are fermions, the Pauli exclusion principle forbids these particles from having exactly the same quantum numbers.

Ionization

Ionization is the process by which an atom or a molecule acquires a negative or positive charge by gaining or losing electrons.

Ionization energy

The ionization energy of an atom or molecule describes the amount of energy required to remove an electron from the atom or molecule in the gaseous state. X + energy ? X^+ + e^-

The term ionization potential has been used in the past but is not recommended.

Kinetic energy	In physics, the kinetic energy of an object is the energy which it possesses due to its motion. It is defined as the work needed to accelerate a body of a given mass from rest to its stated velocity. Having gained this energy during its acceleration, the body maintains this kinetic energy unless its speed changes.
Photon	A photon is an elementary particle, the quantum of light and all other forms of electromagnetic radiation, and the force carrier for the electromagnetic force, even when static via virtual photons. The effects of this force are easily observable at both the microscopic and macroscopic level, because the photon has zero rest mass; this allows long distance interactions. Like all elementary particles, photons are currently best explained by quantum mechanics and exhibit wave-particle duality, exhibiting properties of both waves and particles.
Spectroscopy	Spectroscopy is the study of the interaction between matter and radiated energy. Historically, spectroscopy originated through the study of visible light dispersed according to its wavelength, e.g., by a prism. Later the concept was expanded greatly to comprise any interaction with radiative energy as a function of its wavelength or frequency.
Period	In the periodic table of the elements, elements are arranged in a series of rows (or periods) so that those with similar properties appear in a column. Elements of the same period have the same number of electron shells; with each group across a period, the elements have one more proton and electron and become less metallic. This arrangement reflects the periodic recurrence of similar properties as the atomic number increases.
Scanning tunneling microscope	A scanning tunneling microscope is an instrument for imaging surfaces at the atomic level. Its development in 1981 earned its inventors, Gerd Binnig and Heinrich Rohrer (at IBM Zürich), the Nobel Prize in Physics in 1986. For an Scanning tunneling microscope, good resolution is considered to be 0.1 nm lateral resolution and 0.01 nm depth resolution. With this resolution, individual atoms within materials are routinely imaged and manipulated.
Solvent	A solvent is a substance that dissolves a solute (a chemically different liquid, solid or gas), resulting in a solution. A solvent is usually a liquid but can also be a solid or a gas. The maximum quantity of solute that can dissolve in a specific volume of solvent varies with temperature.
Component	In thermodynamics, a component is a chemically-independent constituent of a system. The number of components represents the minimum number of independent species necessary to define the composition of all phases of the system. Calculating the number of components in a system is necessary, for example, when applying Gibbs' phase rule in determination of the number of degrees of freedom of a system.
Mixing	In industrial process engineering, mixing is a unit operation that involves manipulating a heterogeneous physical system, with the intent to make it more homogeneous.

6. Quantum Mechanics and Molecular Structure

CHAPTER HIGHLIGHTS & NOTES: KEY TERMS, PEOPLE, PLACES, CONCEPTS

Carbon	Carbon fiber, alternatively graphite fiber, carbon graphite or CF, is a material consisting of fibers about 5-10 μm in diameter and composed mostly of carbon atoms. The carbon atoms are bonded together in crystals that are more or less aligned parallel to the long axis of the fiber. The crystal alignment gives the fiber high strength-to-volume ratio (making it strong for its size).
Quantum	In physics, a quantum is the minimum amount of any physical entity involved in an interaction. Behind this, one finds the fundamental notion that a physical property may be 'quantized,' referred to as 'the hypothesis of quantization'. This means that the magnitude can take on only certain discrete values.

CHAPTER QUIZ: KEY TERMS, PEOPLE, PLACES, CONCEPTS

1. The _________ is a subatomic particle with a negative elementary electric charge. _________s belong to the first generation of the lepton particle family, and are generally thought to be elementary particles because they have no known components or substructure. The _________ has a mass that is approximately 1/1836 that of the proton.

a. Compton wavelength
b. Electron
c. Bohr model
d. Bohr magneton

2. _________, also called quantum vacuum _________, is the lowest possible energy that a quantum mechanical physical system may have; it is the energy of its ground state. All quantum mechanical systems undergo fluctuations even in their ground state and have an associated _________, a consequence of their wave-like nature. The uncertainty principle requires every physical system to have a _________ greater than the minimum of its classical potential well.

a. Background field method
b. Zero-point energy
c. Berezin integral
d. Beta function

3. . In chemistry, a _________ is a mathematical function describing the wave-like behavior of an electron in a molecule. This function can be used to calculate chemical and physical properties such as the probability of finding an electron in any specific region. The term orbital was introduced by Robert S. Mulliken in 1932 as an abbreviation for one-electron orbital wave function.

a. Bond hardening
b. Bond softening
c. Molecular orbital

4. _________ is the measure of the probability of an electron being present at a specific location.

In molecules, regions of _________ are usually found around the atom, and its bonds. In de-localized or conjugated systems, such as phenol, benzene and compounds such as hemoglobin and chlorophyll, the _________ covers an entire region, i.e., in benzene they are found above and below the planar ring.

a. Electron density
b. Compton scattering
c. Bohr model
d. Bohr magneton

5. _________ fiber, alternatively graphite fiber, _________ graphite or CF, is a material consisting of fibers about 5-10 μm in diameter and composed mostly of _________ atoms. The _________ atoms are bonded together in crystals that are more or less aligned parallel to the long axis of the fiber. The crystal alignment gives the fiber high strength-to-volume ratio (making it strong for its size).

a. Carbon
b. Benzotriyne
c. Bilayer graphene
d. Carbide-derived carbon

ANSWER KEY
6. Quantum Mechanics and Molecular Structure

1. b
2. b
3. c
4. a
5. a

---

7. Bonding in Organic Molecules

CHAPTER OUTLINE: KEY TERMS, PEOPLE, PLACES, CONCEPTS

- Organic chemistry
- Functional group
- Hydrocarbon
- Alkane
- Atom
- Carbon
- Hydrogen
- Hydrogen atom
- Cycloalkane
- Naphtha
- Cyclohexane
- Distortion
- Molecule
- Chirality
- Isomer
- Polarization
- Alkene
- Alkyne
- Radical
- Unsaturated hydrocarbon
- Combustion

7. Bonding in Organic Molecules

CHAPTER OUTLINE: KEY TERMS, PEOPLE, PLACES, CONCEPTS

- Electron
- Valence electron
- Cracking
- Polyene
- Petroleum
- Aromatic hydrocarbon
- Hydrodealkylation
- Alkyl
- Buckminsterfullerene
- Fullerene
- Alcohol
- Halide
- Atmosphere
- Halogen
- Organic compound
- Carbon monoxide
- Methanol
- Water vapor
- Phenol
- Primary alcohol
- Methane

7. Bonding in Organic Molecules

CHAPTER OUTLINE: KEY TERMS, PEOPLE, PLACES, CONCEPTS

	Condensation
	Condensation reaction
	Epoxide
	Ether
	Oxygen
	Aldehyde
	Ketone
	Carboxylic acid
	Hydrogenation
	Triglyceride
	Absorption
	Glycerol
	Amino acid
	Amide
	Amine
	Insecticide
	Pesticide
	Herbicide

7. Bonding in Organic Molecules

Organic chemistry	Organic chemistry is a chemistry subdiscipline involving the scientific study of the structure, properties, and reactions of organic compounds and organic materials, i.e., matter in its various forms that contain carbon atoms. Study of structure includes using spectroscopy and other physical and chemical methods to determine the chemical composition and constitution of organic compounds and materials. Study of properties includes both physical properties and chemical properties, and uses similar methods as well as methods to evaluate chemical reactivity, with the aim to understand the behavior of the organic matter in its pure form (when possible), but also in solutions, mixtures, and fabricated forms.
Functional group	In organic chemistry, functional groups are lexicon-specific groups of atoms or bonds within molecules that are responsible for the characteristic chemical reactions of those molecules. The same functional group will undergo the same or similar chemical reaction(s) regardless of the size of the molecule it is a part of. However, its relative reactivity can be modified by nearby functional groups.
Hydrocarbon	In organic chemistry, a hydrocarbon is an organic compound consisting entirely of hydrogen and carbon. Hydrocarbons from which one hydrogen atom has been removed are functional groups, called hydrocarbyls. Aromatic hydrocarbons (arenes), alkanes, alkenes, cycloalkanes and alkyne-based compounds are different types of hydrocarbons.
Alkane	In organic chemistry, an alkane, or paraffin, is a saturated hydrocarbon. Alkanes consist only of hydrogen and carbon atoms, all bonds are single bonds, and the carbon atoms are not joined in cyclic structures but instead form an open chain. They have the general chemical formula C_nH_{2n+2}.
Atom	The atom is a basic unit of matter that consists of a dense central nucleus surrounded by a cloud of negatively charged electrons. The atomic nucleus contains a mix of positively charged protons and electrically neutral neutrons, which means 'uncuttable' or 'the smallest indivisible particle of matter'. Although the Indian and Greek concepts of the atom were based purely on philosophy, modern science has retained the name coined by Democritus.
Carbon	Carbon fiber, alternatively graphite fiber, carbon graphite or CF, is a material consisting of fibers about 5-10 µm in diameter and composed mostly of carbon atoms. The carbon atoms are bonded together in crystals that are more or less aligned parallel to the long axis of the fiber. The crystal alignment gives the fiber high strength-to-volume ratio (making it strong for its size).
Hydrogen	Hydrogen is a chemical element with chemical symbol H and atomic number 1. With an atomic weight of 1.00794 u, hydrogen is the lightest element and its monatomic form (H) is the most abundant chemical substance, constituting roughly 75% of the Universe's baryonic mass. Non-remnant stars are mainly composed of hydrogen in its plasma state.

7. Bonding in Organic Molecules

Hydrogen atom

A hydrogen atom is an atom of the chemical element hydrogen. The electrically neutral atom contains a single positively charged proton and a single negatively charged electron bound to the nucleus by the Coulomb force. Atomic hydrogen constitutes about 75% of the elemental mass of the universe.

Cycloalkane

Cycloalkanes are types of hydrocarbon compounds that have one or more rings of carbon atoms in the chemical structure of their molecules. Alkanes are types of organic hydrocarbon compounds that have only single chemical bonds in their chemical structure. Cycloalkanes consist of only carbon (C) and hydrogen (H) atoms and are saturated because there are no multiple C-C bonds to hydrogenate (add more hydrogen to).

Naphtha

Naphtha normally refers to a number of flammable liquid mixtures of hydrocarbons, i.e. a component of natural gas condensate or a distillation product from petroleum, coal tar, or peat boiling in a certain range and containing certain hydrocarbons. It is a broad term covering among the lightest and most volatile fractions of the liquid hydrocarbons in petroleum. Naphtha is a colorless to reddish-brown volatile aromatic liquid, very similar to gasoline.

Cyclohexane

Cyclohexane is a cycloalkane with the molecular formula C_6H_{12}. Cyclohexane is used as a nonpolar solvent for the chemical industry, and also as a raw material for the industrial production of adipic acid and caprolactam, both of which being intermediates used in the production of nylon. On an industrial scale, cyclohexane is produced by reacting benzene with hydrogen.

Distortion

Distortion is the alteration of the original shape (or other characteristic) of something, such as an object, image, sound or waveform. Distortion is usually unwanted, and so engineers strive to eliminate distortion, or minimize it. In some situations, however, distortion may be desirable.

Molecule

A molecule is an electrically neutral group of two or more atoms held together by chemical bonds. Molecules are distinguished from ions by their lack of electrical charge. However, in quantum physics, organic chemistry, and biochemistry, the term molecule is often used less strictly, also being applied to polyatomic ions.

Chirality

The term chiral describes an object, especially a molecule, which has or produces a non-superimposeable mirror image of itself. In chemistry, such a molecule is called an enantiomer or is said to exhibit chirality or enantiomerism. The term 'chiral' comes from the Greek word for the human hand, which itself exhibits such non-superimposeability of the left hand precisely over the right.

Isomer

In chemistry, isomers (; from Greek ?s?µe???, isomerès; isos = 'equal', méros = 'part') are molecules with the same molecular formula but different chemical structures. That is, isomers contain the same number of atoms of each element, but have different arrangements of their atoms in space.

Polarization	Polarization is a property of waves that can oscillate with more than one orientation. Electromagnetic waves, such as light, and gravitational waves exhibit polarization; sound waves in a gas or liquid do not have polarization because the medium vibrates only along the direction in which the waves are travelling. By convention, the polarization of light is described by specifying the orientation of the wave's electric field at a point in space over one period of the oscillation.
Alkene	In organic chemistry, an alkene, olefin, or olefine is an unsaturated chemical compound containing at least one carbon-carbon double bond. The simplest acyclic alkenes, with only one double bond and no other functional groups, known as mono-enes, form a homologous series of hydrocarbons with the general formula C_nH_{2n}. They have two hydrogen atoms less than the corresponding alkane (with the same number of carbon atoms).
Alkyne	In organic chemistry, an alkyne is an unsaturated hydrocarbon which has at least one carbon--carbon triple bond between two carbon atoms. The simplest acyclic alkynes with only one triple bond and no other functional groups form a homologous series with the general chemical formula C_nH_{2n-2}. Alkynes are traditionally known as acetylenes, although the name acetylene also refers specifically to C_2H_2, known formally as ethyne using IUPAC nomenclature.
Radical	In chemistry, a radical is an atom, molecule, or ion that has unpaired valence electrons or an open electron shell, and therefore may be seen as having one or more 'dangling' covalent bonds. With some exceptions, these 'dangling' bonds make free radicals highly chemically reactive towards other substances, or even towards themselves: their molecules will often spontaneously dimerize or polymerize if they come in contact with each other. Most radicals are reasonably stable only at very low concentrations in inert media or in vacuum.
Unsaturated hydrocarbon	Unsaturated hydrocarbons are hydrocarbons that have double or triple covalent bonds between adjacent carbon atoms. Those with at least one carbon to carbon double bond are called alkenes and those with at least one carbon to carbon triple bond are called alkynes. The position of the double or triple bond is shown by a number written either at the start of the name, or just before the -ene or -yne suffix (e.g. pent-2-ene and 2-butyne).
Combustion	Combustion or burning is the sequence of exothermic chemical reactions between a fuel and an oxidant accompanied by the production of heat and conversion of chemical species. The release of heat can produce light in the form of either glowing or a flame. In a complete combustion reaction, a compound reacts with an oxidizing element, such as oxygen or fluorine, and the products are compounds of each element in the fuel with the oxidizing element.
Electron	The electron is a subatomic particle with a negative elementary electric charge.

Electrons belong to the first generation of the lepton particle family, and are generally thought to be elementary particles because they have no known components or substructure. The electron has a mass that is approximately 1/1836 that of the proton.

Valence electron

In chemistry, a valence electron is an electron that is associated with an atom, and that can participate in the formation of a chemical bond; in a single covalent bond, both atoms in the bond contribute one valence electron in order to form a shared pair. The presence of valence electrons can determine the element's chemical properties and whether it may bond with other elements: For a main group element, a valence electron can only be in the outermost electron shell. In a transition metal, a valence electron can also be in an inner shell.

Cracking

In petroleum geology and chemistry, cracking is the process whereby complex organic molecules such as kerogens or heavy hydrocarbons are broken down into simpler molecules such as light hydrocarbons, by the breaking of carbon-carbon bonds in the precursors. The rate of cracking and the end products are strongly dependent on the temperature and presence of catalysts. Cracking is the breakdown of a large alkane into smaller, more useful alkanes and alkenes.

Polyene

Polyenes are poly-unsaturated organic compounds that contain one or more sequences of alternating double and single carbon-carbon bonds. These double carbon-carbon bonds interact in a process known as conjugation, which results in an overall lower energy state of the molecule.

Organic compounds with two carbon-carbon double bonds are dienes; those with three such double bonds are trienes; those with four are tetraenes, etc.

Petroleum

Petroleum (L. petroleum, from Greek: p?t?a + Latin: oleum (oil)) is a naturally occurring, smelly, yellow-to-black liquid consisting of a complex mixture of hydrocarbons of various molecular weights and other liquid organic compounds, that are found in geologic formations beneath the Earth's surface. The name Petroleum covers both naturally occurring unprocessed crude oils and petroleum products that are made up of refined crude oil. A fossil fuel, it is formed when large quantities of dead organisms, usually zooplankton and algae, are buried underneath sedimentary rock and undergo intense heat and pressure.

Aromatic hydrocarbon

An aromatic hydrocarbon or arene is a hydrocarbon with alternating double and single bonds between carbon atoms forming rings. The term 'aromatic' was assigned before the physical mechanism determining aromaticity was discovered, and was derived from the fact that many of the compounds have a sweet scent. The configuration of six carbon atoms in aromatic compounds is known as a benzene ring, after the simplest possible such hydrocarbon, benzene.

Hydrodealkylation

Hydrodealkylation is a chemical reaction that often involves reacting an aromatic hydrocarbon, such as toluene, in the presence of hydrogen gas to form a simpler aromatic hydrocarbon devoid of functional groups. An example is the conversion of 1,2,4-trimethylbenzene to xylene.

Alkyl	In chemistry, an alkyl substituent is an alkane missing one hydrogen. An acyclic alkyl has the general formula C_nH_{2n+1}. A cycloalkyl is derived from a cycloalkane by removal of a hydrogen atom from a ring and has the general formula C_nH_{2n-1}.
Buckminsterfullerene	Buckminsterfullerene is a spherical fullerene molecule with the formula C_{60}. It has a cage-like fused -ring structure (truncated icosahedron) which resembles a soccer ball, made of twenty hexagons and twelve pentagons, with a carbon atom at each vertex of each polygon and a bond along each polygon edge. It was first generated in 1985 by Harold Kroto, James R. Heath, Sean O'Brien, Robert Curl, and Richard Smalley at Rice University.
Fullerene	A fullerene is any molecule composed entirely of carbon, in the form of a hollow sphere, ellipsoid, tube, and many other shapes. Spherical fullerenes are also called buckyballs, and they resemble the balls used in football (soccer). Cylindrical ones are called carbon nanotubes or buckytubes.
Alcohol	In chemistry, an alcohol is an organic compound in which the hydroxyl functional group is bound to a carbon atom. In particular, this carbon center should be saturated, having single bonds to three other atoms. An important class of alcohols are the simple acyclic alcohols, the general formula for which is $C_nH_{2n+1}OH$. Of those, ethanol (C_2H_5OH) is the type of alcohol found in alcoholic beverages, and in common speech the word alcohol refers specifically to ethanol.
Halide	A halide is a binary compound, of which one part is a halogen atom and the other part is an element or radical that is less electronegative than the halogen, to make a fluoride, chloride, bromide, iodide, or astatide compound. Many salts are halides. All Group 1 metals form halides which are white solids at room temperature.
Atmosphere	The standard atmosphere is an international reference pressure defined as 101325 Pa and used as a unit of pressure.
Halogen	The halogens or halogen elements are a group in the periodic table consisting of five chemically related elements, fluorine, chlorine (Cl), bromine (Br), iodine (I), and astatine (At). The artificially created element 117 (ununseptium) may also be a halogen. In the modern IUPAC nomenclature, this group is known as group 17.
Organic compound	An organic compound is any member of a large class of gaseous, liquid, or solid chemical compounds whose molecules contain carbon. For historical reasons discussed below, a few types of carbon-containing compounds such as carbides, carbonates, simple oxides of carbon (such as CO and CO_2), and cyanides are considered inorganic. The distinction between 'organic' and 'inorganic' carbon compounds, while 'useful in organizing the vast subject of chemistry...

7. Bonding in Organic Molecules

CHAPTER HIGHLIGHTS & NOTES: KEY TERMS, PEOPLE, PLACES, CONCEPTS

Carbon monoxide	Carbon monoxide is a colorless, odorless, and tasteless gas that is slightly less dense than air. It is toxic to humans and animals when encountered in higher concentrations, although it is also produced in normal animal metabolism in low quantities, and is thought to have some normal biological functions. In the atmosphere, it is spatially variable, short lived, having a role in the formation of ground-level ozone.
Methanol	Methanol, also known as methyl alcohol, wood alcohol, wood naphtha or wood spirits, is a chemical with the formula CH_3OH . Methanol acquired the name 'wood alcohol' because it was once produced chiefly as a byproduct of the destructive distillation of wood. Modern methanol is produced in a catalytic industrial process directly from carbon monoxide, carbon dioxide, and hydrogen.
Water vapor	Water vapor or aqueous vapor is the gas phase of water. It is one state of water within the hydrosphere. Water vapor can be produced from the evaporation or boiling of liquid water or from the sublimation of ice.
Phenol	Phenol -- also known as carbolic acid -- is an aromatic organic compound with the molecular formula C_6H_5OH. It is a white crystalline solid that is volatile. The molecule consists of a phenyl group ($-C_6H_5$) bonded to a hydroxyl group (-OH). It is mildly acidic, but requires careful handling due to its propensity to cause burns.
Primary alcohol	A primary alcohol is an alcohol which has the hydroxyl group connected to a primary carbon atom. It can also be defined as a molecule containing a "$-CH_2OH$" group. In contrast, a secondary alcohol has a formula "-CHROH" and a tertiary alcohol has a formula "$-CR_2OH$", where "R" indicates a carbon-containing group.
Methane	Methane is a chemical compound with the chemical formula CH4 (one atom of carbon and four atoms of hydrogen). It is the simplest alkane and the main component of natural gas. The relative abundance of methane makes it an attractive fuel.
Condensation	Condensation is the change of the physical state of matter from gas phase into liquid phase, and is the reverse of vaporization. It can also be defined as the change in the state of water vapor to water/any liquid when in contact with any surface. When the transition happens from the gaseous phase into the solid phase directly, the change is called deposition.
Condensation reaction	A condensation reaction, also commonly referred to as dehydration synthesis, is a chemical reaction in which two molecules or moieties combine to form a larger molecule, together with the loss of a small molecule. Possible small molecules lost are water, hydrogen chloride, methanol, or acetic acid.

Epoxide

An epoxide is a cyclic ether with three ring atoms. This ring approximately defines an equilateral triangle, which makes it highly strained. The strained ring makes epoxides more reactive than other ethers.

Ether

Ethers are a class of organic compounds that contain an ether group -- an oxygen atom connected to two alkyl or aryl groups -- of general formula R-O-R'. A typical example is the solvent and anesthetic diethyl ether, commonly referred to simply as 'ether' (CH_3-CH_2-O-CH_2-CH_3). Ethers are common in organic chemistry and pervasive in biochemistry, as they are common linkages in carbohydrates and lignin.

Oxygen

Oxygen is a chemical element with symbol O and atomic number 8. It is a member of the chalcogen group on the periodic table and is a highly reactive nonmetallic element and oxidizing agent that readily forms compounds (notably oxides) with most elements. By mass, oxygen is the third-most abundant element in the universe, after hydrogen and helium At STP, two atoms of the element bind to form dioxygen, a diatomic gas that is colorless, odorless, and tasteless; with the formula O2.

Many major classes of organic molecules in living organisms, such as proteins, nucleic acids, carbohydrates, and fats, contain oxygen, as do the major inorganic compounds that are constituents of animal shells, teeth, and bone.

Aldehyde

An aldehyde is an organic compound containing a formyl group. This functional group, with the structure R-CHO, consists of a carbonyl center (a carbon double bonded to oxygen) bonded to hydrogen and an R group, which is any generic alkyl or side chain. The group without R is called the aldehyde group or formyl group.

Ketone

In chemistry, a ketone is an organic compound with the structure RC(=O)R', where R and R' can be a variety of carbon-containing substituents. Ketones feature a carbonyl group (C=O) bonded to two other carbon atoms. Many ketones are known and many are of great importance in industry and in biology.

Carboxylic acid

A carboxylic acid is an organic acid characterized by the presence of at least one carboxyl group. The general formula of a carboxylic acid is R-COOH, where R is some monovalent functional group. A carboxyl group (or carboxy) is a functional group consisting of a carbonyl (RR'C=O) and a hydroxyl (R-O-H), which has the formula -C(=O)OH, usually written as -COOH or -CO_2H.

Carboxylic acids are Brønsted-Lowry acids because they are proton (H^+) donors.

Hydrogenation

Hydrogenation - to treat with hydrogen - is a chemical reaction between molecular hydrogen and another compound or element, usually in the presence of a catalyst. The process is commonly employed to reduce or saturate organic compounds.

7. Bonding in Organic Molecules

CHAPTER HIGHLIGHTS & NOTES: KEY TERMS, PEOPLE, PLACES, CONCEPTS

Triglyceride	A triglyceride is an ester derived from glycerol and three fatty acids. Triglycerides are a blood lipid that help enable the bidirectional transference of adipose fat and blood glucose from the liver. There are many triglycerides: depending on the oil source, some are highly unsaturated, some less so.
Absorption	In chemistry, absorption is a physical or chemical phenomenon or a process in which atoms, molecules, or ions enter some bulk phase - gas, liquid, or solid material. This is a different process from adsorption, since molecules undergoing absorption are taken up by the volume, not by the surface (as in the case for adsorption). A more general term is sorption, which covers absorption, adsorption, and ion exchange.
Glycerol	Glycerol is a simple polyol (sugar alcohol) compound. It is a colorless, odorless, viscous liquid that is widely used in pharmaceutical formulations. Glycerol has three hydroxyl groups that are responsible for its solubility in water and its hygroscopic nature.
Amino acid	Amino acids are biologically important organic compounds made from amine ($-NH_2$) and carboxylic acid (-COOH) functional groups, along with a side-chain specific to each amino acid. The key elements of an amino acid are carbon, hydrogen, oxygen, and nitrogen, though other elements are found in the side-chains of certain amino acids. About 500 amino acids are known and can be classified in many ways.
Amide	An amide, also known as an '-acid amide', is a compound with the functional group $R_nE_xNR'_2$ (R and R' refer to H or organic groups). Most common are 'organic amides' (n = 1, E = C, x = 1), but many other important types of amides are known including phosphor amides (n = 2, E = P, x = 1 and many related formulas) and sulfonamides (E = S, x= 2). The term amide refers both to classes of compounds and to the functional group ($R_nE(O)_xNR'_2$) within those compounds.
Amine	Amines are organic compounds and functional groups that contain a basic nitrogen atom with a lone pair. Amines are derivatives of ammonia, wherein one or more hydrogen atoms have been replaced by a substituent such as an alkyl or aryl group. Important amines include amino acids, biogenic amines, trimethylamine, and aniline; see Category:Amines for a list of amines.
Insecticide	An insecticide is a chemical used against insects. They include ovicides and larvicides used against the eggs and larvae of insects, respectively. Insecticides are used in agriculture, medicine, industry, and general home use.
Pesticide	Pesticides are substances meant for preventing, destroying or mitigating any pest. They are a class of biocide. The most common use of pesticides is as plant protection products (also known as crop protection products), which in general protect plants from damaging influences such as weeds, diseases or insects.
Herbicide	Herbicides, also commonly known as weedkillers, are pesticides used to kill unwanted plants.

7. Bonding in Organic Molecules

CHAPTER HIGHLIGHTS & NOTES: KEY TERMS, PEOPLE, PLACES, CONCEPTS

Selective herbicides kill specific targets, while leaving the desired crop relatively unharmed. Some of these act by interfering with the growth of the weed and are often synthetic mimics of natural plant hormones.

CHAPTER QUIZ: KEY TERMS, PEOPLE, PLACES, CONCEPTS

1. In organic chemistry, an _________, olefin, or olefine is an unsaturated chemical compound containing at least one carbon-carbon double bond. The simplest acyclic _________s, with only one double bond and no other functional groups, known as mono-enes, form a homologous series of hydrocarbons with the general formula C_nH_{2n}. They have two hydrogen atoms less than the corresponding alkane (with the same number of carbon atoms).

   a. Alkene
   b. Chitobiose
   c. 1-Deoxynojirimycin
   d. Framycetin

2. The term chiral describes an object, especially a molecule, which has or produces a non-superimposeable mirror image of itself. In chemistry, such a molecule is called an enantiomer or is said to exhibit _________ or enantiomerism. The term 'chiral' comes from the Greek word for the human hand, which itself exhibits such non-superimposeability of the left hand precisely over the right.

   a. Chirality
   b. Daylight
   c. Lidar
   d. Tropospheric scatter

3. _________ is the alteration of the original shape (or other characteristic) of something, such as an object, image, sound or waveform. _________ is usually unwanted, and so engineers strive to eliminate _________, or minimize it. In some situations, however, _________ may be desirable.

   a. Distortion
   b. Bandwidth-limited pulse
   c. Beam diameter
   d. Beam divergence

4. . _________s are biologically important organic compounds made from amine ($-NH_2$) and carboxylic acid ($-COOH$) functional groups, along with a side-chain specific to each _________. The key elements of an _________ are carbon, hydrogen, oxygen, and nitrogen, though other elements are found in the side-chains of certain _________s. About 500 _________s are known and can be classified in many ways.

a. Zwitterion
b. Carbanion
c. Bifluoride
d. Amino acid

5. An _________ is a chemical used against insects. They include ovicides and larvicides used against the eggs and larvae of insects, respectively. _________s are used in agriculture, medicine, industry, and general home use.

a. Biocide
b. Insecticide
c. Herbicide
d. Background noise

ANSWER KEY
7. Bonding in Organic Molecules

1. a
2. a
3. a
4. d
5. b

---

8. Bonding in Transition Metal Compounds and Coordination Complexes

CHAPTER OUTLINE: KEY TERMS, PEOPLE, PLACES, CONCEPTS

______ Lanthanide contraction

______ Periodic table

______ Period

______ Enthalpy

______ Oxidation state

______ Ligand

______ Electron

______ Molecule

______ Hydroxide

______ Coordination complex

______ Atom

______ Coordination sphere

______ Substitution reaction

______ Amino acid

______ Heme

______ Electron configuration

______ Electron pair

______ Energy level

______ Magnetic susceptibility

______ Spectrochemical series

______ Molecular orbital

8. Bonding in Transition Metal Compounds and Coordination Complexes

CHAPTER OUTLINE: KEY TERMS, PEOPLE, PLACES, CONCEPTS

______________	Wave function
______________	Metalloid
______________	Atomic orbital
______________	Electron density
______________	Donor

CHAPTER HIGHLIGHTS & NOTES: KEY TERMS, PEOPLE, PLACES, CONCEPTS

Lanthanide contraction	Lanthanide contraction is a term used in chemistry to describe the greater than expected decrease in ionic radii of the elements in the lanthanide series from atomic number 57, lanthanum, to 71, lutetium, which results in smaller than otherwise expected ionic radii for the subsequent elements starting with 72, hafnium. The term was coined by the Norwegian geochemist Victor Goldschmidt in his series 'Geochemische Verteilungsgesetze Der Elemente'.
Periodic table	The periodic table is a tabular arrangement of the chemical elements, organized on the basis of their atomic numbers, electron configurations, and recurring chemical properties. Elements are presented in order of increasing atomic number (the number of protons in the nucleus). The standard form of the table consists of a grid of elements laid out in 18 columns and 7 rows, with a double row of elements below that.
Period	In the periodic table of the elements, elements are arranged in a series of rows (or periods) so that those with similar properties appear in a column. Elements of the same period have the same number of electron shells; with each group across a period, the elements have one more proton and electron and become less metallic. This arrangement reflects the periodic recurrence of similar properties as the atomic number increases.
Enthalpy	Enthalpy is a measure of the total energy of a thermodynamic system. It includes the system's internal energy and thermodynamic potential (a state function), as well as its volume and pressure (the energy required to 'make room for it' by displacing its environment, which is an extensive quantity). The unit of measurement for enthalpy in the International System of Units (SI) is the joule, but other historical, conventional units are still in use, such as the British thermal unit and the calorie.

Oxidation state	The oxidation state, often called the oxidation number, is an indicator of the degree of oxidation of an atom in a chemical compound. The formal oxidation state is the hypothetical charge that an atom would have if all bonds to atoms of different elements were 100% ionic. Oxidation states are typically represented by integers, which can be positive, negative, or zero.
Ligand	In coordination chemistry, a ligand is an ion or molecule that binds to a central metal atom to form a coordination complex. The bonding between metal and ligand generally involves formal donation of one or more of the ligand's electron pairs. The nature of metal-ligand bonding can range from covalent to ionic.
Electron	The electron is a subatomic particle with a negative elementary electric charge. Electrons belong to the first generation of the lepton particle family, and are generally thought to be elementary particles because they have no known components or substructure. The electron has a mass that is approximately 1/1836 that of the proton.
Molecule	A molecule is an electrically neutral group of two or more atoms held together by chemical bonds. Molecules are distinguished from ions by their lack of electrical charge. However, in quantum physics, organic chemistry, and biochemistry, the term molecule is often used less strictly, also being applied to polyatomic ions.
Hydroxide	Hydroxide is a diatomic anion with chemical formula OH^-. It consists of an oxygen and a hydrogen atom held together by a covalent bond, and carries a negative electric charge. It is an important but usually minor constituent of water.
Coordination complex	In chemistry, a coordination complex or metal complex, consists of an atom or ion, and a surrounding array of bound molecules or anions, that are in turn known as ligands or complexing agents. Many metal-containing compounds (especially transition metals) consist of coordination complexes.
Atom	The atom is a basic unit of matter that consists of a dense central nucleus surrounded by a cloud of negatively charged electrons. The atomic nucleus contains a mix of positively charged protons and electrically neutral neutrons, which means 'uncuttable' or 'the smallest indivisible particle of matter'. Although the Indian and Greek concepts of the atom were based purely on philosophy, modern science has retained the name coined by Democritus.
Coordination sphere	In coordination chemistry, the coordination sphere refers to a central atom or ion and an array of molecules or anions, the ligands, around. Molecules that are attached noncovalently to the ligands are called the second coordination sphere.
Substitution reaction	Substitution reaction is also known as single displacement reaction and single replacement reaction. In a substitution reaction, a functional group in a particular chemical compound is replaced by another group.

8. Bonding in Transition Metal Compounds and Coordination Complexes

CHAPTER HIGHLIGHTS & NOTES: KEY TERMS, PEOPLE, PLACES, CONCEPTS

Amino acid	Amino acids are biologically important organic compounds made from amine (-NH_2) and carboxylic acid (-COOH) functional groups, along with a side-chain specific to each amino acid. The key elements of an amino acid are carbon, hydrogen, oxygen, and nitrogen, though other elements are found in the side-chains of certain amino acids. About 500 amino acids are known and can be classified in many ways.
Heme	A haem or heme is a chemical compound of a type known as a prosthetic group consisting of an Fe^{2+} (ferrous) ion contained in the centre of a large heterocyclic organic ring called a porphyrin, made up of four pyrrolic groups joined together by methine bridges. Not all porphyrins contain iron, but a substantial fraction of porphyrin-containing metalloproteins have heme as their prosthetic group; these are known as hemoproteins. Hemes are most commonly recognized in their presence as components of hemoglobin, the red pigment in blood, but they are also components of a number of other hemo-proteins such as myoglobin, cytochrome, endothelial nitric oxide synthase, catalase, etc.
Electron configuration	In atomic physics and quantum chemistry, the electron configuration is the distribution of electrons of an atom or molecule in atomic or molecular orbitals. For example, the electron configuration of the neon atom is $1s^2\ 2s^2\ 2p^6$. Electronic configurations describe electrons as each moving independently in an orbital, in an average field created by all other orbitals.
Electron pair	In chemistry, an electron pair consists of two electrons that occupy the same orbital but have opposite spins. The electron pair concept was introduced in a 1916 paper of Gilbert N. Lewis. Because electrons are fermions, the Pauli exclusion principle forbids these particles from having exactly the same quantum numbers.
Energy level	A quantum mechanical system or particle that is bound--that is, confined spatially--can only take on certain discrete values of energy. This contrasts with classical particles, which can have any energy. These discrete values are called energy levels.
Magnetic susceptibility	In electromagnetism, the magnetic susceptibility χ is a dimensionless proportionality constant that indicates the degree of magnetization of a material in response to an applied magnetic field. A related term is magnetizability, the proportion between magnetic moment and magnetic flux density. A closely related parameter is the permeability, which expresses the total magnetization of material and volume.
Spectrochemical series	A spectrochemical series is a list of ligands ordered on ligand strength and a list of metal ions based on oxidation number, group and its identity.

Molecular orbital

In chemistry, a molecular orbital is a mathematical function describing the wave-like behavior of an electron in a molecule. This function can be used to calculate chemical and physical properties such as the probability of finding an electron in any specific region. The term orbital was introduced by Robert S. Mulliken in 1932 as an abbreviation for one-electron orbital wave function.

Wave function

A wave function or wavefunction in quantum mechanics describes the quantum state of a particle and how it behaves. Typically, its values are complex numbers and, for a single particle, it is a function of space and time. The Schrödinger equation describes how the wave function evolves over time.

Metalloid

A metalloid is a chemical element that has properties that are in between or a mixture of those of metals and nonmetals and is consequently difficult to classify unambiguously as either a metal or a nonmetal. There is no standard definition of a metalloid, nor is there agreement as to which elements are appropriately classified as such. Despite this lack of specificity the term remains in use in chemistry literature.

Atomic orbital

An atomic orbital is a mathematical function that describes the wave-like behavior of either one electron or a pair of electrons in an atom. This function can be used to calculate the probability of finding any electron of an atom in any specific region around the atom's nucleus. The term may also refer to the physical region or space where the electron can be calculated to be present, as defined by the particular mathematical form of the orbital.

Electron density

Electron density is the measure of the probability of an electron being present at a specific location.

In molecules, regions of electron density are usually found around the atom, and its bonds. In de-localized or conjugated systems, such as phenol, benzene and compounds such as hemoglobin and chlorophyll, the electron density covers an entire region, i.e., in benzene they are found above and below the planar ring.

Donor

In semiconductor physics, a donor is a dopant atom that, when added to a semiconductor, can form a n-type region.

For example, when silicon, having four valence electrons, needs to be doped as an n-type semiconductor, elements from group V like phosphorus (P) or arsenic (As) can be used because they have five valence electrons. A dopant with five valence electrons is also called a pentavalent impurity.

8. Bonding in Transition Metal Compounds and Coordination Complexes

1. In the periodic table of the elements, elements are arranged in a series of rows (or _________s) so that those with similar properties appear in a column. Elements of the same _________ have the same number of electron shells; with each group across a _________, the elements have one more proton and electron and become less metallic. This arrangement reflects the periodic recurrence of similar properties as the atomic number increases.

   a. Chemical Galaxy
   b. Period
   c. History of the periodic table
   d. Metalloid

2. _________ is a term used in chemistry to describe the greater than expected decrease in ionic radii of the elements in the lanthanide series from atomic number 57, lanthanum, to 71, lutetium, which results in smaller than otherwise expected ionic radii for the subsequent elements starting with 72, hafnium. The term was coined by the Norwegian geochemist Victor Goldschmidt in his series 'Geochemische Verteilungsgesetze Der Elemente'.

   a. Cerium anomaly
   b. Bexlosteride
   c. Lanthanide contraction
   d. Finasteride

3. _________s are biologically important organic compounds made from amine ($-NH_2$) and carboxylic acid (-COOH) functional groups, along with a side-chain specific to each _________. The key elements of an _________ are carbon, hydrogen, oxygen, and nitrogen, though other elements are found in the side-chains of certain _________s. About 500 _________s are known and can be classified in many ways.

   a. Zwitterion
   b. Carbanion
   c. Amino acid
   d. Bisulfide

4. In semiconductor physics, a _________ is a dopant atom that, when added to a semiconductor, can form a n-type region.

   For example, when silicon, having four valence electrons, needs to be doped as an n-type semiconductor, elements from group V like phosphorus (P) or arsenic (As) can be used because they have five valence electrons. A dopant with five valence electrons is also called a pentavalent impurity.

   a. Chalcogel
   b. Donor
   c. Ceration
   d. Congelation

5. . In chemistry, a _________ or metal complex, consists of an atom or ion, and a surrounding array of bound molecules or anions, that are in turn known as ligands or complexing agents.

Many metal-containing compounds (especially transition metals) consist of coordination complexes.

a. 18-Electron rule
b. Coordination complex
c. Bioorganometallic chemistry
d. Calcareous sinter

ANSWER KEY

8. Bonding in Transition Metal Compounds and Coordination Complexes

---

1. b
2. c
3. c
4. b
5. b

---

9. The Gaseous State

CHAPTER OUTLINE: KEY TERMS, PEOPLE, PLACES, CONCEPTS

_______________ Statistical mechanics

_______________ Molecule

_______________ Volume

_______________ Effusion

_______________ Degree

_______________ Absolute zero

_______________ Entropy

_______________ Ideal gas

_______________ Gas laws

_______________ Ideal gas law

_______________ Mole

_______________ Partial pressure

_______________ Component

_______________ Total pressure

_______________ Mole fraction

_______________ Kinetic theory

_______________ Equilibrium constant

_______________ Molecular beam

_______________ Period

_______________ Intermolecular force

_______________ Thermal equilibrium

9. The Gaseous State

CHAPTER OUTLINE: KEY TERMS, PEOPLE, PLACES, CONCEPTS

______	Energy level
______	Compressibility
______	Compressibility factor
______	Real gas
______	Lennard-Jones potential
______	Atom
______	Gaseous diffusion
______	Diffusion
______	Mean free path
______	Nuclear chemistry
______	Displacement
______	Ammonium perchlorate

CHAPTER HIGHLIGHTS & NOTES: KEY TERMS, PEOPLE, PLACES, CONCEPTS

Statistical mechanics

Statistical mechanics or statistical thermodynamics is a branch of physics that applies probability theory, which contains mathematical tools for dealing with large populations, to the study of the thermodynamic behavior of systems composed of a large number of particles. Statistical mechanics provides a framework for relating the microscopic properties of individual atoms and molecules to the macroscopic bulk properties of materials that can be observed in everyday life, thereby explaining thermodynamics as a result of the classical- and quantum-mechanical descriptions of statistics and mechanics at the microscopic level.

Statistical mechanics provides a molecular-level interpretation of macroscopic thermodynamic quantities such as work, heat, free energy, and entropy.

Molecule

A molecule is an electrically neutral group of two or more atoms held together by chemical bonds. Molecules are distinguished from ions by their lack of electrical charge. However, in quantum physics, organic chemistry, and biochemistry, the term molecule is often used less strictly, also being applied to polyatomic ions.

Volume

In thermodynamics, the volume of a system is an important extensive parameter for describing its thermodynamic state. The specific volume, an intensive property, is the system's volume per unit of mass. Volume is a function of state and is interdependent with other thermodynamic properties such as pressure and temperature.

Effusion

Effusion is the process in which a gas escapes through a small hole. This occurs if the diameter of the hole is considerably smaller than the mean free path of the molecules. According to Graham's law, the rate at which gases effuse (i.e., how many molecules pass through the hole per second) is dependent on their molecular weight.

Degree

The term degree is used in several scales of temperature. The symbol ° is usually used, followed by the initial letter of the unit, for example "°C" for degree(s) Celsius. A degree can be defined as a set change in temperature measured against a given scale, for example, one degree Celsius is one hundredth of the temperature change between the point at which water starts to change state from Solid to liquid state and the point at which it starts to change from its gaseous state to liquid.

Absolute zero

Absolute zero is the lowest temperature possible. More formally, it is the temperature at which entropy reaches its minimum value. The laws of thermodynamics state that absolute zero cannot be reached using only thermodynamic means.

Entropy

In thermodynamics, entropy is a measure of the number of specific ways in which a thermodynamic system may be arranged, often taken to be a measure of disorder, or a measure of progressing towards thermodynamic equilibrium. The entropy of an isolated system never decreases, because isolated systems spontaneously evolve towards thermodynamic equilibrium, which is the state of maximum entropy.

Entropy was originally defined for a thermodynamically reversible process

as $$\Delta S = \int \frac{dQ_{rev}}{T}$$

where the entropy is found from the uniform thermodynamic temperature of a closed system dividing an incremental reversible transfer of heat into that system .

Ideal gas

An ideal gas is a theoretical gas composed of a set of randomly moving, non-interacting point particles. The ideal gas concept is useful because it obeys the ideal gas law, a simplified equation of state, and is amenable to analysis under statistical mechanics.

9. The Gaseous State

Gas laws

The early gas laws were developed at the end of the 18th century, when scientists began to realize that relationships between the pressure, volume and temperature of a sample of gas could be obtained which would hold for all gases. Gases behave in a similar way over a wide variety of conditions because to a good approximation they all have molecules which are widely spaced, and nowadays the equation of state for an ideal gas is derived from kinetic theory. The earlier gas laws are now considered as special cases of the ideal gas equation, with one or more of the variables held constant.

Ideal gas law

The ideal gas law is the equation of state of a hypothetical ideal gas. It is a good approximation to the behaviour of many gases under many conditions, although it has several limitations. It was first stated by Émile Clapeyron in 1834 as a combination of Boyle's law and Charles's law.

Mole

Mole is a unit of measurement used in chemistry to express amounts of a chemical substance, defined as the amount of any substance that contains as many elementary entities (e.g., atoms, molecules, ions, electrons) as there are atoms in 12 grams of pure carbon-12, the isotope of carbon with relative atomic mass 12. This corresponds to the Avogadro constant, which has a value of $6.02214129(27)\times10^{23}$ elementary entities of the substance. It is one of the base units in the International System of Units, and has the unit symbol mol and corresponds with the dimension symbol N. In honour of the unit, chemists often celebrate October 23 (a reference to the 10^{23} part of Avogadro's number) as 'Mole Day'.

The mole is widely used in chemistry instead of units of mass or volume as a convenient way to express amounts of reactants or of products of chemical reactions.

Partial pressure

In a mixture of gases, each gas has a partial pressure which is the hypothetical pressure of that gas if it alone occupied the volume of the mixture at the same temperature. The total pressure of an ideal gas mixture is the sum of the partial pressures of each individual gas in the mixture.

It relies on the following isotherm relation: $V_x \times p_{tot} = V_{tot} \times p_x$ •V_x is the partial volume of any individual gas component (X)•V_{tot} is the total volume in gas mixture•p_x is the partial pressure of gas X•p_{tot} is the total pressure of gas mixture•n_x is the amount of substance of a gas (X)•n_{tot} is the total amount of substance in gas mixture

The partial pressure of a gas is a measure of thermodynamic activity of the gas's molecules.

Component

In thermodynamics, a component is a chemically-independent constituent of a system. The number of components represents the minimum number of independent species necessary to define the composition of all phases of the system.

Total pressure	In physics, the term total pressure may indicate two different quantities, both having the dimensions of a pressure: $p_0 = p + q + \rho g z$ where ? is the density of the fluid, g is the local acceleration due to gravity, and z is the height above a datum.If the variation in height above the datum is zero, or so small it can be ignored, the above equation reduces to the following simplified form: $p_0 = p + q$.In a mixture of ideal gases, total pressure refers to the sum of each gas' partial pressure..
Mole fraction	In chemistry, the mole fraction x_i is defined as the amount of a constituent n_i divided by the total amount of all constituents in a mixture n_{tot}: $x_i = \frac{n_i}{n_{tot}}$ The sum of all the mole fractions is equal to 1: $\sum_{i=1}^{N} n_i = n_{tot}; \sum_{i=1}^{N} x_i = 1$ The mole fraction is also called the amount fraction. It is identical to the number fraction, which is defined as the number of molecules of a constituent N_i divided by the total number of all molecules N_{tot}. It is one way of expressing the composition of a mixture with a dimensionless quantity (mass fraction is another).
Kinetic theory	The kinetic theory of gases describes a gas as a large number of small particles, all of which are in constant, random motion. The rapidly moving particles constantly collide with each other and with the walls of the container. Kinetic theory explains macroscopic properties of gases, such as pressure, temperature, viscosity, thermal conductivity, and volume, by considering their molecular composition and motion.
Equilibrium constant	For a general chemical equilibrium $\alpha A + \beta B ... \rightleftharpoons \rho R + \sigma S ...$ the thermodynamic equilibrium constant can be defined such that, at equilibrium, $K^\ominus = \frac{\{R\}^\rho \{S\}^\sigma ...}{\{A\}^\alpha \{B\}^\beta ...}$ where curly brackets denote the thermodynamic activities of the chemical species. The logarithm of this expression appears in the formula for the Gibbs free energy change for the reaction. If deviations from ideal behaviour are neglected, the activities may be replaced by concentrations, [A], and a concentration quotient, K_c.

9. The Gaseous State

CHAPTER HIGHLIGHTS & NOTES: KEY TERMS, PEOPLE, PLACES, CONCEPTS

Molecular beam

A molecular beam is produced by allowing a gas at higher pressure to expand through a small orifice into a chamber at lower pressure to form a beam of particles moving at approximately equal velocities, with very few collisions between the particles. Molecular beam is useful for fabricating thin films in molecular beam epitaxy and artificial structures such as quantum wells, quantum wires, and quantum dots. Molecular beams have also been applied as crossed molecular beams.

Period

In the periodic table of the elements, elements are arranged in a series of rows (or periods) so that those with similar properties appear in a column. Elements of the same period have the same number of electron shells; with each group across a period, the elements have one more proton and electron and become less metallic. This arrangement reflects the periodic recurrence of similar properties as the atomic number increases.

Intermolecular force

Intermolecular forces are forces of attraction or repulsion which act between neighboring particles . They are weak compared to the intramolecular forces, the forces which keep a molecule together. For example, the covalent bond present within HCl molecules is much stronger than the forces present between the neighboring molecules, which exist when the molecules are sufficiently close to each other.

Thermal equilibrium

In physics, the phrase thermal equilibrium is used sometimes in the common parlance of the ordinary language of physical discourse, and sometimes as a specialized technical term in thermodynamics.

As common parlance, the phrase refers to steady states of temperature, which may be spatial or temporal. The meaning varies from occasion to occasion, as with all ordinary language usages.

Energy level

A quantum mechanical system or particle that is bound--that is, confined spatially--can only take on certain discrete values of energy. This contrasts with classical particles, which can have any energy. These discrete values are called energy levels.

Compressibility

In thermodynamics and fluid mechanics, compressibility is a measure of the relative volume change of a fluid or solid as a response to a pressure change.

$$\beta = -\frac{1}{V}\frac{\partial V}{\partial p}$$

where V is volume and p is pressure.

Compressibility factor

The compressibility factor, also known as the compression factor, is the ratio of the molar volume of a gas to the molar volume of an ideal gas at the same temperature and pressure. It is a useful thermodynamic property for modifying the ideal gas law to account for the real gas behavior. In general, deviation from ideal behavior becomes more significant the closer a gas is to a phase change, the lower the temperature or the larger the pressure.

Real gas

Real gases - as opposed to a perfect or ideal gas - exhibit properties that cannot be explained entirely using the ideal gas law. To understand the behaviour of real gases, the following must be taken into account:•compressibility effects;•variable specific heat capacity;•van der Waals forces;•non-equilibrium thermodynamic effects;•issues with molecular dissociation and elementary reactions with variable composition.

For most applications, such a detailed analysis is unnecessary, and the ideal gas approximation can be used with reasonable accuracy. On the other hand, real-gas models have to be used near the condensation point of gases, near critical points, at very high pressures, to explain the Joule-Thomson effect and in other less usual cases.

Lennard-Jones potential

The Lennard-Jones potential is a mathematically simple model that approximates the interaction between a pair of neutral atoms or molecules. A form of the potential was first proposed in 1924 by John Lennard-Jones. The most common expressions of the L-J potential are

$$V_{LJ} = 4\varepsilon \left[\left(\frac{\sigma}{r}\right)^{12} - \left(\frac{\sigma}{r}\right)^{6} \right] = \varepsilon \left[\left(\frac{r_m}{r}\right)^{12} - 2\left(\frac{r_m}{r}\right)^{6} \right]$$

where e is the depth of the potential well, s is the finite distance at which the inter-particle potential is zero, r is the distance between the particles, and r_m is the distance at which the potential reaches its minimum.

Atom

The atom is a basic unit of matter that consists of a dense central nucleus surrounded by a cloud of negatively charged electrons. The atomic nucleus contains a mix of positively charged protons and electrically neutral neutrons, which means 'uncuttable' or 'the smallest indivisible particle of matter'. Although the Indian and Greek concepts of the atom were based purely on philosophy, modern science has retained the name coined by Democritus.

Gaseous diffusion

Gaseous diffusion is a technology used to produce enriched uranium by forcing gaseous uranium hexafluoride through semipermeable membranes. This produces a slight separation between the molecules containing uranium-235 (^{235}U) and uranium-238 (^{238}U). By use of a large cascade of many stages, high separations can be achieved.

Diffusion

Diffusion, in acoustics and architectural engineering, is the efficacy by which sound energy is spread evenly in a given environment. A perfectly diffusive sound space is one that has certain key acoustic properties which are the same anywhere in the space. A non-diffuse sound space would have considerably different reverberation time as the listener moved around the room.

9. The Gaseous State

CHAPTER HIGHLIGHTS & NOTES: KEY TERMS, PEOPLE, PLACES, CONCEPTS

Nuclear chemistry	Nuclear chemistry is the subfield of chemistry dealing with radioactivity, nuclear processes and nuclear properties. It is the chemistry of radioactive elements such as the actinides, radium and radon together with the chemistry associated with equipment which are designed to perform nuclear processes. This includes the corrosion of surfaces and the behavior under conditions of both normal and abnormal operation (such as during an accident).
Displacement	In fluid mechanics, displacement occurs when an object is immersed in a fluid, pushing it out of the way and taking its place. The volume of the fluid displaced can then be measured, and from this the volume of the immersed object can be deduced (the volume of the immersed object will be exactly equal to the volume of the displaced fluid). An object that sinks displaces an amount of fluid equal to the object's volume.
Ammonium perchlorate	Ammonium perchlorate is an inorganic compound with the formula NH_4ClO_4. It is the salt of perchloric acid and ammonia. It is a powerful oxidizer, which is why its main use is in solid propellants.

CHAPTER QUIZ: KEY TERMS, PEOPLE, PLACES, CONCEPTS

1. In physics, the term _________ may indicate two different quantities, both having the dimensions of a pressure: $p_0 = p + q + \rho g z$ where ? is the density of the fluid, g is the local acceleration due to gravity, and z is the height above a datum.If the variation in height above the datum is zero, or so small it can be ignored, the above equation reduces to the following simplified form: $p_0 = p + q$ •In a mixture of ideal gases, _________ refers to the sum of each gas' partial pressure..

   a. Booster pump
   b. Total pressure
   c. Cryogenic nitrogen plant
   d. Cryogenic oxygen plant

2. . A _________ is an electrically neutral group of two or more atoms held together by chemical bonds. _________s are distinguished from ions by their lack of electrical charge. However, in quantum physics, organic chemistry, and biochemistry, the term _________ is often used less strictly, also being applied to polyatomic ions.

   a. 3-Deazaneplanocin A
   b. Bioconcentration
   c. Molecule

3. The term _________ is used in several scales of temperature. The symbol ° is usually used, followed by the initial letter of the unit, for example "°C" for _________(s) Celsius. A _________ can be defined as a set change in temperature measured against a given scale, for example, one _________ Celsius is one hundredth of the temperature change between the point at which water starts to change state from Solid to liquid state and the point at which it starts to change from its gaseous state to liquid.

a. CrystaSulf
b. Degree
c. Rectisol
d. Scrubber

4. The _________ is a mathematically simple model that approximates the interaction between a pair of neutral atoms or molecules. A form of the potential was first proposed in 1924 by John Lennard-Jones. The most common expressions of the L-J potential are

$$V_{LJ} = 4\varepsilon \left[\left(\frac{\sigma}{r}\right)^{12} - \left(\frac{\sigma}{r}\right)^{6} \right] = \varepsilon \left[\left(\frac{r_m}{r}\right)^{12} - 2\left(\frac{r_m}{r}\right)^{6} \right]$$

where e is the depth of the potential well, s is the finite distance at which the inter-particle potential is zero, r is the distance between the particles, and r_m is the distance at which the potential reaches its minimum.

a. Lennard-Jones potential
b. Dispersive adhesion
c. Hydrogen bond
d. Hydrophile

5. _________ or statistical thermodynamics is a branch of physics that applies probability theory, which contains mathematical tools for dealing with large populations, to the study of the thermodynamic behavior of systems composed of a large number of particles. _________ provides a framework for relating the microscopic properties of individual atoms and molecules to the macroscopic bulk properties of materials that can be observed in everyday life, thereby explaining thermodynamics as a result of the classical- and quantum-mechanical descriptions of statistics and mechanics at the microscopic level.

_________ provides a molecular-level interpretation of macroscopic thermodynamic quantities such as work, heat, free energy, and entropy.

a. Backdraft
b. Batteryless radio
c. Statistical mechanics
d. Bjerrum plot

ANSWER KEY
9. The Gaseous State

1. b
2. c
3. b
4. a
5. c

---

10. Solids, Liquids, and Phase Transitions

CHAPTER OUTLINE: KEY TERMS, PEOPLE, PLACES, CONCEPTS

Effusion

Mole

Molecule

Solubility

Volume

Compressibility

Coefficient

Thermal expansion

Resistance

Viscosity

Diffusion

Atom

Displacement

Convection

Surface tension

Intermolecular force

Polarizability

Electromagnetic radiation

Electron

Radiation

London dispersion force

10. Solids, Liquids, and Phase Transitions

CHAPTER OUTLINE: KEY TERMS, PEOPLE, PLACES, CONCEPTS

	Electron density
	Kinetic energy
	Hydrogen bond
	Electron pair
	Hydrogen
	Hydrogen atom
	Autoionization
	Condensation
	Evaporation
	Vapor pressure
	Chemical reaction
	Phase transition
	Boiling point
	Phase diagram
	Supercooling
	Superheating
	Melting point
	Critical point
	Meniscus
	Supercritical fluid
	Triple point

10. Solids, Liquids, and Phase Transitions

CHAPTER OUTLINE: KEY TERMS, PEOPLE, PLACES, CONCEPTS

______ Sublimation

______ Bismuth

CHAPTER HIGHLIGHTS & NOTES: KEY TERMS, PEOPLE, PLACES, CONCEPTS

Effusion

Effusion is the process in which a gas escapes through a small hole. This occurs if the diameter of the hole is considerably smaller than the mean free path of the molecules. According to Graham's law, the rate at which gases effuse (i.e., how many molecules pass through the hole per second) is dependent on their molecular weight.

Mole

Mole is a unit of measurement used in chemistry to express amounts of a chemical substance, defined as the amount of any substance that contains as many elementary entities (e.g., atoms, molecules, ions, electrons) as there are atoms in 12 grams of pure carbon-12, the isotope of carbon with relative atomic mass 12. This corresponds to the Avogadro constant, which has a value of $6.02214129(27)\times10^{23}$ elementary entities of the substance. It is one of the base units in the International System of Units, and has the unit symbol mol and corresponds with the dimension symbol N. In honour of the unit, chemists often celebrate October 23 (a reference to the 10^{23} part of Avogadro's number) as 'Mole Day'.

The mole is widely used in chemistry instead of units of mass or volume as a convenient way to express amounts of reactants or of products of chemical reactions.

Molecule

A molecule is an electrically neutral group of two or more atoms held together by chemical bonds. Molecules are distinguished from ions by their lack of electrical charge. However, in quantum physics, organic chemistry, and biochemistry, the term molecule is often used less strictly, also being applied to polyatomic ions.

Solubility

Solubility is the property of a solid, liquid, or gaseous chemical substance called solute to dissolve in a solid, liquid, or gaseous solvent to form a homogeneous solution of the solute in the solvent. The solubility of a substance fundamentally depends on the physical and chemical properties of the solute and solvent as well as on temperature, pressure and the pH of the solution. The extent of the solubility of a substance in a specific solvent is measured as the saturation concentration, where adding more solute does not increase the concentration of the solution and begin to precipitate the excess amount of solute.

Volume

In thermodynamics, the volume of a system is an important extensive parameter for describing its thermodynamic state. The specific volume, an intensive property, is the system's volume per unit of mass. Volume is a function of state and is interdependent with other thermodynamic properties such as pressure and temperature.

Compressibility

In thermodynamics and fluid mechanics, compressibility is a measure of the relative volume change of a fluid or solid as a response to a pressure change.

$$\beta = -\frac{1}{V}\frac{\partial V}{\partial p}$$

where V is volume and p is pressure.

Coefficient

In mathematics, a coefficient is a multiplicative factor in some term of an expression ; it is usually a number, but in any case does not involve any variables of the expression. For instance in $7x^2 - 3xy + 1.5 + y$

the first two terms respectively have the coefficients 7 and -3. The third term 1.5 is a constant. The final term does not have any explicitly written coefficient, but is considered to have coefficient 1, since multiplying by that factor would not change the term.

Thermal expansion

Thermal expansion is the tendency of matter to change in volume in response to a change in temperature.

When a substance is heated, its particles begin moving more and thus usually maintain a greater average separation. Materials which contract with increasing temperature are unusual; this effect is limited in size, and only occurs within limited temperature ranges .

Resistance

In the context of ecological stability, resistance is the property of communities or populations to remain 'essentially unchanged' when subject to disturbance. The inverse of resistance is sensitivity.

Viscosity

The viscosity of a fluid is a measure of its resistance to gradual deformation by shear stress or tensile stress. For liquids, it corresponds to the informal notion of 'thickness'. For example, honey has a higher viscosity than water.

Diffusion

Diffusion, in acoustics and architectural engineering, is the efficacy by which sound energy is spread evenly in a given environment. A perfectly diffusive sound space is one that has certain key acoustic properties which are the same anywhere in the space. A non-diffuse sound space would have considerably different reverberation time as the listener moved around the room.

Atom

The atom is a basic unit of matter that consists of a dense central nucleus surrounded by a cloud of negatively charged electrons. The atomic nucleus contains a mix of positively charged protons and electrically neutral neutrons, which means 'uncuttable' or 'the smallest indivisible particle of matter'.

10. Solids, Liquids, and Phase Transitions

CHAPTER HIGHLIGHTS & NOTES: KEY TERMS, PEOPLE, PLACES, CONCEPTS

Displacement	In fluid mechanics, displacement occurs when an object is immersed in a fluid, pushing it out of the way and taking its place. The volume of the fluid displaced can then be measured, and from this the volume of the immersed object can be deduced (the volume of the immersed object will be exactly equal to the volume of the displaced fluid). An object that sinks displaces an amount of fluid equal to the object's volume.
Convection	Convection is the concerted, collective movement of groups or aggregates of molecules within fluids and rheids, either through advection or through diffusion or as a combination of both of them. Convection of mass cannot take place in solids, since neither bulk current flows nor significant diffusion can take place in solids. Diffusion of heat can take place in solids, but that is called heat conduction.
Surface tension	Surface tension is a contractive tendency of the surface of a liquid that allows it to resist an external force. It is revealed, for example, in the floating of some objects on the surface of water, even though they are denser than water, and in the ability of some insects (e.g. water striders) to run on the water surface. This property is caused by cohesion of similar molecules, and is responsible for many of the behaviors of liquids.
Intermolecular force	Intermolecular forces are forces of attraction or repulsion which act between neighboring particles . They are weak compared to the intramolecular forces, the forces which keep a molecule together. For example, the covalent bond present within HCl molecules is much stronger than the forces present between the neighboring molecules, which exist when the molecules are sufficiently close to each other.
Polarizability	Polarizability is the ability for a molecule to be polarized. It is a property of matter. Polarizabilities determine the dynamical response of a bound system to external fields, and provide insight into a molecule's internal structure.
Electromagnetic radiation	Electromagnetic radiation is one of the fundamental phenomena of electromagnetism, behaving as waves propagating through space, and also as photon particles traveling through space, carrying radiant energy. In a vacuum, it propagates at a characteristic speed, the speed of light, normally in straight lines. EMR is emitted and absorbed by charged particles.
Electron	The electron is a subatomic particle with a negative elementary electric charge. Electrons belong to the first generation of the lepton particle family, and are generally thought to be elementary particles because they have no known components or substructure. The electron has a mass that is approximately 1/1836 that of the proton.
Radiation	In physics, radiation is a process in which energetic particles or energetic waves travel through a vacuum, or through matter-containing media that are not required for their propagation.

Waves of a mass filled medium itself, such as water waves or sound waves, are usually not considered to be forms of 'radiation' in this sense.

Radiation can be classified as either ionizing or non-ionizing according to whether it ionizes or does not ionize ordinary chemical matter.

London dispersion force

London dispersion forces are a type of force acting between atoms and molecules. They are part of the van der Waals forces. The London dispersion force is named after the German-American physicist Fritz London.

Electron density

Electron density is the measure of the probability of an electron being present at a specific location.

In molecules, regions of electron density are usually found around the atom, and its bonds. In de-localized or conjugated systems, such as phenol, benzene and compounds such as hemoglobin and chlorophyll, the electron density covers an entire region, i.e., in benzene they are found above and below the planar ring.

Kinetic energy

In physics, the kinetic energy of an object is the energy which it possesses due to its motion. It is defined as the work needed to accelerate a body of a given mass from rest to its stated velocity. Having gained this energy during its acceleration, the body maintains this kinetic energy unless its speed changes.

Hydrogen bond

A hydrogen bond is the electromagnetic attractive interaction between polar molecules in which hydrogen is bound to a highly electronegative atom, such as nitrogen (N), oxygen (O) or fluorine (F). The name hydrogen bond is something of a misnomer, as it is not a true bond but a particularly strong dipole-dipole attraction, and should not be confused with a covalent bond.

These hydrogen-bond attractions can occur between molecules (intermolecular) or within different parts of a single molecule (intramolecular).

Electron pair

In chemistry, an electron pair consists of two electrons that occupy the same orbital but have opposite spins. The electron pair concept was introduced in a 1916 paper of Gilbert N. Lewis.

Because electrons are fermions, the Pauli exclusion principle forbids these particles from having exactly the same quantum numbers.

Hydrogen

Hydrogen is a chemical element with chemical symbol H and atomic number 1. With an atomic weight of 1.00794 u, hydrogen is the lightest element and its monatomic form (H) is the most abundant chemical substance, constituting roughly 75% of the Universe's baryonic mass. Non-remnant stars are mainly composed of hydrogen in its plasma state.

10. Solids, Liquids, and Phase Transitions

CHAPTER HIGHLIGHTS & NOTES: KEY TERMS, PEOPLE, PLACES, CONCEPTS

Hydrogen atom	A hydrogen atom is an atom of the chemical element hydrogen. The electrically neutral atom contains a single positively charged proton and a single negatively charged electron bound to the nucleus by the Coulomb force. Atomic hydrogen constitutes about 75% of the elemental mass of the universe.
Autoionization	Autoionization is a process by which atoms or molecules spontaneously emit one of the shell electrons, thus going from a state with charge Z to a state with charge Z?+?1, for example from an electrically neutral state to a singly ionized state. Atoms can autoionize when either two or more valence electrons are excited or one or more inner-shell electrons are missing. In the latter case, it is called the Auger effect.
Condensation	Condensation is the change of the physical state of matter from gas phase into liquid phase, and is the reverse of vaporization. It can also be defined as the change in the state of water vapor to water/any liquid when in contact with any surface. When the transition happens from the gaseous phase into the solid phase directly, the change is called deposition.
Evaporation	Evaporation is a type of vaporization of a liquid that occurs from the surface of a liquid into a gaseous phase that is not saturated with the evaporating substance. The other type of vaporization is boiling, which, instead, occurs within the entire mass of the liquid and can also take place when the vapor phase is saturated, such as when steam is produced in a boiler. Evaporation that occurs directly from the solid phase below the melting point, as commonly observed with ice at or below freezing or moth crystals (napthalene or paradichlorobenzine), is called sublimation.
Vapor pressure	Vapor pressure or equilibrium vapor pressure is the pressure exerted by a vapor in thermodynamic equilibrium with its condensed phases at a given temperature in a closed system. The equilibrium vapor pressure is an indication of a liquid's evaporation rate. It relates to the tendency of particles to escape from the liquid (or a solid).
Chemical reaction	A chemical reaction is a process that leads to the transformation of one set of chemical substances to another. Classically, chemical reactions encompass changes that only involve the positions of electrons in the forming and breaking of chemical bonds between atoms, with no change to the nuclei (no change to the elements present), and can often be described by a chemical equation. Nuclear chemistry is a sub-discipline of chemistry that involves the chemical reactions of unstable and radioactive elements where both electronic and nuclear changes may both occur.
Phase transition	A phase transition is the transformation of thermodynamic system from one phase or state of matter to another. A phase of a thermodynamic system and the states of matter have uniform physical properties.

Boiling point

The boiling point of a substance is the temperature at which the vapor pressure of the liquid equals the pressure surrounding the liquid and the liquid changes into a vapor.

A liquid in a vacuum has a lower boiling point than when that liquid is at atmospheric pressure. A liquid at high-pressure has a higher boiling point than when that liquid is at atmospheric pressure.

Phase diagram

A phase diagram in physical chemistry, engineering, mineralogy, and materials science is a type of chart used to show conditions at which thermodynamically distinct phases can occur at equilibrium. In mathematics and physics, 'phase diagram' is used with a different meaning: a synonym for a phase space.

Supercooling

Supercooling, also known as undercooling, is the process of lowering the temperature of a liquid or a gas below its freezing point without it becoming a solid.

A liquid below its standard freezing point will crystallize in the presence of a seed crystal or nucleus around which a crystal structure can form creating a solid. However, lacking any such nuclei, the liquid phase can be maintained all the way down to the temperature at which crystal homogeneous nucleation occurs.

Superheating

In physics, superheating is the phenomenon in which a liquid is heated to a temperature higher than its boiling point, without boiling. Superheating is achieved by heating a homogeneous substance in a clean container, free of nucleation sites, while taking care not to disturb the liquid.

Melting point

The melting point of a solid is the temperature at which it changes state from solid to liquid at atmospheric pressure. At the melting point the solid and liquid phase exist in equilibrium. The melting point of a substance depends (usually slightly) on pressure and is usually specified at standard pressure.

Critical point

In physical chemistry, thermodynamics, chemistry and condensed matter physics, a critical point, also known as a critical state, occurs under conditions at which no phase boundaries exist. There are multiple types of critical points, including vapor-liquid critical points and liquid-liquid critical points.

Meniscus

The meniscus is the curve in the upper surface of a liquid close to the surface of the container or another object, caused by surface tension. It can be either convex or concave, depending on the liquid and the surface.

A convex meniscus occurs when the particles in the liquid have a stronger attraction to each other (cohesion) than to the material of the container (adhesion).

Supercritical fluid

A supercritical fluid is any substance at a temperature and pressure above its critical point, where distinct liquid and gas phases do not exist.

It can effuse through solids like a gas, and dissolve materials like a liquid. In addition, close to the critical point, small changes in pressure or temperature result in large changes in density, allowing many properties of a supercritical fluid to be 'fine-tuned'.

Triple point

In thermodynamics, the triple point of a substance is the temperature and pressure at which the three phases of that substance coexist in thermodynamic equilibrium. For example, the triple point of mercury occurs at a temperature of -38.8344 °C and a pressure of 0.2 mPa.

In addition to the triple point between solid, liquid, and gas, there can be triple points involving more than one solid phase, for substances with multiple polymorphs.

Sublimation

Sublimation is the transition of a substance directly from the solid to the gas phase without passing through an intermediate liquid phase. Sublimation is an endothermic phase transition that occurs at temperatures and pressures below a substance's triple point in its phase diagram. The reverse process of sublimation is desublimation, or deposition.

Bismuth

Bismuth is a chemical element with symbol Bi and atomic number 83. Bismuth, a pentavalent poor metal, chemically resembles arsenic and antimony. Elemental bismuth may occur naturally, although its sulfide and oxide form important commercial ores. The free element is 86% as dense as lead.

CHAPTER QUIZ: KEY TERMS, PEOPLE, PLACES, CONCEPTS

1. _________ is the property of a solid, liquid, or gaseous chemical substance called solute to dissolve in a solid, liquid, or gaseous solvent to form a homogeneous solution of the solute in the solvent. The _________ of a substance fundamentally depends on the physical and chemical properties of the solute and solvent as well as on temperature, pressure and the pH of the solution. The extent of the _________ of a substance in a specific solvent is measured as the saturation concentration, where adding more solute does not increase the concentration of the solution and begin to precipitate the excess amount of solute.

   a. Solubility
   b. Concentrate
   c. Condosity
   d. Crenation

2. . _________ is a unit of measurement used in chemistry to express amounts of a chemical substance, defined as the amount of any substance that contains as many elementary entities (e.g., atoms, molecules, ions, electrons) as there are atoms in 12 grams of pure carbon-12, the isotope of carbon with relative atomic mass 12. This corresponds to the Avogadro constant, which has a value of $6.02214129(27) \times 10^{23}$ elementary entities of the substance.

It is one of the base units in the International System of Units, and has the unit symbol mol and corresponds with the dimension symbol N. In honour of the unit, chemists often celebrate October 23 (a reference to the 10^{23} part of Avogadro's number) as '_________ Day'.

The _________ is widely used in chemistry instead of units of mass or volume as a convenient way to express amounts of reactants or of products of chemical reactions.

a. Katal
b. Mole
c. Bisulfide
d. Buffering agent

3. _________ is a type of vaporization of a liquid that occurs from the surface of a liquid into a gaseous phase that is not saturated with the evaporating substance. The other type of vaporization is boiling, which, instead, occurs within the entire mass of the liquid and can also take place when the vapor phase is saturated, such as when steam is produced in a boiler. _________ that occurs directly from the solid phase below the melting point, as commonly observed with ice at or below freezing or moth crystals (napthalene or paradichlorobenzine), is called sublimation.

a. 3T Cycling
b. Evaporation
c. Beamline
d. Bi-isotropic material

4. A _________ in physical chemistry, engineering, mineralogy, and materials science is a type of chart used to show conditions at which thermodynamically distinct phases can occur at equilibrium. In mathematics and physics, '_________' is used with a different meaning: a synonym for a phase space.

a. Bainite
b. Phase diagram
c. Bimetal
d. Biohydrometallurgy

5. _________s are a type of force acting between atoms and molecules. They are part of the van der Waals forces. The _________ is named after the German-American physicist Fritz London.

a. Buckingham potential
b. London dispersion force
c. Hydrogen bond
d. Hydrophile

ANSWER KEY
10. Solids, Liquids, and Phase Transitions

1. a
2. b
3. b
4. b
5. b

---

11. Solutions

CHAPTER OUTLINE: KEY TERMS, PEOPLE, PLACES, CONCEPTS

Solvent

Component

Homogeneous

Concentration

Mole fraction

Mole

Solute

Aqueous

Volume

Electrolyte

Solubility

Solvation shell

Chemical reaction

Spectator ion

Atom

Ideal solution

Molecule

Titration

Hydroxide

Electron

Oxidation

11. Solutions

CHAPTER OUTLINE. KEY TERMS, PEOPLE, PLACES. CONCEPTS

- Redox
- Disproportionation
- Redox titration
- Vapor pressure
- Boiling-point elevation
- Colligative properties
- Boiling point
- Presence
- Freezing-point depression
- Freezing point
- Osmotic pressure
- Semipermeable membrane
- Reverse osmosis
- Osmosis
- Distillation
- Fractional distillation
- Evaporation
- Thermochemistry
- Acceleration
- Colloid
- Settling

11. Solutions

CHAPTER OUTLINE: KEY TERMS, PEOPLE, PLACES, CONCEPTS

_______________ Brownian motion

_______________ Colloidal particle

CHAPTER HIGHLIGHTS & NOTES: KEY TERMS, PEOPLE, PLACES, CONCEPTS

Solvent

A solvent is a substance that dissolves a solute (a chemically different liquid, solid or gas), resulting in a solution. A solvent is usually a liquid but can also be a solid or a gas. The maximum quantity of solute that can dissolve in a specific volume of solvent varies with temperature.

Component

In thermodynamics, a component is a chemically-independent constituent of a system. The number of components represents the minimum number of independent species necessary to define the composition of all phases of the system.

Calculating the number of components in a system is necessary, for example, when applying Gibbs' phase rule in determination of the number of degrees of freedom of a system.

Homogeneous

Homogeneous as a term in physical chemistry and material science refers to substances and mixtures which are in a single phase. This is in contrast to a substance that is heterogeneous. The definition of homogeneous strongly depends on the context used.

Concentration

In chemistry, concentration is the abundance of a constituent divided by the total volume of a mixture. Several types of mathematical description can be distinguished: mass concentration, molar concentration, number concentration, and volume concentration. The term concentration can be applied to any kind of chemical mixture, but most frequently it refers to solutes and solvents in solutions.

Mole fraction

In chemistry, the mole fraction x_i is defined as the amount of a constituent n_i divided by the total amount of all constituents in a mixture n_{tot}: $x_i = \frac{n_i}{n_{tot}}$

The sum of all the mole fractions is equal to 1: $\sum_{i=1}^{N} n_i = n_{tot}; \sum_{i=1}^{N} x_i = 1$

The mole fraction is also called the amount fraction.

It is identical to the number fraction, which is defined as the number of molecules of a constituent N_i divided by the total number of all molecules N_{tot}. It is one way of expressing the composition of a mixture with a dimensionless quantity (mass fraction is another).

Mole

Mole is a unit of measurement used in chemistry to express amounts of a chemical substance, defined as the amount of any substance that contains as many elementary entities (e.g., atoms, molecules, ions, electrons) as there are atoms in 12 grams of pure carbon-12, the isotope of carbon with relative atomic mass 12. This corresponds to the Avogadro constant, which has a value of $6.02214129(27)\times10^{23}$ elementary entities of the substance. It is one of the base units in the International System of Units, and has the unit symbol mol and corresponds with the dimension symbol N. In honour of the unit, chemists often celebrate October 23 (a reference to the 10^{23} part of Avogadro's number) as 'Mole Day'.

The mole is widely used in chemistry instead of units of mass or volume as a convenient way to express amounts of reactants or of products of chemical reactions.

Solute

A solute is a substance that creates a solution when dissolved in a solvent. For example, when sugar (solute) is dissolved in water (solvent).Solute can change its physical state but solvent and solution are of same phase.e.g sugar is solid before getting dissolved in water, and after dissolution it changes its phase to a liquid.

Etymology: from Latin solutus, past participle of solvere, meaning to loosen.

Aqueous

An aqueous solution is a solution in which the solvent is water. It is usually shown in chemical equations by appending (aq) to the relevant formula. For example, a solution of ordinary table salt, or sodium chloride (NaCl), in water would be represented as NaCl(aq).

Volume

In thermodynamics, the volume of a system is an important extensive parameter for describing its thermodynamic state. The specific volume, an intensive property, is the system's volume per unit of mass. Volume is a function of state and is interdependent with other thermodynamic properties such as pressure and temperature.

Electrolyte

An electrolyte is a compound that ionizes when dissolved in suitable ionizing solvents such as water. This includes most soluble salts, acids, and bases. Some gases, such as hydrogen chloride, under conditions of high temperature or low pressure can also function as electrolytes.

Solubility

Solubility is the property of a solid, liquid, or gaseous chemical substance called solute to dissolve in a solid, liquid, or gaseous solvent to form a homogeneous solution of the solute in the solvent. The solubility of a substance fundamentally depends on the physical and chemical properties of the solute and solvent as well as on temperature, pressure and the pH of the solution.

11. Solutions

CHAPTER HIGHLIGHTS & NOTES: KEY TERMS, PEOPLE, PLACES, CONCEPTS

Solvation shell	A solvation shell is a shell of any chemical species that acts as a solvent and surrounds a solute species. When the solvent is water it is often referred to as a hydration shell or hydration sphere. A classic example is when water molecules form a sphere around a metal ion.
Chemical reaction	A chemical reaction is a process that leads to the transformation of one set of chemical substances to another. Classically, chemical reactions encompass changes that only involve the positions of electrons in the forming and breaking of chemical bonds between atoms, with no change to the nuclei (no change to the elements present), and can often be described by a chemical equation. Nuclear chemistry is a sub-discipline of chemistry that involves the chemical reactions of unstable and radioactive elements where both electronic and nuclear changes may both occur.
Spectator ion	A spectator ion is an ion that exists as a reactant and a product in a chemical equation. Spectator ions can, for example, be observed in the reaction of aqueous solutions of sodium chloride and copper(II) sulfate but does not affect the equilibrium:$2Na^{+}_{(aq)} + 2Cl^{-}_{(aq)} + Cu^{2+}_{(aq)} + SO_4^{2-}_{(aq)}$? $2Na^{+}_{(aq)} + SO_4^{2-}_{(aq)} + CuCl_{2\,(s)}$ The Na^{+} and SO_4^{2-} ions are spectator ions since they remain unchanged on both sides of the equation. They simply 'watch' the other ions react, hence the name.
Atom	The atom is a basic unit of matter that consists of a dense central nucleus surrounded by a cloud of negatively charged electrons. The atomic nucleus contains a mix of positively charged protons and electrically neutral neutrons, which means 'uncuttable' or 'the smallest indivisible particle of matter'. Although the Indian and Greek concepts of the atom were based purely on philosophy, modern science has retained the name coined by Democritus.
Ideal solution	In chemistry, an ideal solution or ideal mixture is a solution with thermodynamic properties analogous to those of a mixture of ideal gases. The enthalpy of solution (or 'enthalpy of mixing') is zero as is the volume change on mixing; the closer to zero the enthalpy of solution is, the more 'ideal' the behavior of the solution becomes. The vapour pressure of the solution obeys Raoult's law, and the activity coefficients (which measure deviation from ideality) are equal to one.
Molecule	A molecule is an electrically neutral group of two or more atoms held together by chemical bonds. Molecules are distinguished from ions by their lack of electrical charge. However, in quantum physics, organic chemistry, and biochemistry, the term molecule is often used less strictly, also being applied to polyatomic ions.
Titration	Titration, also known as titrimetry, is a common laboratory method of quantitative chemical analysis that is used to determine the unknown concentration of an identified analyte. Since volume measurements play a key role in titration, it is also known as volumetric analysis.

11. Solutions

Hydroxide

Hydroxide is a diatomic anion with chemical formula OH^-. It consists of an oxygen and a hydrogen atom held together by a covalent bond, and carries a negative electric charge. It is an important but usually minor constituent of water.

Electron

The electron is a subatomic particle with a negative elementary electric charge. Electrons belong to the first generation of the lepton particle family, and are generally thought to be elementary particles because they have no known components or substructure. The electron has a mass that is approximately 1/1836 that of the proton.

Oxidation

Redox (reduction-oxidation) reactions include all chemical reactions in which atoms have their oxidation state changed; in general, redox reactions involve the transfer of electrons between species.

This can be either a simple redox process, such as the oxidation of carbon to yield carbon dioxide or the reduction of carbon by hydrogen to yield methane (CH_4), or a complex process such as the oxidation of glucose ($C_6H_{12}O_6$) in the human body through a series of complex electron transfer processes.

The term 'redox' comes from two concepts involved with electron transfer: reduction and oxidation.

Redox

Redox reactions include all chemical reactions in which atoms have their oxidation state changed; redox reactions generally involve the transfer of electrons between species.

This can be either a simple redox process, such as the oxidation of carbon to yield carbon dioxide (CO2) or the reduction of carbon by hydrogen to yield methane (CH_4), or a complex process such as the oxidation of glucose ($C_6H_{12}O_6$) in the human body through a series of complex electron transfer processes.

The term 'redox' comes from two concepts involved with electron transfer: reduction and oxidation.

Disproportionation

Disproportionation is a specific type of redox reaction in which a species is simultaneously reduced and oxidized to form two different products.

For example: the UV photolysis of mercury chloride Hg_2Cl_2 ? Hg + $HgCl_2$ is a disproportionation. Mercury (I) is a diatomic dication Hg2+2.

Redox titration

Redox titration is a type of titration based on a redox reaction between the analyte and titrant.

Redox titration may involve the use of a redox indicator and/or a potentiometer.

11. Solutions

Vapor pressure

Vapor pressure or equilibrium vapor pressure is the pressure exerted by a vapor in thermodynamic equilibrium with its condensed phases at a given temperature in a closed system. The equilibrium vapor pressure is an indication of a liquid's evaporation rate. It relates to the tendency of particles to escape from the liquid (or a solid).

Boiling-point elevation

Boiling-point elevation describes the phenomenon that the boiling point of a liquid will be higher when another compound is added, meaning that a solution has a higher boiling point than a pure solvent. This happens whenever a non-volatile solute, such as a salt, is added to a pure solvent, such as water. The boiling point can be measured accurately using an ebullioscope.

Colligative properties

In chemistry, colligative properties are properties of solutions that depend upon the ratio of the number of solute particles to the number of solvent molecules in a solution, and not on the type of chemical species present. This number ratio can be related to the various units for concentration of solutions. Here we shall only consider those properties which result because of the dissolution of nonvolatile solute in a volatile liquid solvent.

Boiling point

The boiling point of a substance is the temperature at which the vapor pressure of the liquid equals the pressure surrounding the liquid and the liquid changes into a vapor.

A liquid in a vacuum has a lower boiling point than when that liquid is at atmospheric pressure. A liquid at high-pressure has a higher boiling point than when that liquid is at atmospheric pressure.

Presence

In filmmaking and television production presence is the 'silence' recorded at a location or space when no dialogue is spoken. This term is often confused with ambience.

Every location has a distinct presence created by the position of the microphone in relation to the space boundaries.

Freezing-point depression

Freezing-point depression describes the process in which adding a solute to a solvent decreases the freezing point of the solvent.

Examples include salt in water, alcohol in water, or the mixing of two solids such as impurities in a finely powdered drug. In such cases, the added compound is the solute, and the original solid can be thought of as the solvent.

Freezing point

Freezing, or Solidification, is a phase transition in which a liquid turns into a solid when its temperature is lowered below its freezing point.

For most substances, the melting and freezing points are the same temperature; however, certain substances possess differing solid-liquid transition temperatures. For example, agar displays a hysteresis in its melting and freezing temperatures.

Osmotic pressure	Osmotic pressure is the pressure which needs to be applied to a solution to prevent the inward flow of water across a semipermeable membrane. It is also defined as the minimum pressure needed to nullify osmosis. The phenomenon of osmotic pressure arises from the tendency of a pure solvent to move through a semi-permeable membrane and into a solution containing a solute to which the membrane is impermeable.
Semipermeable membrane	A semipermeable membrane, also termed a selectively permeable membrane, a partially permeable membrane or a differentially permeable membrane, is a membrane that will allow certain molecules or ions to pass through it by diffusion and occasionally specialized 'facilitated diffusion'. Prof. Sidney Loeb and Srinivasa Sourirajan invented the first practical synthetic semi-permeable membrane.
Reverse osmosis	Reverse osmosis is a water purification technology that uses a semipermeable membrane. This membrane-technology is not properly a filtration method. In RO, an applied pressure is used to overcome osmotic pressure, a colligative property, that is driven by chemical potential, a thermodynamic parameter.
Osmosis	Osmosis is the spontaneous net movement of solvent molecules through a partially permeable membrane into a region of higher solute concentration, in the direction that tends to equalize the solute concentrations on the two sides. It may also be used to describe a physical process in which any solvent moves, without input of energy, across a semipermeable membrane (permeable to the solvent, but not the solute) separating two solutions of different concentrations. Although osmosis does not require input of energy, it does use kinetic energy and can be made to do work.
Distillation	Distillation is a method of separating mixtures based on differences in volatility of components in a boiling liquid mixture. Distillation is a unit operation, or a physical separation process, and not a chemical reaction. Commercially, distillation has a number of applications.
Fractional distillation	Fractional distillation is the separation of a mixture into its component parts, or fractions, such as in separating chemical compounds by their boiling point by heating them to a temperature at which one or more fractions of the compound will vaporize. It is a special type of distillation. Generally the component parts boil at less than 25 °C from each other under a pressure of one atmosphere (atm).
Evaporation	Evaporation is a type of vaporization of a liquid that occurs from the surface of a liquid into a gaseous phase that is not saturated with the evaporating substance. The other type of vaporization is boiling, which, instead, occurs within the entire mass of the liquid and can also take place when the vapor phase is saturated, such as when steam is produced in a boiler.

11. Solutions

CHAPTER HIGHLIGHTS & NOTES: KEY TERMS, PEOPLE, PLACES, CONCEPTS

Thermochemistry

Thermochemistry is the study of the energy and heat associated with chemical reactions and/or physical transformations. A reaction may release or absorb energy, and a phase change may do the same, such as in melting and boiling. Thermochemistry focuses on these energy changes, particularly on the system's energy exchange with its surroundings.

Acceleration

In physics, acceleration is the rate at which the velocity of a body changes with time. Velocity and acceleration are vector quantities, with magnitude, direction, and add according to the parallelogram law. As described by Newton's Second Law, acceleration is caused by a net force; the force, as a vector, is equal to the product of the mass of the object being accelerated (scalar) and the acceleration.

Colloid

A colloid is a substance microscopically dispersed throughout another substance.

The dispersed-phase particles have a diameter of between approximately 1 and 1000 nanometers. Such particles are normally invisible in an optical microscope, though their presence can be confirmed with the use of an ultramicroscope or an electron microscope.

Settling

Settling is the process by which particulates settle to the bottom of a liquid and form a sediment. Particles that experience a force, either due to gravity or due to centrifugal motion will tend to move in a uniform manner in the direction exerted by that force. For gravity settling, this means that the particles will tend to fall to the bottom of the vessel, forming a slurry at the vessel base.

Brownian motion

Brownian motion or pedesis is the presumably random moving of particles suspended in a fluid (a liquid or a gas) resulting from their collision with the quick atoms or molecules in the gas or liquid. The term 'Brownian motion' can also refer to the mathematical model used to describe such random movements, which is often called a particle theory.

In 1827, the botanist Robert Brown, looking through a microscope at particles found in pollen grains in water, noted that the particles moved through the water but was not able to determine the mechanisms that caused this motion.

Colloidal particle

Colloidal particle is a small amount of matter having size typical for colloids and with a clear phase boundary . A group of such particles (aggregate, agglomerate) or being a macromolecule (e.g. solution of polymer molecules is a molecular colloid) or a molecular aggregate (e.g. micelle).

A colloidal sized particle is defined in diameter from 1-1000 nanometers.

1. _________ or equilibrium _________ is the pressure exerted by a vapor in thermodynamic equilibrium with its condensed phases at a given temperature in a closed system. The equilibrium _________ is an indication of a liquid's evaporation rate. It relates to the tendency of particles to escape from the liquid (or a solid).

a. Vapor pressure
b. Basic sediment and water
c. Biochemical engineering
d. Bioheat transfer

2. _________ is the study of the energy and heat associated with chemical reactions and/or physical transformations. A reaction may release or absorb energy, and a phase change may do the same, such as in melting and boiling. _________ focuses on these energy changes, particularly on the system's energy exchange with its surroundings.

a. Bioaerosol
b. Thermochemistry
c. Boiling-point elevation
d. Bolaamphiphile

3. _________ is a water purification technology that uses a semipermeable membrane. This membrane-technology is not properly a filtration method. In RO, an applied pressure is used to overcome osmotic pressure, a colligative property, that is driven by chemical potential, a thermodynamic parameter.

a. Ceramic membrane
b. Diafiltration
c. Dialysis tubing
d. Reverse osmosis

4. _________ is a small amount of matter having size typical for colloids and with a clear phase boundary . A group of such particles (aggregate, agglomerate) or being a macromolecule (e.g. solution of polymer molecules is a molecular colloid) or a molecular aggregate (e.g. micelle).

A colloidal sized particle is defined in diameter from 1-1000 nanometers.

a. 3T Cycling
b. Colloidal particle
c. Beamline
d. Bi-isotropic material

5. . _________ is a type of titration based on a redox reaction between the analyte and titrant.

_________ may involve the use of a redox indicator and/or a potentiometer.

a. Barium diphenylamine sulfonate
b. Complexometric titration

c. Conductometry

d. Redox titration

ANSWER KEY
11. Solutions

---

1. a
2. b
3. d
4. b
5. d

You can take the complete Chapter Practice Test

for 11. Solutions
on all key terms, persons, places, and concepts.

Online 99 Cents

http://www.JustTheFacts101.com

12. Thermodynamic Processes and Thermochemistry

CHAPTER OUTLINE: KEY TERMS, PEOPLE, PLACES, CONCEPTS

	Thermodynamics
	Thermal energy
	Kinetic energy
	Volume
	Closed system
	Isolated system
	Block
	Thermodynamic system
	Thermodynamic process
	Thermodynamic state
	Chemical reaction
	Mechanical equilibrium
	Reversible process
	State function
	Product
	Internal energy
	Heat capacity
	Thermal contact
	Enthalpy
	Heat transfer
	Degree

12. Thermodynamic Processes and Thermochemistry

CHAPTER OUTLINE: KEY TERMS, PEOPLE, PLACES, CONCEPTS

______ Hydrogen atom

______ Molecule

______ Equilibrium constant

______ Chemical equilibrium

______ Concentration

______ Partial pressure

______ Exothermic

______ Exothermic reaction

______ Gibbs free energy

______ Thermochemistry

______ Mole

______ Vaporization

______ Standard state

______ Chemical bond

______ Isobaric process

______ Isochoric process

______ Isothermal process

______ Energy level

Thermodynamics	Thermodynamics is a branch of natural science concerned with heat and its relation to energy and work. It defines macroscopic variables (such as temperature, internal energy, entropy, and pressure) that characterize materials and radiation, and explains how they are related and by what laws they change with time. Thermodynamics describes the average behavior of very large numbers of microscopic constituents, and its laws can be derived from statistical mechanics.
Thermal energy	Thermal energy is the part of the total potential energy and kinetic energy of an object or sample of matter that results in the system temperature. It is represented by the variable Q, and can be measured in Joules. This quantity may be difficult to determine or even meaningless unless the system has attained its temperature only through warming (heating), and not been subjected to work input or output, or any other energy-changing processes.
Kinetic energy	In physics, the kinetic energy of an object is the energy which it possesses due to its motion. It is defined as the work needed to accelerate a body of a given mass from rest to its stated velocity. Having gained this energy during its acceleration, the body maintains this kinetic energy unless its speed changes.
Volume	In thermodynamics, the volume of a system is an important extensive parameter for describing its thermodynamic state. The specific volume, an intensive property, is the system's volume per unit of mass. Volume is a function of state and is interdependent with other thermodynamic properties such as pressure and temperature.
Closed system	The term closed system refers to a physical system that is closed to certain types of transfers in or out of the system. The specification of what types of transfers are excluded, is different in different contexts.
Isolated system	In the natural sciences an isolated system is a physical system without any external exchange - neither matter nor energy can enter or exit, but can only move around inside. Truly isolated systems cannot exist in nature, other than allegedly the universe itself, and they are thus hypothetical concepts only. It obeys, in particular, to the first of the conservation laws: its total energy - mass stays constant.
Block	A block of the periodic table of elements is a set of adjacent groups. The term appears to have been first used (in French) by Charles Janet. The respective highest-energy electrons in each element in a block belong to the same atomic orbital type.
Thermodynamic system	A thermodynamic system is a precisely specified macroscopic region of the universe, defined by boundaries or walls of particular natures, together with the physical surroundings of that region, which determine processes that are allowed to affect the interior of the region, studied using the principles of thermodynamics.

All space in the universe outside the thermodynamic system is known as the surroundings, the environment, or a reservoir. A system is separated from its surroundings by a boundary, which may be notional or real but, by convention, delimits a finite volume.

Thermodynamic process

A thermodynamic process is the energetic development of a thermodynamic system proceeding from an initial state to a final state. Paths through the space of thermodynamic variables are often specified by holding certain thermodynamic variables constant. A state function is a thermodynamic variable which depends only on the current state of the system, not the path taken to reach that state.

Thermodynamic state

For thermodynamics, a thermodynamic state of a system is fully identified by values of a suitable set of parameters known as state variables, state parameters or thermodynamic variables. Once such a set of values of thermodynamic variables has been specified for a system, the values of all thermodynamic properties of the system are uniquely determined.

Thermodynamics sets up an idealized formalism that can be summarized by a system of postulates of thermodynamics.

Chemical reaction

A chemical reaction is a process that leads to the transformation of one set of chemical substances to another. Classically, chemical reactions encompass changes that only involve the positions of electrons in the forming and breaking of chemical bonds between atoms, with no change to the nuclei (no change to the elements present), and can often be described by a chemical equation. Nuclear chemistry is a sub-discipline of chemistry that involves the chemical reactions of unstable and radioactive elements where both electronic and nuclear changes may both occur.

Mechanical equilibrium

A standard definition of static equilibrium is:A system of particles is in static equilibrium when all the particles of the system are at rest and the total force on each particle is permanently zero.

This is a strict definition, and often the term static equilibrium is used in a more relaxed manner interchangeably with mechanical equilibrium, as defined next.

A standard definition of mechanical equilibrium for a particle is:The net force acting upon the particle is zero. This implies the object may be motionless or moving at constant speed in a straight line.R = ? F = 0

The necessary conditions for mechanical equilibrium for a system of particles are:(i) the vector sum of all external forces is zero and(ii) the sum of the moments of all external forces about any line is zero.

As applied to a rigid body, the necessary and sufficient conditions become:A rigid body is in mechanical equilibrium when the sum of all forces on all particles of the system is zero, and also the sum of all torques on all particles of the system is zero.R = ? F = 0$M^R{}_O$ = ? M_O = ? (r x F) = 0

A rigid body in mechanical equilibrium is undergoing neither linear nor rotational acceleration; however it could be translating constant velocity in a straight line or rotating with constant angular momentum but not necessarily at constant angular velocity.

Reversible process

In thermodynamics, a reversible process, or reversible cycle if the process is cyclic, is a process that can be 'reversed' by means of infinitesimal changes in some property of the system without entropy production . Due to these infinitesimal changes, the system is in thermodynamic equilibrium throughout the entire process. Since it would take an infinite amount of time for the reversible process to finish, perfectly reversible processes are impossible.

State function

In thermodynamics, a state function, function of state, state quantity, or state variable is a property of a system that depends only on the current state of the system, not on the way in which the system acquired that state . A state function describes the equilibrium state of a system. For example, internal energy, enthalpy, and entropy are state quantities because they describe quantitatively an equilibrium state of a thermodynamic system, irrespective of how the system arrived in that state.

Product

Product are formed during chemical reactions as reagents are consumed. Products have lower energy than the reagents and are produced during the reaction according to the second law of thermodynamics. The released energy comes from changes in chemical bonds between atoms in reagent molecules and may be given off in the form of heat or light.

Internal energy

In thermodynamics, the internal energy is the total energy contained by a thermodynamic system. It is the energy needed to create the system but excludes the energy to displace the system's surroundings, any energy associated with a move as a whole, or due to external force fields. Internal energy has two major components, kinetic energy and potential energy.

Heat capacity

Heat capacity, or thermal capacity, is the measurable physical quantity of heat energy required to change the temperature of an object or body by a given amount. The SI unit of heat capacity is joule per kelvin, $\frac{J}{K}$ and the dimensional form is $M^1L^2T^{-2}T^{-1}$.

Heat capacity is an extensive property of matter, meaning it is proportional to the size of the system.

Thermal contact

In heat transfer and thermodynamics, a thermodynamic system is said to be in thermal contact with another system if it can exchange energy with it through the process of heat.

Perfect thermal isolation is an idealization as real systems are always in thermal contact with their environment to some extent. The area available for heat flow through interstitial gaps often is 2 to 4 orders of magnitude greater than the contact area; heat flow through gaps can't be neglected especially if the solids are relatively poor conductors or interface medium is a good conductor.

Enthalpy

Enthalpy is a measure of the total energy of a thermodynamic system. It includes the system's internal energy and thermodynamic potential (a state function), as well as its volume and pressure (the energy required to 'make room for it' by displacing its environment, which is an extensive quantity). The unit of measurement for enthalpy in the International System of Units (SI) is the joule, but other historical, conventional units are still in use, such as the British thermal unit and the calorie.

Heat transfer

Heat transfer is a discipline of thermal engineering that concerns the generation, use, conversion, and exchange of thermal energy and heat between physical systems. As such, heat transfer is involved in almost every sector of the economy. Heat transfer is classified into various mechanisms, such as thermal conduction, thermal convection, thermal radiation, and transfer of energy by phase changes.

Degree

The term degree is used in several scales of temperature. The symbol ° is usually used, followed by the initial letter of the unit, for example "°C" for degree(s) Celsius. A degree can be defined as a set change in temperature measured against a given scale, for example, one degree Celsius is one hundredth of the temperature change between the point at which water starts to change state from Solid to liquid state and the point at which it starts to change from its gaseous state to liquid.

Hydrogen atom

A hydrogen atom is an atom of the chemical element hydrogen. The electrically neutral atom contains a single positively charged proton and a single negatively charged electron bound to the nucleus by the Coulomb force. Atomic hydrogen constitutes about 75% of the elemental mass of the universe.

Molecule

A molecule is an electrically neutral group of two or more atoms held together by chemical bonds. Molecules are distinguished from ions by their lack of electrical charge. However, in quantum physics, organic chemistry, and biochemistry, the term molecule is often used less strictly, also being applied to polyatomic ions.

Equilibrium constant

For a general chemical equilibrium $\alpha A + \beta B ... \rightleftharpoons \rho R + \sigma S ...$

the thermodynamic equilibrium constant can be defined such that, at equilibrium, $K^{\ominus} = \frac{\{R\}^{\rho}\{S\}^{\sigma}...}{\{A\}^{\alpha}\{B\}^{\beta}...}$

where curly brackets denote the thermodynamic activities of the chemical species.

The logarithm of this expression appears in the formula for the Gibbs free energy change for the reaction. If deviations from ideal behaviour are neglected, the activities may be replaced by concentrations, [A], and a concentration quotient, K_c.

Chemical equilibrium

In a chemical reaction, chemical equilibrium is the state in which both reactants and products are present at concentrations which have no further tendency to change with time. Usually, this state results when the forward reaction proceeds at the same rate as the reverse reaction. The reaction rates of the forward and backward reactions are generally not zero, but equal.

Concentration

In chemistry, concentration is the abundance of a constituent divided by the total volume of a mixture. Several types of mathematical description can be distinguished: mass concentration, molar concentration, number concentration, and volume concentration. The term concentration can be applied to any kind of chemical mixture, but most frequently it refers to solutes and solvents in solutions.

Partial pressure

In a mixture of gases, each gas has a partial pressure which is the hypothetical pressure of that gas if it alone occupied the volume of the mixture at the same temperature. The total pressure of an ideal gas mixture is the sum of the partial pressures of each individual gas in the mixture.

It relies on the following isotherm relation: $V_x \times p_{tot} = V_{tot} \times p_x$ •V_x is the partial volume of any individual gas component (X)•V_{tot} is the total volume in gas mixture•p_x is the partial pressure of gas X•p_{tot} is the total pressure of gas mixture•n_x is the amount of substance of a gas (X)•n_{tot} is the total amount of substance in gas mixture

The partial pressure of a gas is a measure of thermodynamic activity of the gas's molecules.

Exothermic

In thermodynamics, the term exothermic describes a process or reaction that releases energy from the system, usually in the form of heat, but also in a form of light (e.g. a spark, flame, or flash), electricity (e.g. a battery), or sound (e.g. explosion heard when burning hydrogen). Its etymology stems from the prefix exo (derived from the Greek word ???, exo, 'outside') and the Greek word thermasi (meaning 'to heat'). The term exothermic was first coined by Marcellin Berthelot.

Exothermic reaction

An exothermic reaction is a chemical reaction that releases energy in the form of light or heat. It is the opposite of an endothermic reaction.

Expressed in a chemical equation: reactants ? products + energy

Gibbs free energy

In thermodynamics, the Gibbs free energy is a thermodynamic potential that measures the 'usefulness' or process-initiating work obtainable from a thermodynamic system at a constant temperature and pressure (isothermal, isobaric). Just as in mechanics, where potential energy is defined as capacity to do work, similarly different potentials have different meanings.

12. Thermodynamic Processes and Thermochemistry

Thermochemistry

Thermochemistry is the study of the energy and heat associated with chemical reactions and/or physical transformations. A reaction may release or absorb energy, and a phase change may do the same, such as in melting and boiling. Thermochemistry focuses on these energy changes, particularly on the system's energy exchange with its surroundings.

Mole

Mole is a unit of measurement used in chemistry to express amounts of a chemical substance, defined as the amount of any substance that contains as many elementary entities (e.g., atoms, molecules, ions, electrons) as there are atoms in 12 grams of pure carbon-12, the isotope of carbon with relative atomic mass 12. This corresponds to the Avogadro constant, which has a value of $6.02214129(27)\times10^{23}$ elementary entities of the substance. It is one of the base units in the International System of Units, and has the unit symbol mol and corresponds with the dimension symbol N. In honour of the unit, chemists often celebrate October 23 (a reference to the 10^{23} part of Avogadro's number) as 'Mole Day'.

The mole is widely used in chemistry instead of units of mass or volume as a convenient way to express amounts of reactants or of products of chemical reactions.

Vaporization

Vaporization of an element or compound is a phase transition from the liquid phase to gas phase. There are two types of vaporization: evaporation and boiling.

Evaporation is a phase transition from the liquid phase to gas phase that occurs at temperatures below the boiling temperature at a given pressure.

Standard state

In chemistry, the standard state of a material is a reference point used to calculate its properties under different conditions. In principle, the choice of standard state is arbitrary, although the International Union of Pure and Applied Chemistry (IUPAC) recommends a conventional set of standard states for general use. IUPAC recommends using a standard pressure $p^o = 10^5$ Pa.

Chemical bond

A chemical bond is an attraction between atoms that allows the formation of chemical substances that contain two or more atoms. The bond is caused by the electrostatic force of attraction between opposite charges, either between electrons and nuclei, or as the result of a dipole attraction. The strength of chemical bonds varies considerably; there are 'strong bonds' such as covalent or ionic bonds and 'weak bonds' such as dipole-dipole interactions, the London dispersion force and hydrogen bonding.

Isobaric process

An isobaric process' is a thermodynamic process in which the pressure stays constant: ?P = 0. The term derives from the Greek iso-, (equal), and baros (weight). The heat transferred to the system does work but also changes the internal energy of the system: $Q = \Delta U + W$

According to the first law of thermodynamics, where W is work done on the system, U is internal energy, and Q is heat. Pressure-volume work by the closed system is defined as:

$$W = \int p\, dV$$

where ? means change over the whole process, whereas d denotes a differential.

Isochoric process

An isochoric process, also called a constant-volume process, an isovolumetric process, or an isometric process, is a thermodynamic process during which the volume of the closed system undergoing such a process remains constant. An isochoric process is exemplified by the heating or the cooling of the contents of a sealed, inelastic container: The thermodynamic process is the addition or removal of heat; the isolation of the contents of the container establishes the closed system; and the inability of the container to deform imposes the constant-volume condition. •Property database.

Isothermal process

An isothermal process is a change of a system, in which the temperature remains constant: ?T = 0. This typically occurs when a system is in contact with an outside thermal reservoir (heat bath), and the change occurs slowly enough to allow the system to continually adjust to the temperature of the reservoir through heat exchange. In contrast, an adiabatic process is where a system exchanges no heat with its surroundings (Q = 0). In other words, in an isothermal process, the value ?T = 0 but Q ? 0, while in an adiabatic process, ?T ? 0 but Q = 0.

Energy level

A quantum mechanical system or particle that is bound--that is, confined spatially--can only take on certain discrete values of energy. This contrasts with classical particles, which can have any energy. These discrete values are called energy levels.

CHAPTER QUIZ: KEY TERMS, PEOPLE, PLACES, CONCEPTS

1. In thermodynamics, a _________, or reversible cycle if the process is cyclic, is a process that can be 'reversed' by means of infinitesimal changes in some property of the system without entropy production . Due to these infinitesimal changes, the system is in thermodynamic equilibrium throughout the entire process. Since it would take an infinite amount of time for the _________ to finish, perfectly _________es are impossible.

a. Cryogenic nitrogen plant
b. Reversible process
c. Gas slug
d. Beat

2. . An _________ is a change of a system, in which the temperature remains constant: ?T = 0. This typically occurs when a system is in contact with an outside thermal reservoir (heat bath), and the change occurs slowly enough to allow the system to continually adjust to the temperature of the reservoir through heat exchange.

In contrast, an adiabatic process is where a system exchanges no heat with its surroundings (Q = 0). In other words, in an _________, the value ?T = 0 but Q ? 0, while in an adiabatic process, ?T ? 0 but Q = 0.

a. Cryogenic nitrogen plant
b. Cryogenic oxygen plant
c. Isothermal process
d. Beat

3. A _________ is an electrically neutral group of two or more atoms held together by chemical bonds. _________s are distinguished from ions by their lack of electrical charge. However, in quantum physics, organic chemistry, and biochemistry, the term _________ is often used less strictly, also being applied to polyatomic ions.

a. 3-Deazaneplanocin A
b. Molecule
c. Biophysical chemistry
d. Chemical biology

4. _________ is the study of the energy and heat associated with chemical reactions and/or physical transformations. A reaction may release or absorb energy, and a phase change may do the same, such as in melting and boiling. _________ focuses on these energy changes, particularly on the system's energy exchange with its surroundings.

a. Bioaerosol
b. Thermochemistry
c. Boiling-point elevation
d. Bolaamphiphile

5. In a mixture of gases, each gas has a _________ which is the hypothetical pressure of that gas if it alone occupied the volume of the mixture at the same temperature. The total pressure of an ideal gas mixture is the sum of the _________s of each individual gas in the mixture.

It relies on the following isotherm relation: $V_x \times p_{tot} = V_{tot} \times p_x$ •V_x is the partial volume of any individual gas component (X)•V_{tot} is the total volume in gas mixture•p_x is the _________ of gas X•p_{tot} is the total pressure of gas mixture•n_x is the amount of substance of a gas (X)•n_{tot} is the total amount of substance in gas mixture

The _________ of a gas is a measure of thermodynamic activity of the gas's molecules.

a. Binding constant
b. Partial pressure
c. Bromley equation
d. Buffer solution

ANSWER KEY
12. Thermodynamic Processes and Thermochemistry

1. b
2. c
3. b
4. b
5. b

13. Spontaneous Processes and Thermodynamic Equilibrium

CHAPTER OUTLINE: KEY TERMS, PEOPLE, PLACES, CONCEPTS

- Entropy
- Gibbs free energy
- State function
- Thermodynamics
- Thermodynamic state
- Thermochemistry
- Chemical reaction
- Molecule
- Second law of thermodynamics
- Thermal contact
- Carnot cycle
- Efficiency
- Isothermal process
- Phase transition
- Ideal gas
- Isentropic process
- Absolute zero
- Mole
- Third law of thermodynamics
- Standard state
- Degree

13. Spontaneous Processes and Thermodynamic Equilibrium

CHAPTER OUTLINE: KEY TERMS, PEOPLE, PLACES, CONCEPTS

Heat engine

CHAPTER HIGHLIGHTS & NOTES: KEY TERMS, PEOPLE, PLACES, CONCEPTS

Entropy

In thermodynamics, entropy is a measure of the number of specific ways in which a thermodynamic system may be arranged, often taken to be a measure of disorder, or a measure of progressing towards thermodynamic equilibrium. The entropy of an isolated system never decreases, because isolated systems spontaneously evolve towards thermodynamic equilibrium, which is the state of maximum entropy.

Entropy was originally defined for a thermodynamically reversible process as

$$\Delta S = \int \frac{dQ_{rev}}{T}$$

where the entropy is found from the uniform thermodynamic temperature of a closed system dividing an incremental reversible transfer of heat into that system .

Gibbs free energy

In thermodynamics, the Gibbs free energy is a thermodynamic potential that measures the 'usefulness' or process-initiating work obtainable from a thermodynamic system at a constant temperature and pressure (isothermal, isobaric). Just as in mechanics, where potential energy is defined as capacity to do work, similarly different potentials have different meanings. The Gibbs free energy is the maximum amount of non-expansion work that can be extracted from a closed system; this maximum can be attained only in a completely reversible process.

State function

In thermodynamics, a state function, function of state, state quantity, or state variable is a property of a system that depends only on the current state of the system, not on the way in which the system acquired that state . A state function describes the equilibrium state of a system. For example, internal energy, enthalpy, and entropy are state quantities because they describe quantitatively an equilibrium state of a thermodynamic system, irrespective of how the system arrived in that state.

Thermodynamics

Thermodynamics is a branch of natural science concerned with heat and its relation to energy and work. It defines macroscopic variables (such as temperature, internal energy, entropy, and pressure) that characterize materials and radiation, and explains how they are related and by what laws they change with time.

Thermodynamic state	For thermodynamics, a thermodynamic state of a system is fully identified by values of a suitable set of parameters known as state variables, state parameters or thermodynamic variables. Once such a set of values of thermodynamic variables has been specified for a system, the values of all thermodynamic properties of the system are uniquely determined. Thermodynamics sets up an idealized formalism that can be summarized by a system of postulates of thermodynamics.
Thermochemistry	Thermochemistry is the study of the energy and heat associated with chemical reactions and/or physical transformations. A reaction may release or absorb energy, and a phase change may do the same, such as in melting and boiling. Thermochemistry focuses on these energy changes, particularly on the system's energy exchange with its surroundings.
Chemical reaction	A chemical reaction is a process that leads to the transformation of one set of chemical substances to another. Classically, chemical reactions encompass changes that only involve the positions of electrons in the forming and breaking of chemical bonds between atoms, with no change to the nuclei (no change to the elements present), and can often be described by a chemical equation. Nuclear chemistry is a sub-discipline of chemistry that involves the chemical reactions of unstable and radioactive elements where both electronic and nuclear changes may both occur.
Molecule	A molecule is an electrically neutral group of two or more atoms held together by chemical bonds. Molecules are distinguished from ions by their lack of electrical charge. However, in quantum physics, organic chemistry, and biochemistry, the term molecule is often used less strictly, also being applied to polyatomic ions.
Second law of thermodynamics	The second law of thermodynamics states that the entropy of an isolated system never decreases, because isolated systems spontaneously evolve toward thermodynamic equilibrium--the state of maximum entropy. Equivalently, perpetual motion machines of the second kind are impossible. The second law is an empirically validated postulate of thermodynamics, but it can be understood and explained using the underlying quantum statistical mechanics, together with the assumption of low-entropy initial conditions in the distant past of a system results from an infinitesimal transfer of heat to a closed system divided by the common temperature of the system and the surroundings which supply the heat.
Thermal contact	In heat transfer and thermodynamics, a thermodynamic system is said to be in thermal contact with another system if it can exchange energy with it through the process of heat. Perfect thermal isolation is an idealization as real systems are always in thermal contact with their environment to some extent. The area available for heat flow through interstitial gaps often is 2 to 4 orders of magnitude greater than the contact area; heat flow through gaps can't be neglected especially if the solids are relatively poor conductors or interface medium is a good conductor.

13. Spontaneous Processes and Thermodynamic Equilibrium

CHAPTER HIGHLIGHTS & NOTES: KEY TERMS, PEOPLE, PLACES, CONCEPTS

Carnot cycle	The Carnot cycle is a theoretical thermodynamic cycle proposed by Nicolas Léonard Sadi Carnot in 1823 and expanded by in the 1830s and 40s. It can be shown that it is the most efficient cycle for converting a given amount of thermal energy into work, or conversely, creating a temperature difference (e.g. refrigeration) by doing a given amount of work. Every single thermodynamic system exists in a particular state.
Efficiency	Efficiency in general, describes the extent to which time, effort or cost is well used for the intended task or purpose. It is often used with the specific purpose of relaying the capability of a specific application of effort to produce a specific outcome effectively with a minimum amount or quantity of waste, expense, or unnecessary effort. 'Efficiency' has widely varying meanings in different disciplines.
Isothermal process	An isothermal process is a change of a system, in which the temperature remains constant: ?T = 0. This typically occurs when a system is in contact with an outside thermal reservoir (heat bath), and the change occurs slowly enough to allow the system to continually adjust to the temperature of the reservoir through heat exchange. In contrast, an adiabatic process is where a system exchanges no heat with its surroundings (Q = 0). In other words, in an isothermal process, the value ?T = 0 but Q ? 0, while in an adiabatic process, ?T ? 0 but Q = 0.
Phase transition	A phase transition is the transformation of thermodynamic system from one phase or state of matter to another. A phase of a thermodynamic system and the states of matter have uniform physical properties. During a phase transition of a given medium certain properties of the medium change, often discontinuously, as a result of some external condition, such as temperature, pressure, and others.
Ideal gas	An ideal gas is a theoretical gas composed of a set of randomly moving, non-interacting point particles. The ideal gas concept is useful because it obeys the ideal gas law, a simplified equation of state, and is amenable to analysis under statistical mechanics. At normal conditions such as standard temperature and pressure, most real gases behave qualitatively like an ideal gas.
Isentropic process	In thermodynamics, an isentropic process or isoentropic process (?s?? = 'equal' ; e?t??p?a entropy = 'disorder'(Greek)) is one in which, for purposes of engineering analysis and calculation, one may assume that the process takes place from initiation to completion without an increase or decrease in the entropy of the system, i.e., the entropy of the system remains constant. It can be proven that any reversible adiabatic process is an isentropic process. A simple more common definition of isentropic would be 'No change in entropy'.

Absolute zero

Absolute zero is the lowest temperature possible. More formally, it is the temperature at which entropy reaches its minimum value. The laws of thermodynamics state that absolute zero cannot be reached using only thermodynamic means.

Mole

Mole is a unit of measurement used in chemistry to express amounts of a chemical substance, defined as the amount of any substance that contains as many elementary entities (e.g., atoms, molecules, ions, electrons) as there are atoms in 12 grams of pure carbon-12, the isotope of carbon with relative atomic mass 12. This corresponds to the Avogadro constant, which has a value of $6.02214129(27) \times 10^{23}$ elementary entities of the substance. It is one of the base units in the International System of Units, and has the unit symbol mol and corresponds with the dimension symbol N. In honour of the unit, chemists often celebrate October 23 (a reference to the 10^{23} part of Avogadro's number) as 'Mole Day'.

The mole is widely used in chemistry instead of units of mass or volume as a convenient way to express amounts of reactants or of products of chemical reactions.

Third law of thermodynamics

The third law of thermodynamics is sometimes stated as follows:'

The entropy of a perfect crystal, at absolute zero kelvin, is exactly equal to zero. '

At zero kelvin the system must be in a state with the minimum possible energy, and this statement of the third law holds true if the perfect crystal has only one minimum energy state. Entropy is related to the number of possible microstates, and with only one microstate available at zero kelvin, the entropy is exactly zero.

Standard state

In chemistry, the standard state of a material is a reference point used to calculate its properties under different conditions. In principle, the choice of standard state is arbitrary, although the International Union of Pure and Applied Chemistry (IUPAC) recommends a conventional set of standard states for general use. IUPAC recommends using a standard pressure $p^o = 10^5$ Pa.

Degree

The term degree is used in several scales of temperature. The symbol ° is usually used, followed by the initial letter of the unit, for example "°C" for degree(s) Celsius. A degree can be defined as a set change in temperature measured against a given scale, for example, one degree Celsius is one hundredth of the temperature change between the point at which water starts to change state from Solid to liquid state and the point at which it starts to change from its gaseous state to liquid.

Heat engine

In thermodynamics, a heat engine is a system that performs the conversion of heat or thermal energy to mechanical work. It does this by bringing a working substance from a higher state temperature to a lower state temperature. A heat 'source' generates thermal energy that brings the working substance to the high temperature state.

13. Spontaneous Processes and Thermodynamic Equilibrium

CHAPTER QUIZ: KEY TERMS, PEOPLE, PLACES, CONCEPTS

1. In thermodynamics, the _________ is a thermodynamic potential that measures the 'usefulness' or process-initiating work obtainable from a thermodynamic system at a constant temperature and pressure (isothermal, isobaric). Just as in mechanics, where potential energy is defined as capacity to do work, similarly different potentials have different meanings. The _________ is the maximum amount of non-expansion work that can be extracted from a closed system; this maximum can be attained only in a completely reversible process.

   a. CALPHAD
   b. Thermodynamic free energy
   c. Gibbs free energy
   d. Flue-gas desulfurization

2. _________ is a branch of natural science concerned with heat and its relation to energy and work. It defines macroscopic variables (such as temperature, internal energy, entropy, and pressure) that characterize materials and radiation, and explains how they are related and by what laws they change with time. _________ describes the average behavior of very large numbers of microscopic constituents, and its laws can be derived from statistical mechanics.

   a. 4A Molecular Sieve
   b. Basic sediment and water
   c. Biochemical engineering
   d. Thermodynamics

3. In thermodynamics, _________ is a measure of the number of specific ways in which a thermodynamic system may be arranged, often taken to be a measure of disorder, or a measure of progressing towards thermodynamic equilibrium. The _________ of an isolated system never decreases, because isolated systems spontaneously evolve towards thermodynamic equilibrium, which is the state of maximum _________.

   _________ was originally defined for a thermodynamically reversible process as $\Delta S = \int \frac{dQ_{rev}}{T}$

   where the _________ is found from the uniform thermodynamic temperature of a closed system dividing an incremental reversible transfer of heat into that system .

   a. Boltzmann brain
   b. Configuration entropy
   c. Entropy
   d. Flue-gas desulfurization

4. . In thermodynamics, a _________, function of state, state quantity, or state variable is a property of a system that depends only on the current state of the system, not on the way in which the system acquired that state . A _________ describes the equilibrium state of a system. For example, internal energy, enthalpy, and entropy are state quantities because they describe quantitatively an equilibrium state of a thermodynamic system, irrespective of how the system arrived in that state.

   a. Backdraft

b. State function
c. Binodal
d. Bjerrum plot

5. For thermodynamics, a _________ of a system is fully identified by values of a suitable set of parameters known as state variables, state parameters or thermodynamic variables. Once such a set of values of thermodynamic variables has been specified for a system, the values of all thermodynamic properties of the system are uniquely determined.

   Thermodynamics sets up an idealized formalism that can be summarized by a system of postulates of thermodynamics.

   a. Backdraft
   b. Batteryless radio
   c. Thermodynamic state
   d. Bjerrum plot

ANSWER KEY
13. Spontaneous Processes and Thermodynamic Equilibrium

1. c
2. d
3. c
4. b
5. c

---

14. Chemical Equilibrium

CHAPTER OUTLINE: KEY TERMS, PEOPLE, PLACES, CONCEPTS

Chemical reaction

Equilibrium constant

Thermodynamic equilibrium

Concentration

Partial pressure

Product

Chemical equilibrium

Steady state

Coefficient

Water gas

Carbon

Carbon monoxide

Hydrogen

Methane

Ideal solution

Thermodynamics

Activity coefficient

Reaction quotient

Hemoglobin

Molecule

Oxygen

14. Chemical Equilibrium

CHAPTER OUTLINE: KEY TERMS, PEOPLE, PLACES, CONCEPTS

	Saturation
	Volume
	Exothermic
	Exothermic reaction
	Vapor pressure
	Reaction rate
	Solute
	Extraction
	Solvent
	Chromatography

CHAPTER HIGHLIGHTS & NOTES: KEY TERMS, PEOPLE, PLACES, CONCEPTS

Chemical reaction	A chemical reaction is a process that leads to the transformation of one set of chemical substances to another. Classically, chemical reactions encompass changes that only involve the positions of electrons in the forming and breaking of chemical bonds between atoms, with no change to the nuclei (no change to the elements present), and can often be described by a chemical equation. Nuclear chemistry is a sub-discipline of chemistry that involves the chemical reactions of unstable and radioactive elements where both electronic and nuclear changes may both occur.
Equilibrium constant	For a general chemical equilibrium $\alpha A + \beta B ... \rightleftharpoons \rho R + \sigma S ...$ the thermodynamic equilibrium constant can be defined such that, at equilibrium, $K^{\ominus} = \frac{\{R\}^{\rho}\{S\}^{\sigma}...}{\{A\}^{\alpha}\{B\}^{\beta}...}$

where curly brackets denote the thermodynamic activities of the chemical species. The logarithm of this expression appears in the formula for the Gibbs free energy change for the reaction. If deviations from ideal behaviour are neglected, the activities may be replaced by concentrations, [A], and a concentration quotient, K_c.

Thermodynamic equilibrium

In thermodynamics, a thermodynamic system is in thermodynamic equilibrium when it is in thermal equilibrium, mechanical equilibrium, radiative equilibrium, and chemical equilibrium. Equilibrium means a state of balance. In a state of thermodynamic equilibrium, there are no net flows of matter or of energy, no phase changes, and no unbalanced potentials (or driving forces), within the system.

Concentration

In chemistry, concentration is the abundance of a constituent divided by the total volume of a mixture. Several types of mathematical description can be distinguished: mass concentration, molar concentration, number concentration, and volume concentration. The term concentration can be applied to any kind of chemical mixture, but most frequently it refers to solutes and solvents in solutions.

Partial pressure

In a mixture of gases, each gas has a partial pressure which is the hypothetical pressure of that gas if it alone occupied the volume of the mixture at the same temperature. The total pressure of an ideal gas mixture is the sum of the partial pressures of each individual gas in the mixture.

It relies on the following isotherm relation: $V_x \times p_{tot} = V_{tot} \times p_x$ •V_x is the partial volume of any individual gas component (X)•V_{tot} is the total volume in gas mixture•p_x is the partial pressure of gas X•p_{tot} is the total pressure of gas mixture•n_x is the amount of substance of a gas (X)•n_{tot} is the total amount of substance in gas mixture

The partial pressure of a gas is a measure of thermodynamic activity of the gas's molecules.

Product

Product are formed during chemical reactions as reagents are consumed. Products have lower energy than the reagents and are produced during the reaction according to the second law of thermodynamics. The released energy comes from changes in chemical bonds between atoms in reagent molecules and may be given off in the form of heat or light.

Chemical equilibrium

In a chemical reaction, chemical equilibrium is the state in which both reactants and products are present at concentrations which have no further tendency to change with time. Usually, this state results when the forward reaction proceeds at the same rate as the reverse reaction. The reaction rates of the forward and backward reactions are generally not zero, but equal.

Steady state

In chemistry, a steady state is a situation in which all state variables are constant in spite of ongoing processes that strive to change them. For an entire system to be at steady state, i.e.

for all state variables of a system to be constant, there must be a flow through the system (compare mass balance). One of the most simple examples of such a system is the case of a bathtub with the tap open but without the bottom plug: after a certain time the water flows in and out at the same rate, so the water level (the state variable being Volume) stabilizes and the system is at steady state.

Coefficient

In mathematics, a coefficient is a multiplicative factor in some term of an expression ; it is usually a number, but in any case does not involve any variables of the expression. For instance in $7x^2 - 3xy + 1.5 + y$

the first two terms respectively have the coefficients 7 and -3. The third term 1.5 is a constant. The final term does not have any explicitly written coefficient, but is considered to have coefficient 1, since multiplying by that factor would not change the term.

Water gas

Water gas is a synthesis gas, containing carbon monoxide and hydrogen. It is a useful product but requires careful handling because of the risk of carbon monoxide poisoning. The gas is made by passing steam over a red-hot carbon fuel such as coke:H_2O + C ? H_2 + CO (?H = +131 kJ/mol)

The reaction is endothermic so the fuel must be continually re-heated to keep the reaction going.

Carbon

Carbon fiber, alternatively graphite fiber, carbon graphite or CF, is a material consisting of fibers about 5-10 μm in diameter and composed mostly of carbon atoms. The carbon atoms are bonded together in crystals that are more or less aligned parallel to the long axis of the fiber. The crystal alignment gives the fiber high strength-to-volume ratio (making it strong for its size).

Carbon monoxide

Carbon monoxide is a colorless, odorless, and tasteless gas that is slightly less dense than air. It is toxic to humans and animals when encountered in higher concentrations, although it is also produced in normal animal metabolism in low quantities, and is thought to have some normal biological functions. In the atmosphere, it is spatially variable, short lived, having a role in the formation of ground-level ozone.

Hydrogen

Hydrogen is a chemical element with chemical symbol H and atomic number 1. With an atomic weight of 1.00794 u, hydrogen is the lightest element and its monatomic form (H) is the most abundant chemical substance, constituting roughly 75% of the Universe's baryonic mass. Non-remnant stars are mainly composed of hydrogen in its plasma state.

At standard temperature and pressure, hydrogen is a colorless, odorless, tasteless, non-toxic, nonmetallic, highly combustible diatomic gas with the molecular formula H_2.

Methane

Methane is a chemical compound with the chemical formula CH4 (one atom of carbon and four atoms of hydrogen). It is the simplest alkane and the main component of natural gas.

14. Chemical Equilibrium

Ideal solution	In chemistry, an ideal solution or ideal mixture is a solution with thermodynamic properties analogous to those of a mixture of ideal gases. The enthalpy of solution (or 'enthalpy of mixing') is zero as is the volume change on mixing; the closer to zero the enthalpy of solution is, the more 'ideal' the behavior of the solution becomes. The vapour pressure of the solution obeys Raoult's law, and the activity coefficients (which measure deviation from ideality) are equal to one.
Thermodynamics	Thermodynamics is a branch of natural science concerned with heat and its relation to energy and work. It defines macroscopic variables (such as temperature, internal energy, entropy, and pressure) that characterize materials and radiation, and explains how they are related and by what laws they change with time. Thermodynamics describes the average behavior of very large numbers of microscopic constituents, and its laws can be derived from statistical mechanics.
Activity coefficient	An activity coefficient is a factor used in thermodynamics to account for deviations from ideal behaviour in a mixture of chemical substances. In an ideal mixture, the interactions between each pair of chemical species are the same (or more formally, the enthalpy change of solution is zero) and, as a result, properties of the mixtures can be expressed directly in terms of simple concentrations or partial pressures of the substances present e.g. Raoult's law. Deviations from ideality are accommodated by modifying the concentration by an activity coefficient.
Reaction quotient	In chemistry, a reaction quotient: Q_r is a function of the activities or concentrations of the chemical species involved in a chemical reaction. In the special case that the reaction is at equilibrium the reaction quotient is equal to the equilibrium constant. A general chemical reaction in which a moles of a reactant A and ß moles of a reactant B react to give s moles of a product S and t moles of a product T can be written asaA + ßB sS + tT The reaction is written as an equilibrium even though in many cases it may appear to have gone to completion.
Hemoglobin	Hemoglobin; also spelled haemoglobin and abbreviated Hb or Hgb, is the iron-containing oxygen-transport metalloprotein in the red blood cells of all vertebrates as well as the tissues of some invertebrates. Hemoglobin in the blood carries oxygen from the respiratory organs (lungs or gills) to the rest of the body (i.e. the tissues) where it releases the oxygen to burn nutrients to provide energy to power the functions of the organism, and collects the resultant carbon dioxide to bring it back to the respiratory organs to be dispensed from the organism. In mammals, the protein makes up about 97% of the red blood cells' dry content (by weight), and around 35% of the total content (including water).
Molecule	A molecule is an electrically neutral group of two or more atoms held together by chemical bonds. Molecules are distinguished from ions by their lack of electrical charge.

Oxygen	Oxygen is a chemical element with symbol O and atomic number 8. It is a member of the chalcogen group on the periodic table and is a highly reactive nonmetallic element and oxidizing agent that readily forms compounds (notably oxides) with most elements. By mass, oxygen is the third-most abundant element in the universe, after hydrogen and helium At STP, two atoms of the element bind to form dioxygen, a diatomic gas that is colorless, odorless, and tasteless; with the formula O2. Many major classes of organic molecules in living organisms, such as proteins, nucleic acids, carbohydrates, and fats, contain oxygen, as do the major inorganic compounds that are constituents of animal shells, teeth, and bone.
Saturation	In chemistry, saturation has diverse meanings, all based on reaching a maximum capacity. •In physical chemistry, saturation is the point at which a solution of a substance can dissolve no more of that substance and additional amounts of it will appear as a separate phase (as a precipitate if solid or as effervescence or inclusion if gaseous). This point of maximum concentration, the saturation point, depends on the temperature and pressure of the solution as well as the chemical nature of the substances involved.
Volume	In thermodynamics, the volume of a system is an important extensive parameter for describing its thermodynamic state. The specific volume, an intensive property, is the system's volume per unit of mass. Volume is a function of state and is interdependent with other thermodynamic properties such as pressure and temperature.
Exothermic	In thermodynamics, the term exothermic describes a process or reaction that releases energy from the system, usually in the form of heat, but also in a form of light (e.g. a spark, flame, or flash), electricity (e.g. a battery), or sound (e.g. explosion heard when burning hydrogen). Its etymology stems from the prefix exo (derived from the Greek word ???, exo, 'outside') and the Greek word thermasi (meaning 'to heat'). The term exothermic was first coined by Marcellin Berthelot.
Exothermic reaction	An exothermic reaction is a chemical reaction that releases energy in the form of light or heat. It is the opposite of an endothermic reaction. Expressed in a chemical equation: reactants ? products + energy
Vapor pressure	Vapor pressure or equilibrium vapor pressure is the pressure exerted by a vapor in thermodynamic equilibrium with its condensed phases at a given temperature in a closed system. The equilibrium vapor pressure is an indication of a liquid's evaporation rate. It relates to the tendency of particles to escape from the liquid (or a solid).
Reaction rate	The reaction rate or speed of reaction for a reactant or product in a particular reaction is intuitively defined as how fast or slow a reaction takes place.

For example, the oxidative rusting of iron under Earth's atmosphere is a slow reaction that can take many years, but the combustion of cellulose in a fire is a reaction that takes place in fractions of a second.

Chemical kinetics is the part of physical chemistry that studies reaction rates.

Solute

A solute is a substance that creates a solution when dissolved in a solvent. For example, when sugar (solute) is dissolved in water (solvent).Solute can change its physical state but solvent and solution are of same phase.e.g sugar is solid before getting dissolved in water, and after dissolution it changes its phase to a liquid.

Etymology: from Latin solutus, past participle of solvere, meaning to loosen.

Extraction

Extraction in chemistry is a separation process consisting in the separation of a substance from a matrix. It may refer to Liquid-liquid extraction, and Solid phase extraction.

Other techniques include Supercritical carbon dioxide extraction, ultrasonic extraction, heat reflux extraction, microwave-assisted extraction, DIC (instant controlled pressure drop).

Solvent

A solvent is a substance that dissolves a solute (a chemically different liquid, solid or gas), resulting in a solution. A solvent is usually a liquid but can also be a solid or a gas. The maximum quantity of solute that can dissolve in a specific volume of solvent varies with temperature.

Chromatography

Chromatography is the collective term for a set of laboratory techniques for the separation of mixtures. The mixture is dissolved in a fluid called the mobile phase, which carries it through a structure holding another material called the stationary phase. The various constituents of the mixture travel at different speeds, causing them to separate.

1. _________ is a colorless, odorless, and tasteless gas that is slightly less dense than air. It is toxic to humans and animals when encountered in higher concentrations, although it is also produced in normal animal metabolism in low quantities, and is thought to have some normal biological functions. In the atmosphere, it is spatially variable, short lived, having a role in the formation of ground-level ozone.

   a. Benzoquinonetetracarboxylic dianhydride
   b. Carbon monoxide
   c. Barium acetylacetonate
   d. Cerium acetylacetonate

2. A _________ is a substance that dissolves a solute (a chemically different liquid, solid or gas), resulting in a solution. A _________ is usually a liquid but can also be a solid or a gas. The maximum quantity of solute that can dissolve in a specific volume of _________ varies with temperature.

   a. Bioorthogonal chemistry
   b. Solvent
   c. Carbothermic reaction
   d. Ceramide phosphoethanolamine synthase

3. _________ are formed during chemical reactions as reagents are consumed. _________s have lower energy than the reagents and are produced during the reaction according to the second law of thermodynamics. The released energy comes from changes in chemical bonds between atoms in reagent molecules and may be given off in the form of heat or light.

   a. Bioorthogonal chemistry
   b. Carbonylation
   c. Product
   d. Ceramide phosphoethanolamine synthase

4. _________ in chemistry is a separation process consisting in the separation of a substance from a matrix. It may refer to Liquid-liquid _________, and Solid phase _________.

   Other techniques include Supercritical carbon dioxide _________, ultrasonic _________, heat reflux _________, microwave-assisted _________, DIC (instant controlled pressure drop).

   a. Biomonitoring
   b. Extraction
   c. Bradford protein assay
   d. Bulk material analyzer

5. . A _________ is a substance that creates a solution when dissolved in a solvent. For example, when sugar (_________) is dissolved in water (solvent)._________ can change its physical state but solvent and solution are of same phase.e.g sugar is solid before getting dissolved in water, and after dissolution it changes its phase to a liquid.

Etymology: from Latin solutus, past participle of solvere, meaning to loosen.

a. Bunsen solubility coefficient
b. Concentrate
c. Condosity
d. Solute

ANSWER KEY
14. Chemical Equilibrium

1. b
2. b
3. c
4. b
5. d

---

15. Acid—Base Equilibria

CHAPTER OUTLINE: KEY TERMS, PEOPLE, PLACES, CONCEPTS

- Hydroxide
- Hydrogen
- Amphoterism
- Acceptor
- Chemical bond
- Electron
- Electron pair
- Acid anhydride
- Anhydride
- Activity coefficient
- Autoionization
- Aqueous
- Coefficient
- Concentration
- Dissociation
- Equilibrium constant
- Homogeneous
- Hydronium
- Molecule
- Product
- Leveling effect

15. Acid—Base Equilibria

CHAPTER OUTLINE: KEY TERMS, PEOPLE, PLACES, CONCEPTS

	Conjugate acid
	Solvent
	Strength
	Galvanic cell
	PH meter
	Electrolyte
	Oxoacid
	Weak base
	Hydrolysis
	Buffer solution
	Buffer
	Titration
	Titration curve
	Volume
	Equivalence point
	Ideal solution
	Thermodynamics
	Blood plasma
	Plasma
	Organic acid
	Atom

Resonance

CHAPTER HIGHLIGHTS & NOTES: KEY TERMS, PEOPLE, PLACES, CONCEPTS

Hydroxide

Hydroxide is a diatomic anion with chemical formula OH^-. It consists of an oxygen and a hydrogen atom held together by a covalent bond, and carries a negative electric charge. It is an important but usually minor constituent of water.

Hydrogen

Hydrogen is a chemical element with chemical symbol H and atomic number 1. With an atomic weight of 1.00794 u, hydrogen is the lightest element and its monatomic form (H) is the most abundant chemical substance, constituting roughly 75% of the Universe's baryonic mass. Non-remnant stars are mainly composed of hydrogen in its plasma state.

At standard temperature and pressure, hydrogen is a colorless, odorless, tasteless, non-toxic, nonmetallic, highly combustible diatomic gas with the molecular formula H_2.

Amphoterism

In chemistry, an amphoteric species is a molecule or ion that can react as an acid as well as a base. Many metals (such as zinc, tin, lead, aluminium, and beryllium) and most metalloids form amphoteric oxides or hydroxides. Amphoterism depends on the oxidation state of the oxide.

Acceptor

In semiconductor physics, an acceptor is a dopant atom that when added to a semiconductor can form a p-type region.

For example, when silicon, having four valence electrons, needs to be doped as a p-type semiconductor, elements from group III like boron (B) or aluminium (Al), having three valence electrons, can be used. The latter elements are also called trivalent impurities.

Chemical bond

A chemical bond is an attraction between atoms that allows the formation of chemical substances that contain two or more atoms. The bond is caused by the electrostatic force of attraction between opposite charges, either between electrons and nuclei, or as the result of a dipole attraction. The strength of chemical bonds varies considerably; there are 'strong bonds' such as covalent or ionic bonds and 'weak bonds' such as dipole-dipole interactions, the London dispersion force and hydrogen bonding.

Electron

The electron is a subatomic particle with a negative elementary electric charge.

Electrons belong to the first generation of the lepton particle family, and are generally thought to be elementary particles because they have no known components or substructure. The electron has a mass that is approximately 1/1836 that of the proton.

Electron pair

In chemistry, an electron pair consists of two electrons that occupy the same orbital but have opposite spins. The electron pair concept was introduced in a 1916 paper of Gilbert N. Lewis.

Because electrons are fermions, the Pauli exclusion principle forbids these particles from having exactly the same quantum numbers.

Acid anhydride

Commonly an acid anhydride is an organic compound that has two acyl groups bound to the same oxygen atom. Most commonly, the acyl groups are derived from the same carboxylic acid, the formula of the anhydride being $(RC(O))_2O$. Symmetrical acid anhydrides of this type are named by replacing the word acid in the name of the parent carboxylic acid by the word anhydride. Thus, $(CH_3CO)_2O$ is called acetic anhydride.

Anhydride

Commonly an acid anhydride is an organic compound that has two acyl groups bound to the same oxygen atom. For the inorganic equivalent, see Acidic oxide. Most commonly, the acyl groups are derived from the same carboxylic acid, the formula of the anhydride being $(RC(O))_2O$. Symmetrical acid anhydrides of this type are named by replacing the word acid in the name of the parent carboxylic acid by the word anhydride.

Activity coefficient

An activity coefficient is a factor used in thermodynamics to account for deviations from ideal behaviour in a mixture of chemical substances. In an ideal mixture, the interactions between each pair of chemical species are the same (or more formally, the enthalpy change of solution is zero) and, as a result, properties of the mixtures can be expressed directly in terms of simple concentrations or partial pressures of the substances present e.g. Raoult's law. Deviations from ideality are accommodated by modifying the concentration by an activity coefficient.

Autoionization

Autoionization is a process by which atoms or molecules spontaneously emit one of the shell electrons, thus going from a state with charge Z to a state with charge Z?+?1, for example from an electrically neutral state to a singly ionized state.

Atoms can autoionize when either two or more valence electrons are excited or one or more inner-shell electrons are missing. In the latter case, it is called the Auger effect.

Aqueous

An aqueous solution is a solution in which the solvent is water. It is usually shown in chemical equations by appending (aq) to the relevant formula. For example, a solution of ordinary table salt, or sodium chloride (NaCl), in water would be represented as NaCl(aq).

Coefficient

In mathematics, a coefficient is a multiplicative factor in some term of an expression ; it is usually a number, but in any case does not involve any variables of the expression. For instance in

$$7x^2 - 3xy + 1.5 + y$$

the first two terms respectively have the coefficients 7 and -3. The third term 1.5 is a constant. The final term does not have any explicitly written coefficient, but is considered to have coefficient 1, since multiplying by that factor would not change the term.

Concentration

In chemistry, concentration is the abundance of a constituent divided by the total volume of a mixture. Several types of mathematical description can be distinguished: mass concentration, molar concentration, number concentration, and volume concentration. The term concentration can be applied to any kind of chemical mixture, but most frequently it refers to solutes and solvents in solutions.

Dissociation

Dissociation in chemistry and biochemistry is a general process in which ionic compounds separate or split into smaller particles, ions, or radicals, usually in a reversible manner. For instance, when a Brønsted-Lowry acid is put in water, a covalent bond between an electronegative atom and a hydrogen atom is broken by heterolytic fission, which gives a proton and a negative ion. Dissociation is the opposite of association and recombination.

Equilibrium constant

For a general chemical equilibrium $\alpha A + \beta B ... \rightleftharpoons \rho R + \sigma S ...$

the thermodynamic equilibrium constant can be defined such that, at equilibrium,

$$K^{\ominus} = \frac{\{R\}^{\rho}\{S\}^{\sigma}...}{\{A\}^{\alpha}\{B\}^{\beta}...}$$

where curly brackets denote the thermodynamic activities of the chemical species. The logarithm of this expression appears in the formula for the Gibbs free energy change for the reaction. If deviations from ideal behaviour are neglected, the activities may be replaced by concentrations, [A], and a concentration quotient, K_c.

Homogeneous

Homogeneous as a term in physical chemistry and material science refers to substances and mixtures which are in a single phase. This is in contrast to a substance that is heterogeneous. The definition of homogeneous strongly depends on the context used.

Hydronium

The hydronium cation, also known as hydroxonium is the positively charged polyatomic ion with the chemical formula H3O+. Hydronium, a type of oxonium ion, is formed by the protonation of water (H2O). This cation is often used to represent the nature of the proton in aqueous solution, where the proton is highly solvated (bound to a solvent).

Molecule

A molecule is an electrically neutral group of two or more atoms held together by chemical bonds. Molecules are distinguished from ions by their lack of electrical charge.

15. Acid—Base Equilibria

Product	Product are formed during chemical reactions as reagents are consumed. Products have lower energy than the reagents and are produced during the reaction according to the second law of thermodynamics. The released energy comes from changes in chemical bonds between atoms in reagent molecules and may be given off in the form of heat or light.
Leveling effect	Leveling effect or solvent leveling refers to the effect of solvent on the properties of acids and bases. The strength of a strong acid is limited ('leveled') by the basicity of the solvent. Similarly the strength of a strong base is leveled by the acidity of the solvent.
Conjugate acid	A conjugate acid, within the Brønsted-Lowry theory, is a species formed by the reception of a proton, by a base - in other words, the base with a hydrogen ion added to it - while a conjugate base is formed by the removal of a proton from an acid: the conjugate base of an acid is that acid with a hydrogen ion removed. Visually, this can be represented as:A conjugate acid of the base ? Base + H+A conjugate base of the acid ? Acid - H+ The Brønsted-Lowry model is based on the idea that acids are proton donors and bases are proton acceptors; the conjugate base or conjugate acid is merely what is left after an acid has lost a proton or a base has gained a proton, respectively.
Solvent	A solvent is a substance that dissolves a solute (a chemically different liquid, solid or gas), resulting in a solution. A solvent is usually a liquid but can also be a solid or a gas. The maximum quantity of solute that can dissolve in a specific volume of solvent varies with temperature.
Strength	In explosive materials, strength is the parameter determining the ability of the explosive to move the surrounding material. It is related to the total gas yield of the reaction, and the amount of heat produced. Cf.
Galvanic cell	A galvanic cell, or voltaic cell or Alessandro Volta respectively, is an electrochemical cell that derives electrical energy from spontaneous redox reactions taking place within the cell. It generally consists of two different metals connected by a salt bridge, or individual half-cells separated by a porous membrane. Volta was the inventor of the voltaic pile, the first electrical battery.
PH meter	A pH meter is an electronic device used for measuring the pH of a liquid (though special probes are sometimes used to measure the pH of semi-solid substances). A typical pH meter consists of a special measuring probe (a glass electrode) connected to an electronic meter that measures and displays the pH reading.

Electrolyte	An electrolyte is a compound that ionizes when dissolved in suitable ionizing solvents such as water. This includes most soluble salts, acids, and bases. Some gases, such as hydrogen chloride, under conditions of high temperature or low pressure can also function as electrolytes.
Oxoacid	An oxoacid is an acid that contains oxygen. To be more specific, it is an acid that:•contains oxygen•contains at least one other element•has at least one hydrogen atom bound to oxygen•forms an ion by the loss of one or more protons. The name oxyacid is sometimes used.
Weak base	In chemistry, a weak base is a chemical base that does not ionize fully in an aqueous solution. As Brønsted-Lowry bases are proton acceptors, a weak base may also be defined as a chemical base in which protonation is incomplete. This results in a relatively low pH compared to strong bases.
Hydrolysis	Hydrolysis usually means the cleavage of chemical bonds by the addition of water. Where a carbohydrate is broken into its component sugar molecules by hydrolysis this is termed saccharification. Generally, hydrolysis or saccharification is a step in the degradation of a substance.
Buffer solution	A buffer is an aqueous solution consisting of a mixture of a weak acid and its conjugate base or a weak base and its conjugate acid. Its pH changes very little when a small amount of strong acid or base is added to it and thus it is used to prevent changes in the pH of a solution. Buffer solutions are used as a means of keeping pH at a nearly constant value in a wide variety of chemical applications.
Buffer	In a fiber optic cable, a buffer is one type of component used to encapsulate one or more optical fibers for the purpose of providing such functions as mechanical isolation, protection from physical damage and fiber identification. The buffer may take the form of a miniature conduit, contained within the cable and called a 'loose buffer', or 'loose buffer tube'. A loose buffer may contain more than one fiber, and sometimes contains a lubricating gel.
Titration	Titration, also known as titrimetry, is a common laboratory method of quantitative chemical analysis that is used to determine the unknown concentration of an identified analyte. Since volume measurements play a key role in titration, it is also known as volumetric analysis. A reagent, called the titrant or titrator is prepared as a standard solution.
Titration curve	Titrations are often recorded on graphs called titration curves, which generally contain the volume of the titrant as the independent variable and the pH of the solution as the dependent variable .

15. Acid—Base Equilibria

The equivalence point on the graph is where all of the starting solution (usually an acid) has been neutralized by the titrant (usually a base). It can be calculated precisely by finding the second derivative of the titration curve and computing the points of inflection (where the graph changes concavity); however, in most cases, simple visual inspection of the curve will suffice (in the curve given to the right, both equivalence points are visible, after roughly 15 and 30 mL of NaOH solution has been titrated into the oxalic acid solution.

Volume

In thermodynamics, the volume of a system is an important extensive parameter for describing its thermodynamic state. The specific volume, an intensive property, is the system's volume per unit of mass. Volume is a function of state and is interdependent with other thermodynamic properties such as pressure and temperature.

Equivalence point

The equivalence point, or stoichiometric point, of a chemical reaction is the point at which an added titrant is stoichiometrically equal to the number of moles of substance present in the sample: the smallest amount of titrant that is sufficient to fully neutralize or react with the analyte. In some cases there are multiple equivalence points, which are multiples of the first equivalence point, such as in the titration of a diprotic acid.

Acid-Base Equivalence Point - the point at which chemically equivalent quantities of acid and base have been mixed, can be found by means of an indicator

In a reaction, the equivalence of the reactants as well as products is conserved.

Ideal solution

In chemistry, an ideal solution or ideal mixture is a solution with thermodynamic properties analogous to those of a mixture of ideal gases. The enthalpy of solution (or 'enthalpy of mixing') is zero as is the volume change on mixing; the closer to zero the enthalpy of solution is, the more 'ideal' the behavior of the solution becomes. The vapour pressure of the solution obeys Raoult's law, and the activity coefficients (which measure deviation from ideality) are equal to one.

Thermodynamics

Thermodynamics is a branch of natural science concerned with heat and its relation to energy and work. It defines macroscopic variables (such as temperature, internal energy, entropy, and pressure) that characterize materials and radiation, and explains how they are related and by what laws they change with time. Thermodynamics describes the average behavior of very large numbers of microscopic constituents, and its laws can be derived from statistical mechanics.

Blood plasma

Blood plasma is the straw-colored/pale-yellow liquid component of blood that normally holds the blood cells in whole blood in suspension. It makes up about 55% of total blood volume. It is the intravascular fluid part of extracellular fluid (all body fluid outside of cells).

Plasma

Plasma is one of the four fundamental states of matter (the others being solid, liquid, and gas). It comprises the major component of the Sun.

15. Acid—Base Equilibria

CHAPTER HIGHLIGHTS & NOTES: KEY TERMS, PEOPLE, PLACES, CONCEPTS

Organic acid

An organic acid is an organic compound with acidic properties. The most common organic acids are the carboxylic acids, whose acidity is associated with their carboxyl group -COOH. Sulfonic acids, containing the group $-SO_2OH$, are relatively stronger acids. Alcohols, with -OH, can act as acids but they are usually very weak.

Atom

The atom is a basic unit of matter that consists of a dense central nucleus surrounded by a cloud of negatively charged electrons. The atomic nucleus contains a mix of positively charged protons and electrically neutral neutrons, which means 'uncuttable' or 'the smallest indivisible particle of matter'. Although the Indian and Greek concepts of the atom were based purely on philosophy, modern science has retained the name coined by Democritus.

Resonance

In physics, resonance is the tendency of a system to oscillate with greater amplitude at some frequencies than at others. Frequencies at which the response amplitude is a relative maximum are known as the system's resonant frequencies, or resonance frequencies. At these frequencies, even small periodic driving forces can produce large amplitude oscillations, because the system stores vibrational energy.

CHAPTER QUIZ: KEY TERMS, PEOPLE, PLACES, CONCEPTS

1. In semiconductor physics, an _________ is a dopant atom that when added to a semiconductor can form a p-type region.

   For example, when silicon, having four valence electrons, needs to be doped as a p-type semiconductor, elements from group III like boron (B) or aluminium (Al), having three valence electrons, can be used. The latter elements are also called trivalent impurities.

   a. Chalcogel
   b. SEAgel
   c. Ceration
   d. Acceptor

2. _________ are formed during chemical reactions as reagents are consumed. _________s have lower energy than the reagents and are produced during the reaction according to the second law of thermodynamics. The released energy comes from changes in chemical bonds between atoms in reagent molecules and may be given off in the form of heat or light.

   a. Bioorthogonal chemistry
   b. Product
   c. Carbothermic reaction
   d. Ceramide phosphoethanolamine synthase

3. The _________ is a subatomic particle with a negative elementary electric charge. _________s belong to the first generation of the lepton particle family, and are generally thought to be elementary particles because they have no known components or substructure. The _________ has a mass that is approximately 1/1836 that of the proton.

a. Compton wavelength
b. Electron
c. Bohr model
d. Bohr magneton

4. _________ as a term in physical chemistry and material science refers to substances and mixtures which are in a single phase. This is in contrast to a substance that is heterogeneous. The definition of _________ strongly depends on the context used.

a. Homogeneous
b. Creosote
c. Mixture
d. Binder

5. _________ is a diatomic anion with chemical formula OH^-. It consists of an oxygen and a hydrogen atom held together by a covalent bond, and carries a negative electric charge. It is an important but usually minor constituent of water.

a. Base
b. Base modifying agent
c. Calcium oxide
d. Hydroxide

ANSWER KEY
15. Acid—Base Equilibria

1. d
2. b
3. b
4. a
5. d

---

16. Solubility and Precipitation Equilibria

CHAPTER OUTLINE: KEY TERMS, PEOPLE, PLACES, CONCEPTS

- Solubility
- Solvation
- Dissolution
- Solute
- Solvent
- Volume
- Ideal solution
- Product
- Precipitation
- Hydroxide
- Coordination complex
- Ligand
- Atom
- Molecule
- Equilibrium constant
- Amphoterism

16. Solubility and Precipitation Equilibria

CHAPTER HIGHLIGHTS & NOTES: KEY TERMS, PEOPLE, PLACES, CONCEPTS

Solubility	Solubility is the property of a solid, liquid, or gaseous chemical substance called solute to dissolve in a solid, liquid, or gaseous solvent to form a homogeneous solution of the solute in the solvent. The solubility of a substance fundamentally depends on the physical and chemical properties of the solute and solvent as well as on temperature, pressure and the pH of the solution. The extent of the solubility of a substance in a specific solvent is measured as the saturation concentration, where adding more solute does not increase the concentration of the solution and begin to precipitate the excess amount of solute.
Solvation	Solvation, also sometimes called dissolution, is the process of attraction and association of molecules of a solvent with molecules or ions of a solute. As ions dissolve in a solvent they spread out and become surrounded by solvent molecules.
Dissolution	Dissolution is the process by which a solute forms a solution in a solvent. The solute, in the case of solids, has its crystalline structure disintegrated as separate ions, atoms, and molecules form. For liquids and gases, the molecules must be adaptable with those of the solvent for a solution to form.
Solute	A solute is a substance that creates a solution when dissolved in a solvent. For example, when sugar (solute) is dissolved in water (solvent).Solute can change its physical state but solvent and solution are of same phase.e.g sugar is solid before getting dissolved in water, and after dissolution it changes its phase to a liquid. Etymology: from Latin solutus, past participle of solvere, meaning to loosen.
Solvent	A solvent is a substance that dissolves a solute (a chemically different liquid, solid or gas), resulting in a solution. A solvent is usually a liquid but can also be a solid or a gas. The maximum quantity of solute that can dissolve in a specific volume of solvent varies with temperature.
Volume	In thermodynamics, the volume of a system is an important extensive parameter for describing its thermodynamic state. The specific volume, an intensive property, is the system's volume per unit of mass. Volume is a function of state and is interdependent with other thermodynamic properties such as pressure and temperature.
Ideal solution	In chemistry, an ideal solution or ideal mixture is a solution with thermodynamic properties analogous to those of a mixture of ideal gases. The enthalpy of solution (or 'enthalpy of mixing') is zero as is the volume change on mixing; the closer to zero the enthalpy of solution is, the more 'ideal' the behavior of the solution becomes. The vapour pressure of the solution obeys Raoult's law, and the activity coefficients (which measure deviation from ideality) are equal to one.
Product	Product are formed during chemical reactions as reagents are consumed. Products have lower energy than the reagents and are produced during the reaction according to the second law of thermodynamics. The released energy comes from changes in chemical bonds between atoms in reagent molecules and may be given off in the form of heat or light.

Precipitation

Precipitation is the formation of a solid in a solution or inside another solid during a chemical reaction or by diffusion in a solid. When the reaction occurs in a liquid solution, the solid formed is called the precipitate. The chemical that causes the solid to form is called the precipitant.

Hydroxide

Hydroxide is a diatomic anion with chemical formula OH^-. It consists of an oxygen and a hydrogen atom held together by a covalent bond, and carries a negative electric charge. It is an important but usually minor constituent of water.

Coordination complex

In chemistry, a coordination complex or metal complex, consists of an atom or ion, and a surrounding array of bound molecules or anions, that are in turn known as ligands or complexing agents. Many metal-containing compounds (especially transition metals) consist of coordination complexes.

Ligand

In coordination chemistry, a ligand is an ion or molecule that binds to a central metal atom to form a coordination complex. The bonding between metal and ligand generally involves formal donation of one or more of the ligand's electron pairs. The nature of metal-ligand bonding can range from covalent to ionic.

Atom

The atom is a basic unit of matter that consists of a dense central nucleus surrounded by a cloud of negatively charged electrons. The atomic nucleus contains a mix of positively charged protons and electrically neutral neutrons, which means 'uncuttable' or 'the smallest indivisible particle of matter'. Although the Indian and Greek concepts of the atom were based purely on philosophy, modern science has retained the name coined by Democritus.

Molecule

A molecule is an electrically neutral group of two or more atoms held together by chemical bonds. Molecules are distinguished from ions by their lack of electrical charge. However, in quantum physics, organic chemistry, and biochemistry, the term molecule is often used less strictly, also being applied to polyatomic ions.

Equilibrium constant

For a general chemical equilibrium $\alpha A + \beta B ... \rightleftharpoons \rho R + \sigma S ...$

the thermodynamic equilibrium constant can be defined such that, at equilibrium,

$$K^{\ominus} = \frac{\{R\}^{\rho}\{S\}^{\sigma}...}{\{A\}^{\alpha}\{B\}^{\beta}...}$$

where curly brackets denote the thermodynamic activities of the chemical species. The logarithm of this expression appears in the formula for the Gibbs free energy change for the reaction. If deviations from ideal behaviour are neglected, the activities may be replaced by concentrations, [A], and a concentration quotient, K_c.

16. Solubility and Precipitation Equilibria

CHAPTER HIGHLIGHTS & NOTES: KEY TERMS, PEOPLE, PLACES, CONCEPTS

Amphoterism	In chemistry, an amphoteric species is a molecule or ion that can react as an acid as well as a base. Many metals (such as zinc, tin, lead, aluminium, and beryllium) and most metalloids form amphoteric oxides or hydroxides. Amphoterism depends on the oxidation state of the oxide.

CHAPTER QUIZ: KEY TERMS, PEOPLE, PLACES, CONCEPTS

1. _________ is the process by which a solute forms a solution in a solvent. The solute, in the case of solids, has its crystalline structure disintegrated as separate ions, atoms, and molecules form. For liquids and gases, the molecules must be adaptable with those of the solvent for a solution to form.

   a. Bioaerosol
   b. Dissolution
   c. Boiling-point elevation
   d. Bolaamphiphile

2. _________, also sometimes called dissolution, is the process of attraction and association of molecules of a solvent with molecules or ions of a solute. As ions dissolve in a solvent they spread out and become surrounded by solvent molecules.

   a. 3A Molecular sieve
   b. Biochemical cascade
   c. Solvation
   d. Black oxide

3. _________ is a diatomic anion with chemical formula OH^-. It consists of an oxygen and a hydrogen atom held together by a covalent bond, and carries a negative electric charge. It is an important but usually minor constituent of water.

   a. Base
   b. Hydroxide
   c. Calcium oxide
   d. Free base

4. . _________ is the property of a solid, liquid, or gaseous chemical substance called solute to dissolve in a solid, liquid, or gaseous solvent to form a homogeneous solution of the solute in the solvent. The _________ of a substance fundamentally depends on the physical and chemical properties of the solute and solvent as well as on temperature, pressure and the pH of the solution. The extent of the _________ of a substance in a specific solvent is measured as the saturation concentration, where adding more solute does not increase the concentration of the solution and begin to precipitate the excess amount of solute.

   a. Bunsen solubility coefficient

b. Concentrate
c. Solubility
d. Crenation

5. In chemistry, an _________ or ideal mixture is a solution with thermodynamic properties analogous to those of a mixture of ideal gases. The enthalpy of solution (or 'enthalpy of mixing') is zero as is the volume change on mixing; the closer to zero the enthalpy of solution is, the more 'ideal' the behavior of the solution becomes. The vapour pressure of the solution obeys Raoult's law, and the activity coefficients (which measure deviation from ideality) are equal to one.

a. Bunsen solubility coefficient
b. Concentrate
c. Ideal solution
d. Crenation

ANSWER KEY

16. Solubility and Precipitation Equilibria

1. b
2. c
3. b
4. c
5. c

You can take the complete Chapter Practice Test

17. Electrochemistry

CHAPTER OUTLINE: KEY TERMS, PEOPLE, PLACES, CONCEPTS

- Electrochemistry
- Electrode
- Electrolytic cell
- Galvanic cell
- Anode
- Cathode
- Electrochemical cell
- Ammeter
- Salt bridge
- Electrolyte
- Electron
- Half-cell
- Mixing
- Mole
- Oxidation
- Product
- Current
- Charged particle
- Nernst equation
- Electrochemical potential
- Component

17. Electrochemistry

CHAPTER OUTLINE: KEY TERMS, PEOPLE, PLACES, CONCEPTS

- Enthalpy
- Standard hydrogen electrode
- Standard state
- Oxidizing agent
- Reducing agent
- Disproportionation
- Reduction potential
- Chemical species
- Concentration
- Partial pressure
- Equilibrium constant
- PH meter
- Glass electrode
- Organic synthesis
- Cyclic voltammetry
- Aqueous
- Functional group
- Photoelectrochemistry
- Valence band
- Molecular orbital
- Molecule

17. Electrochemistry

CHAPTER OUTLINE: KEY TERMS, PEOPLE, PLACES, CONCEPTS

- Artificial photosynthesis
- Battery
- Atom
- Isotope
- Fuel cell
- Corrosion
- Extractive metallurgy
- Passivation
- Pyrometallurgy
- Metallurgy
- Recovery
- Bayer process
- Smelting
- Dissolution
- Refining
- Bauxite
- Electrolysis
- Magnesium
- Electroplating
- Deposition
- Autoionization

17. Electrochemistry

CHAPTER OUTLINE: KEY TERMS, PEOPLE, PLACES, CONCEPTS

____________ | Spectrophotometer

CHAPTER HIGHLIGHTS & NOTES: KEY TERMS, PEOPLE, PLACES, CONCEPTS

Electrochemistry

Electrochemistry is a branch of chemistry that studies chemical reactions which take place in a solution at the interface of an electron conductor and an ionic conductor (the electrolyte). These reactions involve electron transfer between the electrode and the electrolyte or species in solution.

If a chemical reaction is driven by an externally applied voltage, as in electrolysis, or if a voltage is created by a chemical reaction as in a battery, it is an electrochemical reaction.

Electrode

An electrode is an electrical conductor used to make contact with a nonmetallic part of a circuit . The word was coined by the scientist Michael Faraday from the Greek words elektron (meaning amber, from which the word electricity is derived) and hodos, a way.

Electrolytic cell

An electrolytic cell is an electrochemical cell that undergoes a redox reaction when electrical energy is applied. It is most often used to decompose chemical compounds, in a process called electrolysis--the Greek word lysis means to break up. When electrical energy is added to the system, the chemical energy is increased.

Galvanic cell

A galvanic cell, or voltaic cell or Alessandro Volta respectively, is an electrochemical cell that derives electrical energy from spontaneous redox reactions taking place within the cell. It generally consists of two different metals connected by a salt bridge, or individual half-cells separated by a porous membrane.

Volta was the inventor of the voltaic pile, the first electrical battery.

Anode

An anode is an electrode through which electric current flows into a polarized electrical device. The direction of electric current is, by convention, opposite to the direction of electron flow. In other words, the electrons flow from the anode into, for example, an electrical circuit.

Cathode

A cathode is an electrode through which electric current flows out of a polarized electrical device. The direction of electric current is, by convention, opposite to the direction of electron flow--thus, electrons are considered to flow toward the cathode electrode while current flows away from it. This convention is sometimes remembered using the mnemonic CCD for cathode current departs.

Electrochemical cell

An electrochemical cell is a device capable of either deriving electrical energy from chemical reactions, or facilitating chemical reactions through the introduction of electrical energy. A common example of an electrochemical cell is a standard 1.5-volt 'battery'. (Actually a single 'Galvanic cell'; a battery properly consists of multiple cells, connected in either parallel or series pattern).

Ammeter

An ammeter is a measuring instrument used to measure the electric current in a circuit. Electric currents are measured in amperes (A), hence the name. Instruments used to measure smaller currents, in the milliampere or microampere range, are designated as milliammeters or microammeters.

Salt bridge

A salt bridge, in electrochemistry, is a laboratory device used to connect the oxidation and reduction half-cells of a galvanic cell, a type of electrochemical cell. Salt bridges usually come in two types: glass tube and filter paper.

Electrolyte

An electrolyte is a compound that ionizes when dissolved in suitable ionizing solvents such as water. This includes most soluble salts, acids, and bases. Some gases, such as hydrogen chloride, under conditions of high temperature or low pressure can also function as electrolytes.

Electron

The electron is a subatomic particle with a negative elementary electric charge. Electrons belong to the first generation of the lepton particle family, and are generally thought to be elementary particles because they have no known components or substructure. The electron has a mass that is approximately 1/1836 that of the proton.

Half-cell

A half-cell is a structure that contains a conductive electrode and a surrounding conductive electrolyte separated by a naturally occurring Helmholtz double layer. Chemical reactions within this layer momentarily pump electric charges between the electrode and the electrolyte, resulting in a potential difference between the electrode and the electrolyte. The typical anode reaction involves a metal atom in the electrode dissolved and transported as a positive ion across the double layer, causing the electrolyte to acquire a net positive charge while the electrode acquires a net negative charge.

Mixing

In industrial process engineering, mixing is a unit operation that involves manipulating a heterogeneous physical system, with the intent to make it more homogeneous. Familiar examples include pumping of the water in a swimming pool to homogenize the water temperature, and the stirring of pancake batter to eliminate lumps.

Mole

Mole is a unit of measurement used in chemistry to express amounts of a chemical substance, defined as the amount of any substance that contains as many elementary entities (e.g., atoms, molecules, ions, electrons) as there are atoms in 12 grams of pure carbon-12, the isotope of carbon with relative atomic mass 12. This corresponds to the Avogadro constant, which has a value of $6.02214129(27)\times10^{23}$ elementary entities of the substance.

It is one of the base units in the International System of Units, and has the unit symbol mol and corresponds with the dimension symbol N. In honour of the unit, chemists often celebrate October 23 (a reference to the 10^{23} part of Avogadro's number) as 'Mole Day'.

The mole is widely used in chemistry instead of units of mass or volume as a convenient way to express amounts of reactants or of products of chemical reactions.

Oxidation

Redox (reduction-oxidation) reactions include all chemical reactions in which atoms have their oxidation state changed; in general, redox reactions involve the transfer of electrons between species.

This can be either a simple redox process, such as the oxidation of carbon to yield carbon dioxide or the reduction of carbon by hydrogen to yield methane (CH_4), or a complex process such as the oxidation of glucose ($C_6H_{12}O_6$) in the human body through a series of complex electron transfer processes.

The term 'redox' comes from two concepts involved with electron transfer: reduction and oxidation.

Product

Product are formed during chemical reactions as reagents are consumed. Products have lower energy than the reagents and are produced during the reaction according to the second law of thermodynamics. The released energy comes from changes in chemical bonds between atoms in reagent molecules and may be given off in the form of heat or light.

Current

A current in a fluid is the magnitude and direction of flow within that fluid. An air current presents the same properties specifically for a gaseous medium.

Types of fluid currents include•Boundary current•Current a current in a river or stream•Ocean current•Rip current•Subsurface currents•Turbidity current.

Charged particle

In physics, a charged particle is a particle with an electric charge. It may be either a subatomic particle or an ion. A collection of charged particles, or even a gas containing a proportion of charged particles, is called a plasma, which is called the fourth state of matter because its properties are quite different from solids, liquids and gases (plasma is the most common state of matter in the universe).

Nernst equation

In electrochemistry, the Nernst equation is an equation that relates the equilibrium reduction potential of a half-cell in an electrochemical cell (or the total voltage for a full cell) to the standard electrode potential, temperature, activity, and reaction quotient of the underlying reactions and species used. It is named after the German physical chemist who first formulated it, Walther Nernst.

Electrochemical potential	In electrochemistry, the electrochemical potential, $\bar{\mu}$, sometimes abbreviated to ECP, is a thermodynamic measure that combines the concepts of energy stored in the form of chemical potential and electrostatics. Electrochemical potential is expressed in the unit of J/mol.
Component	In thermodynamics, a component is a chemically-independent constituent of a system. The number of components represents the minimum number of independent species necessary to define the composition of all phases of the system. Calculating the number of components in a system is necessary, for example, when applying Gibbs' phase rule in determination of the number of degrees of freedom of a system.
Enthalpy	Enthalpy is a measure of the total energy of a thermodynamic system. It includes the system's internal energy and thermodynamic potential (a state function), as well as its volume and pressure (the energy required to 'make room for it' by displacing its environment, which is an extensive quantity). The unit of measurement for enthalpy in the International System of Units (SI) is the joule, but other historical, conventional units are still in use, such as the British thermal unit and the calorie.
Standard hydrogen electrode	The standard hydrogen electrode, is a redox electrode which forms the basis of the thermodynamic scale of oxidation-reduction potentials. Its absolute electrode potential is estimated to be 4.44 ± 0.02 V at 25 °C, but to form a basis for comparison with all other electrode reactions, hydrogen's standard electrode potential (E^0) is declared to be zero at all temperatures. Potentials of any other electrodes are compared with that of the standard hydrogen electrode at the same temperature.
Standard state	In chemistry, the standard state of a material is a reference point used to calculate its properties under different conditions. In principle, the choice of standard state is arbitrary, although the International Union of Pure and Applied Chemistry (IUPAC) recommends a conventional set of standard states for general use. IUPAC recommends using a standard pressure $p^o = 10^5$ Pa.
Oxidizing agent	An oxidizing agent is the element or compound in an oxidation-reduction (redox) reaction that accepts an electron from another species. Because the oxidizing agent is gaining electrons, it is said to have been reduced. The oxidizing agent itself is reduced, as it is taking electrons onto itself, but the reactant is oxidized by having its electrons taken away by the oxidizing agent.
Reducing agent	A reducing agent is the element or compound in an oxidation-reduction reaction that donates an electron to another species. Because the reducing agent is losing electrons, we say it has been oxidized.

17. Electrochemistry

CHAPTER HIGHLIGHTS & NOTES: KEY TERMS, PEOPLE, PLACES, CONCEPTS

Disproportionation

Disproportionation is a specific type of redox reaction in which a species is simultaneously reduced and oxidized to form two different products.

For example: the UV photolysis of mercury chloride Hg_2Cl_2 ? Hg + $HgCl_2$ is a disproportionation. Mercury (I) is a diatomic dication Hg2+2.

Reduction potential

Reduction potential is a measure of the tendency of a chemical species to acquire electrons and thereby be reduced. Reduction potential is measured in volts (V), or millivolts (mV). Each species has its own intrinsic reduction potential; the more positive the potential, the greater the species' affinity for electrons and tendency to be reduced.

Chemical species

Chemical species are atoms, molecules, molecular fragments, ions, etc., subjected to a chemical process or to a measurement. Generally, a chemical species can be defined as an ensemble of chemically identical molecular entities that can explore the same set of molecular energy levels on a characteristic or delineated time scale. The term may be applied equally to a set of chemically identical atomic or molecular structural units in a solid array.

Concentration

In chemistry, concentration is the abundance of a constituent divided by the total volume of a mixture. Several types of mathematical description can be distinguished: mass concentration, molar concentration, number concentration, and volume concentration. The term concentration can be applied to any kind of chemical mixture, but most frequently it refers to solutes and solvents in solutions.

Partial pressure

In a mixture of gases, each gas has a partial pressure which is the hypothetical pressure of that gas if it alone occupied the volume of the mixture at the same temperature. The total pressure of an ideal gas mixture is the sum of the partial pressures of each individual gas in the mixture.

It relies on the following isotherm relation: $V_x \times p_{tot} = V_{tot} \times p_x$ •V_x is the partial volume of any individual gas component (X)•V_{tot} is the total volume in gas mixture•p_x is the partial pressure of gas X•p_{tot} is the total pressure of gas mixture•n_x is the amount of substance of a gas (X)•n_{tot} is the total amount of substance in gas mixture

The partial pressure of a gas is a measure of thermodynamic activity of the gas's molecules.

Equilibrium constant

For a general chemical equilibrium $\alpha A + \beta B ... \rightleftharpoons \rho R + \sigma S ...$

the thermodynamic equilibrium constant can be defined such that, at equilibrium,

$$K^{\ominus} = \frac{\{R\}^{\rho}\{S\}^{\sigma}...}{\{A\}^{\alpha}\{B\}^{\beta}...}$$

where curly brackets denote the thermodynamic activities of the chemical species. The logarithm of this expression appears in the formula for the Gibbs free energy change for the reaction. If deviations from ideal behaviour are neglected, the activities may be replaced by concentrations, [A], and a concentration quotient, K_c.

PH meter	A pH meter is an electronic device used for measuring the pH of a liquid (though special probes are sometimes used to measure the pH of semi-solid substances). A typical pH meter consists of a special measuring probe (a glass electrode) connected to an electronic meter that measures and displays the pH reading.
Glass electrode	A glass electrode is a type of ion-selective electrode made of a doped glass membrane that is sensitive to a specific ion. It is an important part of the instrumentation for chemical analysis and physico-chemical studies. In modern practice, widely used membranous ion-selective electrodes (ISE, including glasses) are part of a galvanic cell.
Organic synthesis	Organic synthesis is a special branch of chemical synthesis and is concerned with the construction of organic compounds via organic reactions. Organic molecules can often contain a higher level of complexity compared to purely inorganic compounds, so the synthesis of organic compounds has developed into one of the most important branches of organic chemistry. There are two main areas of research fields within the general area of organic synthesis: total synthesis and methodology.
Cyclic voltammetry	Cyclic voltammetry or CV is a type of potentiodynamic electrochemical measurement. In a cyclic voltammetry experiment the working electrode potential is ramped linearly versus time like linear sweep voltammetry. Cyclic voltammetry takes the experiment a step further than linear sweep voltammetry which ends when it reaches a set potential.
Aqueous	An aqueous solution is a solution in which the solvent is water. It is usually shown in chemical equations by appending (aq) to the relevant formula. For example, a solution of ordinary table salt, or sodium chloride (NaCl), in water would be represented as NaCl(aq).
Functional group	In organic chemistry, functional groups are lexicon-specific groups of atoms or bonds within molecules that are responsible for the characteristic chemical reactions of those molecules. The same functional group will undergo the same or similar chemical reaction(s) regardless of the size of the molecule it is a part of. However, its relative reactivity can be modified by nearby functional groups.
Photoelectrochemistry	Photoelectrochemistry is a subfield of study within physical chemistry concerned with the interaction of light with electrochemical systems. It is active domain of investigation. One of the pioneers of this field of electrochemistry was the German electrochemist Heinz Gerischer.

17. Electrochemistry

CHAPTER HIGHLIGHTS & NOTES: KEY TERMS, PEOPLE, PLACES, CONCEPTS

Valence band

In solids, the valence band is the highest range of electron energies in which electrons are normally present at absolute zero temperature.

The valence electrons are bound to individual atoms, as opposed to conduction electrons, which can move freely within the atomic lattice of the material. On a graph of the electronic band structure of a material, the valence band is located below the conduction band, separated from it in insulators and semiconductors by a band gap.

Molecular orbital

In chemistry, a molecular orbital is a mathematical function describing the wave-like behavior of an electron in a molecule. This function can be used to calculate chemical and physical properties such as the probability of finding an electron in any specific region. The term orbital was introduced by Robert S. Mulliken in 1932 as an abbreviation for one-electron orbital wave function.

Molecule

A molecule is an electrically neutral group of two or more atoms held together by chemical bonds. Molecules are distinguished from ions by their lack of electrical charge. However, in quantum physics, organic chemistry, and biochemistry, the term molecule is often used less strictly, also being applied to polyatomic ions.

Artificial photosynthesis

Artificial photosynthesis is a chemical process that replicates the natural process of photosynthesis, a process that converts sunlight, water, and carbon dioxide into carbohydrates and oxygen. The term is commonly used to refer to any scheme for capturing and storing the energy from sunlight in the chemical bonds of a fuel (a solar fuel). Photocatalytic water splitting converts water into protons (and eventually hydrogen) and oxygen, and is a main research area in artificial photosynthesis.

Battery

An electric battery is a device consisting of one or more electrochemical cells that convert stored chemical energy into electrical energy. Each battery consists of a negative electrode material, a positive electrode material, an electrolyte that allows ions to move between the electrodes, and terminals that allow current to flow out of the battery to perform work.

Primary (single-use or 'disposable') batteries are used once and discarded; the electrode materials are irrevesibly changed during discharge.

Atom

The atom is a basic unit of matter that consists of a dense central nucleus surrounded by a cloud of negatively charged electrons. The atomic nucleus contains a mix of positively charged protons and electrically neutral neutrons, which means 'uncuttable' or 'the smallest indivisible particle of matter'. Although the Indian and Greek concepts of the atom were based purely on philosophy, modern science has retained the name coined by Democritus.

Isotope

Isotopes are variants of a particular chemical element such that, while all isotopes of a given element have the same number of protons in each atom, they differ in neutron number. The term isotope is formed from the Greek roots isos (?s?? 'equal') and topos (t?p?? 'place'), meaning 'the same place'.

Fuel cell	A fuel cell is a device that converts the chemical energy from a fuel into electricity through a chemical reaction with oxygen or another oxidizing agent. Hydrogen is the most common fuel, but hydrocarbons such as natural gas and alcohols like methanol are sometimes used. Fuel cells are different from batteries in that they require a constant source of fuel and oxygen/air to sustain the chemical reaction; however, fuel cells can produce electricity continually for as long as these inputs are supplied.
Corrosion	Corrosion is the gradual destruction of materials by chemical reaction with its environment. In the most common use of the word, this means electrochemical oxidation of metals in reaction with an oxidant such as oxygen. Rusting, the formation of iron oxides, is a well-known example of electrochemical corrosion.
Extractive metallurgy	Extractive metallurgy is the study of the processes used in the separation and concentration of raw materials. The field is an applied science, covering all aspects of the physical and chemical processes used to produce mineral-containing and metallic materials, sometimes for direct use as a finished product, but more often in a form that requires further physical processing which is generally the subject of physical metallurgy, ceramics, and other disciplines within the broad field of materials science. The field of ferrous and non-ferrous extractive metallurgy of encompasses many specialty sub-disciplines, each concerned with various physical and chemical processes that are steps in an overall process of producing a particular material.
Passivation	Passivation, in physical chemistry and engineering, refers to a material becoming 'passive,' that is, being less affected by environmental factors such as air and water. Passivation involves a shielding outer-layer of corrosion, which can be applied as a microcoating, or which occurs spontaneously in nature. As a technique, passivation is the use of a light coat of a protective material, such as metal oxide, to create a shell against corrosion.
Pyrometallurgy	Pyrometallurgy is a branch of extractive metallurgy. It consists of the thermal treatment of minerals and metallurgical ores and concentrates to bring about physical and chemical transformations in the materials to enable recovery of valuable metals. Pyrometallurgical treatment may produce saleable products such as pure metals, or intermediate compounds or alloys, suitable as feed for further processing.
Metallurgy	Metallurgy is a domain of materials science and materials engineering that studies the physical and chemical behavior of metallic elements, their intermetallic compounds, and their mixtures, which are called alloys. Metallurgy is also the technology of metals: the way in which science is applied to the production of metals, and the engineering of metal components for use in products for consumers and manufacturers.

17. Electrochemistry

CHAPTER HIGHLIGHTS & NOTES: KEY TERMS, PEOPLE, PLACES, CONCEPTS

Recovery	Recovery is a process by which deformed grains can reduce their stored energy by the removal or rearrangement of defects in their crystal structure. These defects, primarily dislocations, are introduced by plastic deformation of the material and act to increase the yield strength of a material. Since recovery reduces the dislocation density the process is normally accompanied by a reduction in a materials strength and a simultaneous increase in the ductility.
Bayer process	The Bayer process is the principal industrial means of refining bauxite to produce alumina . Bauxite, the most important ore of aluminium, contains only 30-54% aluminium oxide, (alumina), Al_2O_3, the rest being a mixture of silica, various iron oxides, and titanium dioxide. The aluminium oxide must be purified before it can be refined to aluminium metal.
Smelting	Smelting is a form of extractive metallurgy; its main use is to produce a metal from its ore. This includes production of silver, iron, copper and other base metals from their ores. Smelting uses heat and a chemical reducing agent to decompose the ore, driving off other elements as gasses or slag and leaving just the metal behind.
Dissolution	Dissolution is the process by which a solute forms a solution in a solvent. The solute, in the case of solids, has its crystalline structure disintegrated as separate ions, atoms, and molecules form. For liquids and gases, the molecules must be adaptable with those of the solvent for a solution to form.
Refining	Refining consists of purifying an impure material, in this case a metal. It is to be distinguished from other processes such as smelting and calcining in that those two involve a chemical change to the raw material, whereas in refining, the final material is usually identical chemically to the original one, only it is purer. The processes used are of many types, including pyrometallurgical and hydrometallurgical techniques.
Bauxite	Bauxite is an aluminium ore and is the main source of aluminium. This form of rock consists mostly of the minerals gibbsite $Al(OH)_3$, boehmite ?-AlO(OH), and diaspore a-AlO(OH), in a mixture with the two iron oxides goethite and haematite, the clay mineral kaolinite, and small amounts of anatase TiO_2. Bauxite was named after the village Les Baux in southern France, where it was first recognized as containing aluminium and named by the French geologist Pierre Berthier in 1821.
Electrolysis	In chemistry and manufacturing, electrolysis is a method of using a direct electric current to drive an otherwise non-spontaneous chemical reaction. Electrolysis is commercially highly important as a stage in the separation of elements from naturally occurring sources such as ores using an electrolytic cell.
Magnesium	Magnesium is a chemical element with the symbol Mg and atomic number 12. Its common oxidation number is +2. It is an alkaline earth metal and the eighth most abundant element in the Earth's crust and ninth in the known universe as a whole. Magnesium is the fourth most common element in the Earth as a whole (behind iron, oxygen and silicon), making up 13% of the planet's mass and a large fraction of the planet's mantle.

Electroplating	Electroplating is a process that uses electrical current to reduce dissolved metal cations so that they form a coherent metal coating on an electrode. The term is also used for electrical oxidation of anions onto a solid subtrate, as in the formation silver chloride on silver wire to make silver/silver-chloride electrodes. Electroplating is primarily used to change the surface properties of an object (e.g. abrasion and wear resistance, corrosion protection, lubricity, aesthetic qualities, etc)., but may also be used to build up thickness on undersized parts or to form objects by electroforming.
Deposition	Deposition, also known as desublimation, is a thermodynamic process, a phase transition in which gas transforms into solid. The reverse of deposition is sublimation. One example of deposition is the process by which, in sub-freezing air, water vapor changes directly to ice without first becoming a liquid.
Autoionization	Autoionization is a process by which atoms or molecules spontaneously emit one of the shell electrons, thus going from a state with charge Z to a state with charge Z?+?1, for example from an electrically neutral state to a singly ionized state. Atoms can autoionize when either two or more valence electrons are excited or one or more inner-shell electrons are missing. In the latter case, it is called the Auger effect.
Spectrophotometer	In chemistry, spectrophotometry is the quantitative measurement of the reflection or transmission properties of a material as a function of wavelength. It is more specific than the general term electromagnetic spectroscopy in that spectrophotometry deals with visible light, near-ultraviolet, and near-infrared, but does not cover time-resolved spectroscopic techniques. Spectrophotometry involves the use of a spectrophotometer.

17. Electrochemistry

CHAPTER QUIZ: KEY TERMS, PEOPLE, PLACES, CONCEPTS

1. An _________ is an electrochemical cell that undergoes a redox reaction when electrical energy is applied. It is most often used to decompose chemical compounds, in a process called electrolysis--the Greek word lysis means to break up. When electrical energy is added to the system, the chemical energy is increased.

   a. Bisulfide
   b. Buffering agent
   c. Carbonate alkalinity
   d. Electrolytic cell

2. _________s are variants of a particular chemical element such that, while all _________s of a given element have the same number of protons in each atom, they differ in neutron number. The term _________ is formed from the Greek roots isos (?s?? 'equal') and topos (t?p?? 'place'), meaning 'the same place'. Thus, different _________s of a single element occupy the same position on the periodic table.

   a. Baryon number
   b. Isotope
   c. Binary collision approximation
   d. Binding energy

3. For a general chemical equilibrium $\alpha A + \beta B ... \rightleftharpoons \rho R + \sigma S ...$

   the thermodynamic _________ can be defined such that, at equilibrium, $K^{\ominus} = \frac{\{R\}^{\rho}\{S\}^{\sigma}...}{\{A\}^{\alpha}\{B\}^{\beta}...}$

   where curly brackets denote the thermodynamic activities of the chemical species. The logarithm of this expression appears in the formula for the Gibbs free energy change for the reaction. If deviations from ideal behaviour are neglected, the activities may be replaced by concentrations, [A], and a concentration quotient, K_c.

   a. Binding constant
   b. Binding selectivity
   c. Equilibrium constant
   d. Buffer solution

4. _________ is a form of extractive metallurgy; its main use is to produce a metal from its ore. This includes production of silver, iron, copper and other base metals from their ores. _________ uses heat and a chemical reducing agent to decompose the ore, driving off other elements as gasses or slag and leaving just the metal behind.

   a. Bunker Hill Mine and Smelting Complex
   b. Smelting
   c. Holden/Marolt Mining and Ranching Museum
   d. Binder

5. In thermodynamics, a _________ is a chemically-independent constituent of a system. The number of _________s represents the minimum number of independent species necessary to define the composition of all phases of the system.

   Calculating the number of _________s in a system is necessary, for example, when applying Gibbs' phase rule in determination of the number of degrees of freedom of a system.

   a. Behentrimonium chloride
   b. Cocamidopropyl betaine
   c. Cocamidopropyl hydroxysultaine
   d. Component

ANSWER KEY
17. Electrochemistry

1. d
2. b
3. c
4. b
5. d

---

18. Chemical Kinetics

CHAPTER OUTLINE: KEY TERMS, PEOPLE, PLACES, CONCEPTS

- Reaction mechanism
- Elementary reaction
- Ideal solution
- Thermodynamics
- Coefficient
- Concentration
- Product
- Reaction rate
- Chemical reaction
- Half-life
- Reaction intermediate
- Chemical species
- Detailed balance
- Chemical equilibrium
- Equilibrium thermodynamics
- Rate-determining step
- Reactive intermediate
- Chain reaction
- Initiation
- Equilibrium constant
- Activation energy

18. Chemical Kinetics

CHAPTER OUTLINE: KEY TERMS, PEOPLE, PLACES, CONCEPTS

- ______ Molecule
- ______ Activated complex
- ______ Reaction coordinate
- ______ Transition state
- ______ Atom
- ______ Transient
- ______ Collision theory
- ______ Reaction dynamics
- ______ Cross section
- ______ Steric factor
- ______ Transition state theory
- ______ Battery
- ______ Electrochemistry
- ______ Isotope
- ______ Molecular beam
- ______ Diffusion-controlled reaction
- ______ Catalysis
- ______ Homogeneous catalysis
- ______ Catalytic converter
- ______ Heterogeneous catalysis
- ______ Carbon

18. Chemical Kinetics

CHAPTER OUTLINE: KEY TERMS, PEOPLE, PLACES, CONCEPTS

	Carbon dioxide
	Hydrocarbon
	Nitrogen
	Oxide
	Active site
	Enzyme
	Enzyme catalysis
	Enzyme kinetics
	Substrate
	Turnover number

CHAPTER HIGHLIGHTS & NOTES: KEY TERMS, PEOPLE, PLACES, CONCEPTS

Reaction mechanism

In chemistry, a reaction mechanism is the step by step sequence of elementary reactions by which overall chemical change occurs.

Although only the net chemical change is directly observable for most chemical reactions, experiments can often be designed that suggest the possible sequence of steps in a reaction mechanism. Recently, electrospray ionization mass spectrometry has been used to corroborate the mechanism of several organic reaction proposals.

Elementary reaction

An elementary reaction is a chemical reaction in which one or more of the chemical species react directly to form products in a single reaction step and with a single transition state.

In a unimolecular elementary reaction, a molecule A dissociates or isomerises to form the products $\mathrm{A} \rightarrow \mathrm{products.}$

At constant temperature, the rate of such a reaction is proportional to the concentration of the species A $\frac{d[\mathrm{A}]}{dt} = -k[\mathrm{A}].$

In a bimolecular elementary reaction, two atoms, molecules, ions or radicals, A and B, react together to form the product(s) $\mathrm{A} + \mathrm{B} \rightarrow \mathrm{products}.$

The rate of such a reaction, at constant temperature, is proportional to the product of the concentrations of the species A and B $\frac{d[\mathrm{A}]}{dt} = \frac{d[\mathrm{B}]}{dt} = -k[\mathrm{A}][\mathrm{B}].$

The rate expression for an elementary bimolecular reaction is sometimes referred to as the Law of Mass Action as it was first proposed by Guldberg and Waage in 1864. An example of this type of reaction is a cycloaddition reaction. This rate expression can be derived from first principles by using collision theory for ideal gases.

Ideal solution

In chemistry, an ideal solution or ideal mixture is a solution with thermodynamic properties analogous to those of a mixture of ideal gases. The enthalpy of solution (or 'enthalpy of mixing') is zero as is the volume change on mixing; the closer to zero the enthalpy of solution is, the more 'ideal' the behavior of the solution becomes. The vapour pressure of the solution obeys Raoult's law, and the activity coefficients (which measure deviation from ideality) are equal to one.

Thermodynamics

Thermodynamics is a branch of natural science concerned with heat and its relation to energy and work. It defines macroscopic variables (such as temperature, internal energy, entropy, and pressure) that characterize materials and radiation, and explains how they are related and by what laws they change with time. Thermodynamics describes the average behavior of very large numbers of microscopic constituents, and its laws can be derived from statistical mechanics.

Coefficient

In mathematics, a coefficient is a multiplicative factor in some term of an expression ; it is usually a number, but in any case does not involve any variables of the expression. For instance in $7x^2 - 3xy + 1.5 + y$

the first two terms respectively have the coefficients 7 and -3. The third term 1.5 is a constant. The final term does not have any explicitly written coefficient, but is considered to have coefficient 1, since multiplying by that factor would not change the term.

Concentration

In chemistry, concentration is the abundance of a constituent divided by the total volume of a mixture. Several types of mathematical description can be distinguished: mass concentration, molar concentration, number concentration, and volume concentration.

Product

Product are formed during chemical reactions as reagents are consumed. Products have lower energy than the reagents and are produced during the reaction according to the second law of thermodynamics. The released energy comes from changes in chemical bonds between atoms in reagent molecules and may be given off in the form of heat or light.

Reaction rate

The reaction rate or speed of reaction for a reactant or product in a particular reaction is intuitively defined as how fast or slow a reaction takes place. For example, the oxidative rusting of iron under Earth's atmosphere is a slow reaction that can take many years, but the combustion of cellulose in a fire is a reaction that takes place in fractions of a second.

Chemical kinetics is the part of physical chemistry that studies reaction rates.

Chemical reaction

A chemical reaction is a process that leads to the transformation of one set of chemical substances to another. Classically, chemical reactions encompass changes that only involve the positions of electrons in the forming and breaking of chemical bonds between atoms, with no change to the nuclei (no change to the elements present), and can often be described by a chemical equation. Nuclear chemistry is a sub-discipline of chemistry that involves the chemical reactions of unstable and radioactive elements where both electronic and nuclear changes may both occur.

Half-life

Half-life is the amount of time required for a quantity to fall to half its value as measured at the beginning of the time period. While the term 'half-life' can be used to describe any quantity which follows an exponential decay, it is most often used within the context of nuclear physics and nuclear chemistry--that is, the time required, probabilistically, for half of the unstable, radioactive atoms in a sample to undergo radioactive decay.

The original term, dating to Ernest Rutherford's discovery of the principle in 1907, was 'half-life period', which was shortened to 'half-life' in the early 1950s.

Reaction intermediate

A reaction intermediate or an intermediate is a molecular entity that is formed from the reactants and reacts further to give the directly observed products of a chemical reaction. Most chemical reactions are stepwise, that is they take more than one elementary step to complete. An intermediate is the reaction product of each of these steps, except for the last one, which forms the final product.

Chemical species

Chemical species are atoms, molecules, molecular fragments, ions, etc., subjected to a chemical process or to a measurement. Generally, a chemical species can be defined as an ensemble of chemically identical molecular entities that can explore the same set of molecular energy levels on a characteristic or delineated time scale. The term may be applied equally to a set of chemically identical atomic or molecular structural units in a solid array.

18. Chemical Kinetics

Chemical equilibrium	In a chemical reaction, chemical equilibrium is the state in which both reactants and products are present at concentrations which have no further tendency to change with time. Usually, this state results when the forward reaction proceeds at the same rate as the reverse reaction. The reaction rates of the forward and backward reactions are generally not zero, but equal.
Equilibrium thermodynamics	Equilibrium Thermodynamics is the systematic study of transformations of matter and energy in systems as they approach equilibrium. The word equilibrium implies a state of balance. Equilibrium thermodynamics, in origins, derives from analysis of the Carnot cycle.
Rate-determining step	In chemical kinetics, the rate of a reaction mechanism with several steps is often determined by the slowest step, known as the rate-determining step or rate-limiting step. The experimental rate equation can help to identify which step is rate-determining. In a reaction coordinate, the transition state with the highest energy is the rate-determining step of a given reaction.
Reactive intermediate	In chemistry a reactive intermediate is a short-lived, high energy, highly reactive molecule. When generated in a chemical reaction it will quickly convert into a more stable molecule. Only in exceptional cases can these compounds be isolated and stored, e.g. low temperatures, matrix isolation.
Chain reaction	A chain reaction is a sequence of reactions where a reactive product or by-product causes additional reactions to take place. In a chain reaction, positive feedback leads to a self-amplifying chain of events. Chain reactions are one way in which systems which are in thermodynamic non-equilibrium can release energy or increase entropy in order to reach a state of higher entropy.
Initiation	In chemistry, initiation is a chemical reaction that triggers one or more secondary reactions. Often the initiation reaction generates a reactive intermediate from a stable molecule which is then involved in secondary reactions. In polymerisation, initiation is followed by a chain reaction and termination.
Equilibrium constant	For a general chemical equilibrium $\alpha A + \beta B ... \rightleftharpoons \rho R + \sigma S ...$ the thermodynamic equilibrium constant can be defined such that, at equilibrium, $K^\ominus = \frac{\{R\}^\rho \{S\}^\sigma ...}{\{A\}^\alpha \{B\}^\beta ...}$ where curly brackets denote the thermodynamic activities of the chemical species. The logarithm of this expression appears in the formula for the Gibbs free energy change for the reaction.

Activation energy	In chemistry, activation energy is a term introduced in 1889 by the Swedish scientist Svante Arrhenius that is defined as the minimum energy that must be input to a chemical system, containing potential reactants, in order for a chemical reaction to occur. Activation energy may also be defined as the minimum energy required to start a chemical reaction. The activation energy of a reaction is usually denoted by E_a and given in units of kilojoules per mole.
Molecule	A molecule is an electrically neutral group of two or more atoms held together by chemical bonds. Molecules are distinguished from ions by their lack of electrical charge. However, in quantum physics, organic chemistry, and biochemistry, the term molecule is often used less strictly, also being applied to polyatomic ions.
Activated complex	In chemistry an activated complex is defined by the International Union of Pure and Applied Chemistry as 'that assembly of atoms which corresponds to an arbitrary infinitesimally small region at or near the col of a potential energy surface'. In other words, it refers to a collection of intermediate structures in a chemical reaction that persist while bonds are breaking and new bonds are forming. It therefore represents not one defined state, but rather a range of transient configurations that a collection of atoms passes through in between clearly defined products and reactants.
Reaction coordinate	In chemistry, a reaction coordinate is an abstract one-dimensional coordinate which represents progress along a reaction pathway. It is usually a geometric parameter that changes during the conversion of one or more molecular entities. In molecular dynamics simulations a reaction coordinate is called collective variable.
Transition state	The transition state of a chemical reaction is a particular configuration along the reaction coordinate. It is defined as the state corresponding to the highest potential energy along this reaction coordinate. At this point, assuming a perfectly irreversible reaction, colliding reactant molecules always go on to form products.
Atom	The atom is a basic unit of matter that consists of a dense central nucleus surrounded by a cloud of negatively charged electrons. The atomic nucleus contains a mix of positively charged protons and electrically neutral neutrons, which means 'uncuttable' or 'the smallest indivisible particle of matter'. Although the Indian and Greek concepts of the atom were based purely on philosophy, modern science has retained the name coined by Democritus.
Transient	In acoustics and audio, a transient is a high amplitude, short-duration sound at the beginning of a waveform that occurs in phenomena such as musical sounds, noises or speech. It can sometimes contain a high degree of non-periodic components and a higher magnitude of high frequencies than the harmonic content of that sound. Transients do not necessarily directly depend on the frequency of the tone they initiate.

18. Chemical Kinetics

CHAPTER HIGHLIGHTS & NOTES: KEY TERMS, PEOPLE, PLACES, CONCEPTS

Collision theory	Collision theory is a theory proposed independently by Max Trautz in 1916 and William Lewis in 1918, that qualitatively explains how chemical reactions occur and why reaction rates differ for different reactions. The collision theory states that when suitable particles of the reactant hit each other, only a certain percentage of the collisions cause any noticeable or significant chemical change; these successful changes are called successful collisions. The successful collisions have enough energy, also known as activation energy, at the moment of impact to break the preexisting bonds and form all new bonds.
Reaction dynamics	Reaction dynamics is a field within physical chemistry, studying why chemical reactions occur, how to predict their behavior, and how to control them. It is closely related to chemical kinetics, but is concerned with individual chemical events on atomic length scales and over very brief time periods.
Cross section	A cross section is the effective area that governs the probability of some scattering or absorption event. Together with particle density and path length, it can be used to predict the total scattering probability via the Beer-Lambert law. In nuclear and particle physics, the concept of a cross section is used to express the likelihood of interaction between particles.
Steric factor	Steric factor, P is a term used in collision theory. It is defined as the ratio between the experimental value of the rate constant and the one predicted by collision theory. It can also be defined as the ratio between the preexponential factor and the collision frequency, and it is most often less than unity.
Transition state theory	Transition state theory explains the reaction rates of elementary chemical reactions. The theory assumes a special type of chemical equilibrium (quasi-equilibrium) between reactants and activated transition state complexes. Transition state theory is used primarily to understand qualitatively how chemical reactions take place.
Battery	An electric battery is a device consisting of one or more electrochemical cells that convert stored chemical energy into electrical energy. Each battery consists of a negative electrode material, a positive electrode material, an electrolyte that allows ions to move between the electrodes, and terminals that allow current to flow out of the battery to perform work. Primary (single-use or 'disposable') batteries are used once and discarded; the electrode materials are irrevesibly changed during discharge.
Electrochemistry	Electrochemistry is a branch of chemistry that studies chemical reactions which take place in a solution at the interface of an electron conductor and an ionic conductor (the electrolyte).

	These reactions involve electron transfer between the electrode and the electrolyte or species in solution. If a chemical reaction is driven by an externally applied voltage, as in electrolysis, or if a voltage is created by a chemical reaction as in a battery, it is an electrochemical reaction.
Isotope	Isotopes are variants of a particular chemical element such that, while all isotopes of a given element have the same number of protons in each atom, they differ in neutron number. The term isotope is formed from the Greek roots isos (?s?? 'equal') and topos (t?p?? 'place'), meaning 'the same place'. Thus, different isotopes of a single element occupy the same position on the periodic table.
Molecular beam	A molecular beam is produced by allowing a gas at higher pressure to expand through a small orifice into a chamber at lower pressure to form a beam of particles moving at approximately equal velocities, with very few collisions between the particles. Molecular beam is useful for fabricating thin films in molecular beam epitaxy and artificial structures such as quantum wells, quantum wires, and quantum dots. Molecular beams have also been applied as crossed molecular beams.
Diffusion-controlled reaction	Diffusion-controlled reactions are reactions that occur so quickly that the reaction rate is the rate of transport of the reactants through the reaction medium (usually a solution). As quickly as the reactants encounter each other, they react. The process of chemical reaction can be considered as involving the diffusion of reactants until they encounter each other in the right stoichiometry and form an activated complex which can form the product species.
Catalysis	Catalysis is the increase rate of a chemical reaction due to the participation of a substance called a catalyst. Unlike other reagents in the chemical reaction, a catalyst is not consumed. With a catalyst, less free energy is required to reach the transition state, but the total free energy from reactants to products does not change.
Homogeneous catalysis	In chemistry, homogeneous catalysis is a sequence of reactions that involve a catalyst in the same phase as the reactants. Most commonly, a homogeneous catalyst is codissolved in a solvent with the reactants.
Catalytic converter	A catalytic converter is a vehicle emissions control device which converts toxic byproducts of combustion in the exhaust of an internal combustion engine to less toxic substances by way of catalyzed chemical reactions. The specific reactions vary with the type of catalyst installed. Most present-day vehicles that run on gasoline are fitted with a "three-way" converter, so named because it converts the three main pollutants in automobile exhaust: carbon monoxide, unburned hydrocarbon and oxides of nitrogen.
Heterogeneous catalysis	In chemistry, heterogeneous catalysis refers to the form of catalysis where the phase of the catalyst differs from that of the reactants.

Phase here refers not only to solid, liquid, vs gas, but also immiscible liquids, e.g. oil and water. The great majority of practical heterogeneous catalysts are solids and the great majority of reactants are gases or liquids.

Carbon

Carbon fiber, alternatively graphite fiber, carbon graphite or CF, is a material consisting of fibers about 5-10 μm in diameter and composed mostly of carbon atoms. The carbon atoms are bonded together in crystals that are more or less aligned parallel to the long axis of the fiber. The crystal alignment gives the fiber high strength-to-volume ratio (making it strong for its size).

Carbon dioxide

Carbon dioxide is a naturally occurring chemical compound composed of two oxygen atoms each covalently double bonded to a single carbon atom. It is a gas at standard temperature and pressure and exists in Earth's atmosphere in this state, as a trace gas at a concentration of 0.039 per cent by volume.

As part of the carbon cycle, plants, algae, and cyanobacteria use light energy to photosynthesize carbohydrate from carbon dioxide and water, with oxygen produced as a waste product.

Hydrocarbon

In organic chemistry, a hydrocarbon is an organic compound consisting entirely of hydrogen and carbon. Hydrocarbons from which one hydrogen atom has been removed are functional groups, called hydrocarbyls. Aromatic hydrocarbons (arenes), alkanes, alkenes, cycloalkanes and alkyne-based compounds are different types of hydrocarbons.

Nitrogen

Nitrogen, symbol N, is the chemical element of atomic number 7. At room temperature, it is a gas of diatomic molecules and is colorless and odorless. Nitrogen is a common element in the universe, estimated at about seventh in total abundance in our galaxy and the Solar System. On Earth, the element is primarily found as the free element; it forms about 80% of the Earth's atmosphere.

Oxide

An oxide is a chemical compound that contains at least one oxygen atom and one other element in its chemical formula. Metal oxides typically contain an anion of oxygen in the oxidation state of -2. Most of the Earth's crust consists of solid oxides, the result of elements being oxidized by the oxygen in air or in water. Hydrocarbon combustion affords the two principal carbon oxides: carbon monoxide and carbon dioxide.

Active site

In biology, the active site is the small port of an enzyme where substrate molecules bind and undergo a chemical reaction. This chemical reaction occurs when a substrate collides with and slots into the active site of an enzyme. The active site is usually found in a 3-D groove or pocket of the enzyme, lined with amino acid residues (or nucleotides in RNA enzymes).

Enzyme

Enzymes are large biological molecules responsible for the thousands of metabolic processes that sustain life. They are highly selective catalysts, greatly accelerating both the rate and specificity of metabolic reactions, from the digestion of food to the synthesis of DNA.

Most enzymes are proteins, although some catalytic RNA molecules have been identified. Enzymes adopt a specific three-dimensional structure, and may employ organic (e.g. biotin) and inorganic (e.g. magnesium ion) cofactors to assist in catalysis.

Enzyme catalysis

Enzyme catalysis is the catalysis of chemical reactions by specialized proteins known as enzymes. Catalysis of biochemical reactions in the cell is vital due to the very low reaction rates of the uncatalysed reactions.

The mechanism of enzyme catalysis is similar in principle to other types of chemical catalysis.

Enzyme kinetics

Enzyme kinetics is the study of the chemical reactions that are catalysed by enzymes. In enzyme kinetics, the reaction rate is measured and the effects of varying the conditions of the reaction is investigated. Studying an enzyme's kinetics in this way can reveal the catalytic mechanism of this enzyme, its role in metabolism, how its activity is controlled, and how a drug or an agonist might inhibit the enzyme.

Substrate

In chemistry, a substrate is the chemical species being observed, which reacts with a reagent. This term is highly context-dependent. In particular, in biochemistry, an enzyme substrate is the material upon which an enzyme acts.

Turnover number

Turnover number has two related meanings:

In enzymology, turnover number is defined as the maximum number of molecules of substrate that an enzyme can convert to product per catalytic site per unit of time and can be calculated as follows:

For example, carbonic anhydrase has a turnover number of 400,000 to 600,000 s^{-1}, which means that each carbonic anhydrase molecule can produce up to 600,000 molecules of product (bicarbonate ions) per second.

In other chemical fields, such as organometallic catalysis, turnover number is used with a slightly different meaning: the number of moles of substrate that a mole of catalyst can convert before becoming inactivated. An ideal catalyst would have an infinite turnover number in this sense, because it wouldn't ever be consumed, but in actual practice one often sees turnover numbers which go from 100 up to 40 million for Catalase.

18. Chemical Kinetics

CHAPTER QUIZ: KEY TERMS, PEOPLE, PLACES, CONCEPTS

1. A _________ is the effective area that governs the probability of some scattering or absorption event. Together with particle density and path length, it can be used to predict the total scattering probability via the Beer-Lambert law.

   In nuclear and particle physics, the concept of a _________ is used to express the likelihood of interaction between particles.

   a. Baryon number
   b. Beta decay
   c. Binary collision approximation
   d. Cross section

2. _________ is a theory proposed independently by Max Trautz in 1916 and William Lewis in 1918, that qualitatively explains how chemical reactions occur and why reaction rates differ for different reactions. The _________ states that when suitable particles of the reactant hit each other, only a certain percentage of the collisions cause any noticeable or significant chemical change; these successful changes are called successful collisions. The successful collisions have enough energy, also known as activation energy, at the moment of impact to break the preexisting bonds and form all new bonds.

   a. Bioorthogonal chemistry
   b. Collision theory
   c. Carbothermic reaction
   d. Ceramide phosphoethanolamine synthase

3. A _________ is an electrically neutral group of two or more atoms held together by chemical bonds. _________s are distinguished from ions by their lack of electrical charge. However, in quantum physics, organic chemistry, and biochemistry, the term _________ is often used less strictly, also being applied to polyatomic ions.

   a. 3-Deazaneplanocin A
   b. Molecule
   c. Biophysical chemistry
   d. Chemical biology

4. The _________ or speed of reaction for a reactant or product in a particular reaction is intuitively defined as how fast or slow a reaction takes place. For example, the oxidative rusting of iron under Earth's atmosphere is a slow reaction that can take many years, but the combustion of cellulose in a fire is a reaction that takes place in fractions of a second.

   Chemical kinetics is the part of physical chemistry that studies _________s.

   a. 4A Molecular Sieve
   b. Reaction rate
   c. Biochemical engineering
   d. Bioheat transfer

5. . The _________ is a basic unit of matter that consists of a dense central nucleus surrounded by a cloud of negatively charged electrons.

The atomic nucleus contains a mix of positively charged protons and electrically neutral neutrons, which means 'uncuttable' or 'the smallest indivisible particle of matter'. Although the Indian and Greek concepts of the _________ were based purely on philosophy, modern science has retained the name coined by Democritus.

a. 3-Deazaneplanocin A
b. Atom
c. Calibration curve
d. Bulk material analyzer

ANSWER KEY
18. Chemical Kinetics

---

1. d
2. b
3. b
4. b
5. b

---

19. Nuclear Chemistry

CHAPTER OUTLINE: KEY TERMS, PEOPLE, PLACES, CONCEPTS

- Nuclear chemistry
- Photographic emulsion
- Scintillation counter
- Radiation
- Atomic number
- Neutron number
- Nucleon
- Nuclide
- Atom
- Block
- Current
- Electron
- Gas-filled tube
- Intensity
- Mass number
- Molecule
- Neutron
- Proton
- Atomic mass
- Positron
- Quark

19. Nuclear Chemistry

CHAPTER OUTLINE: KEY TERMS, PEOPLE, PLACES, CONCEPTS

Alpha decay

Beta decay

Neutron emission

Proton emission

Positron emission

Chemical reaction

Neutrino

Radioactive decay

Electron capture

Kinetic energy

Binding energy

Nuclear binding energy

Ideal solution

Nuclear fission

Nuclear power

Nuclear reactor

Nuclear fusion

Exothermic

Helium

Nucleosynthesis

Neutron diffraction

Nuclear chemistry	Nuclear chemistry is the subfield of chemistry dealing with radioactivity, nuclear processes and nuclear properties. It is the chemistry of radioactive elements such as the actinides, radium and radon together with the chemistry associated with equipment which are designed to perform nuclear processes. This includes the corrosion of surfaces and the behavior under conditions of both normal and abnormal operation (such as during an accident).
Photographic emulsion	Photographic emulsion is a light-sensitive colloid. Most commonly, in silver-gelatin photography it consists of silver halide crystals dispersed in gelatin. The emulsion is usually coated onto a substrate of glass, films of cellulose nitrate, cellulose acetate or polyester, paper or fabric.
Scintillation counter	A scintillation counter is an instrument for detecting and measuring ionizing radiation. It consists of a scintillator which generates photons of light in response to incident radiation, a sensitive photomultiplier tube which converts the light to an electrical signal, and the necessary electronics to process the photomultiplier tube output. Scintillation counters are widely used because they can be made inexpensively yet with good quantum efficiency and can measure both the intensity and the energy of incident radiation.
Radiation	In physics, radiation is a process in which energetic particles or energetic waves travel through a vacuum, or through matter-containing media that are not required for their propagation. Waves of a mass filled medium itself, such as water waves or sound waves, are usually not considered to be forms of 'radiation' in this sense. Radiation can be classified as either ionizing or non-ionizing according to whether it ionizes or does not ionize ordinary chemical matter.
Atomic number	In chemistry and physics, the atomic number is the number of protons found in the nucleus of an atom and therefore identical to the charge number of the nucleus. It is conventionally represented by the symbol Z. The atomic number uniquely identifies a chemical element. In an atom of neutral charge, the atomic number is also equal to the number of electrons.
Neutron number	The neutron number, symbol N, is the number of neutrons in a nuclide. Atomic number plus neutron number equals mass number: $Z+N=A$. The difference between the neutron number and the atomic number is known as the neutron excess: $D = N - Z = A - 2Z$. Neutron number is rarely written explicitly in nuclide symbol notation, but appears as a subscript to the right of the element symbol. In order of increasing explicitness and decreasing frequency of usage:

19. Nuclear Chemistry

CHAPTER HIGHLIGHTS & NOTES: KEY TERMS, PEOPLE, PLACES, CONCEPTS

Nucleon	In chemistry and physics, a nucleon is one of the particles that makes up the atomic nucleus. Each atomic nucleus consists of one or more nucleons, and each atom in turn consists of a cluster of nucleons surrounded by one or more electrons. There are two known kinds of nucleon: the neutron and the proton.
Nuclide	A nuclide is an atomic species characterized by the specific constitution of its nucleus, i.e., by its number of protons Z, its number of neutrons N, and its nuclear energy state. The word nuclide was proposed by Truman P. Kohman in 1947. Doctor Kohman originally suggested nuclide as referring to a 'species of nucleus' defined by containing a certain number of neutrons and protons. The word thus was originally intended to focus on the nucleus.
Atom	The atom is a basic unit of matter that consists of a dense central nucleus surrounded by a cloud of negatively charged electrons. The atomic nucleus contains a mix of positively charged protons and electrically neutral neutrons, which means 'uncuttable' or 'the smallest indivisible particle of matter'. Although the Indian and Greek concepts of the atom were based purely on philosophy, modern science has retained the name coined by Democritus.
Block	A block of the periodic table of elements is a set of adjacent groups. The term appears to have been first used (in French) by Charles Janet. The respective highest-energy electrons in each element in a block belong to the same atomic orbital type.
Current	A current in a fluid is the magnitude and direction of flow within that fluid. An air current presents the same properties specifically for a gaseous medium. Types of fluid currents include•Boundary current•Current a current in a river or stream•Ocean current•Rip current•Subsurface currents•Turbidity current.
Electron	The electron is a subatomic particle with a negative elementary electric charge. Electrons belong to the first generation of the lepton particle family, and are generally thought to be elementary particles because they have no known components or substructure. The electron has a mass that is approximately 1/1836 that of the proton.
Gas-filled tube	A gas-filled tube, also known as a discharge tube, is an arrangement of electrodes in a gas within an insulating, temperature-resistant envelope. Gas-filled tubes exploit phenomena related to electric discharge in gases, and operate by ionizing the gas with an applied voltage sufficient to cause electrical conduction by the underlying phenomena of the Townsend discharge. The voltage required to initiate and sustain discharge is dependent on the pressure and composition of the fill gas and geometry of the tube.
Intensity	In physics, intensity is the power transferred per unit area.

In the SI system, it has units watts per metre squared (W/m^2). It is used most frequently with waves (e.g. sound or light), in which case the average power transfer over one period of the wave is used.

Mass number

The mass number, also called atomic mass number or nucleon number, is the total number of protons and neutrons (together known as nucleons) in an atomic nucleus. Because protons and neutrons both are baryons, the mass number A is identical with the baryon number B as of the nucleus as of the whole atom or ion. The mass number is different for each different isotope of a chemical element.

Molecule

A molecule is an electrically neutral group of two or more atoms held together by chemical bonds. Molecules are distinguished from ions by their lack of electrical charge. However, in quantum physics, organic chemistry, and biochemistry, the term molecule is often used less strictly, also being applied to polyatomic ions.

Neutron

The neutron is a subatomic hadron particle that has the symbol n or n0, no net electric charge and a mass slightly larger than that of a proton. With the exception of hydrogen-1, nuclei of atoms consist of protons and neutrons, which are therefore collectively referred to as nucleons. The number of protons in a nucleus is the atomic number and defines the type of element the atom forms.

Proton

The proton is a subatomic particle with the symbol p or p+ and a positive electric charge of 1 elementary charge. One or more protons are present in the nucleus of each atom. The number of protons in each atom is its atomic number.

Atomic mass

The atomic mass is the mass of an atomic particle, sub-atomic particle, or molecule. It may be expressed in unified atomic mass units; by international agreement, 1 atomic mass unit is defined as 1/12 of the mass of a single carbon-12 atom (at rest). When expressed in such units, the atomic mass is called the relative isotopic mass .

Positron

The positron or antielectron is the antiparticle or the antimatter counterpart of the electron. The positron has an electric charge of +1e, a spin of ½, and has the same mass as an electron. When a low-energy positron collides with a low-energy electron, annihilation occurs, resulting in the production of two or more gamma ray photons .

Quark

A quark is an elementary particle and a fundamental constituent of matter. Quarks combine to form composite particles called hadrons, the most stable of which are protons and neutrons, the components of atomic nuclei. Due to a phenomenon known as color confinement, quarks are never directly observed or found in isolation; they can be found only within hadrons, such as baryons, named up, down, strange, charm, bottom, and top .

Alpha decay

Alpha decay, or a-decay, is a type of radioactive decay in which an atomic nucleus emits an alpha particle and thereby transforms into an atom with a mass number 4 less and atomic number 2 less.

For example, uranium-238 decaying through a-particle emission to form thorium-234 can be expressed as: ${}^{238}_{92}\mathrm{U} \rightarrow {}^{234}_{90}\mathrm{Th} + \alpha$

Because an alpha particle is the same as the nucleus of a helium-4 atom - consisting of two protons and two neutrons and thus having mass number 4 and atomic number 2 - this can also be written as: ${}^{238}_{92}\mathrm{U} \rightarrow {}^{234}_{90}\mathrm{Th} + {}^{4}_{2}\mathrm{He}$

Notice how, on either side of the nuclear equation, both the mass number and the atomic number are conserved: the mass number is 238 on the right side and (234 + 4) on the left side, and the atomic number is 92 on the right side and (90 + 2) on the left side.

The alpha particle also has a charge +2, but the charge is usually not written in nuclear equations, which describe nuclear reactions without considering the electrons.

Beta decay

In nuclear physics, beta decay is a type of radioactive decay in which a beta particle (an electron or a positron) is emitted from an atomic nucleus. Beta decay is a process which allows the atom to obtain the optimal ratio of protons and neutrons.

Beta decay is mediated by the weak force.

Neutron emission

Neutron emission is a type of radioactive decay of atoms containing excess neutrons, in which a neutron is simply ejected from the nucleus. Two examples of isotopes which emit neutrons are beryllium-13 (mean life 2.7×10^{-21} s) and helium-5 (7×10^{-22} s).

Neutron emission usually happens from nuclei that are in an excited state, such as the excited O-17* produced from the beta decay of N-17. The neutron emission process itself is controlled by the nuclear force and therefore is extremely fast, sometimes referred to as 'nearly instantaneous'.

Proton emission

Proton emission is a type of radioactive decay in which a proton is ejected from a nucleus.

Proton emission can occur from high-lying excited states in a nucleus following a beta decay, in which case the process is known as beta-delayed proton emission, or can occur from the ground state (or a low-lying isomer) of very proton-rich nuclei, in which case the process is very similar to alpha decay.

For a proton to escape a nucleus, the proton separation energy must be negative - the proton is therefore unbound, and tunnels out of the nucleus in a finite time.

Positron emission

Positron emission or beta plus decay is a particular type of radioactive decay and a subtype of beta decay, in which a proton inside a radionuclide nucleus is converted into a neutron while releasing a positron and an electron neutrino ($?_e$). Positron emission is mediated by the weak force.

Chemical reaction	A chemical reaction is a process that leads to the transformation of one set of chemical substances to another. Classically, chemical reactions encompass changes that only involve the positions of electrons in the forming and breaking of chemical bonds between atoms, with no change to the nuclei (no change to the elements present), and can often be described by a chemical equation. Nuclear chemistry is a sub-discipline of chemistry that involves the chemical reactions of unstable and radioactive elements where both electronic and nuclear changes may both occur.
Neutrino	A neutrino is an electrically neutral, weakly interacting elementary subatomic particle with half-integer spin. The neutrino is denoted by the Greek letter ? (nu). All evidence suggests that neutrinos have mass but that their mass is tiny even by the standards of subatomic particles.
Radioactive decay	Radioactive decay, also known as nuclear decay or radioactivity, is the process by which a nucleus of an unstable atom loses energy by emitting particles of ionizing radiation. A material that spontaneously emits this kind of radiation--which includes the emission of energetic alpha particles, beta particles, and gamma rays--is considered radioactive. Radioactive decay is a stochastic (i.e., random) process at the level of single atoms, in that, according to quantum theory, it is impossible to predict when a particular atom will decay.
Electron capture	Electron capture is a process in which a proton-rich nuclide absorbs an inner atomic electron, thereby changing a nuclear proton to a neutron and simultaneously causing the emission of an electron neutrino. Various photon emissions follow, as the energy of the atom falls to the ground state of the new nuclide. Electron capture is the primary decay mode for isotopes with a relative superabundance of protons in the nucleus, but with insufficient energy difference between the isotope and its prospective daughter (the isobar with one less positive charge) for the nuclide to decay by emitting a positron.
Kinetic energy	In physics, the kinetic energy of an object is the energy which it possesses due to its motion. It is defined as the work needed to accelerate a body of a given mass from rest to its stated velocity. Having gained this energy during its acceleration, the body maintains this kinetic energy unless its speed changes.
Binding energy	Binding energy is the mechanical energy required to disassemble a whole into separate parts. A bound system typically has a lower potential energy than the sum of its constituent parts -- this is what keeps the system together. Often this means that energy is released upon the creation of a bound state.
Nuclear binding energy	Nuclear binding energy is the energy required to split a nucleus of an atom into its component parts. The component parts are neutrons and protons, which are collectively called nucleons.

19. Nuclear Chemistry

CHAPTER HIGHLIGHTS & NOTES: KEY TERMS, PEOPLE, PLACES, CONCEPTS

Ideal solution

In chemistry, an ideal solution or ideal mixture is a solution with thermodynamic properties analogous to those of a mixture of ideal gases. The enthalpy of solution (or 'enthalpy of mixing') is zero as is the volume change on mixing; the closer to zero the enthalpy of solution is, the more 'ideal' the behavior of the solution becomes. The vapour pressure of the solution obeys Raoult's law, and the activity coefficients (which measure deviation from ideality) are equal to one.

Nuclear fission

In nuclear physics and nuclear chemistry, nuclear fission is either a nuclear reaction or a radioactive decay process in which the nucleus of a particle splits into smaller parts . The fission process often produces free neutrons and photons (in the form of gamma rays), and releases a very large amount of energy even by the energetic standards of radioactive decay.

Nuclear fission of heavy elements was discovered on December 17, 1938 by Otto Hahn and his assistant Fritz Strassmann, and explained theoretically in January 1939 by Lise Meitner and her nephew Otto Robert Frisch.

Nuclear power

Nuclear power, or nuclear energy, is the use of exothermic nuclear processes, to generate useful heat and electricity. The term includes nuclear fission, nuclear decay and nuclear fusion. Presently the nuclear fission of elements in the actinide series of the periodic table produce the vast majority of nuclear energy in the direct service of humankind, with nuclear decay processes, primarily in the form of geothermal energy, and radioisotope thermoelectric generators, in niche uses making up the rest.

Nuclear reactor

A nuclear reactor is a device to initiate and control a sustained nuclear chain reaction. Nuclear reactors are used at nuclear power plants for electricity generation and in propulsion of ships. Heat from nuclear fission is passed to a working fluid (water or gas), which runs through turbines.

Nuclear fusion

In nuclear physics, nuclear fusion is a nuclear reaction in which two or more atomic nuclei collide at a very high speed and join to form a new type of atomic nucleus. During this process, matter is not conserved because some of the mass of the fusing nuclei is converted to photons (energy). Fusion is the process that powers active or 'main sequence' stars.

Exothermic

In thermodynamics, the term exothermic describes a process or reaction that releases energy from the system, usually in the form of heat, but also in a form of light (e.g. a spark, flame, or flash), electricity (e.g. a battery), or sound (e.g. explosion heard when burning hydrogen). Its etymology stems from the prefix exo (derived from the Greek word ???, exo, 'outside') and the Greek word thermasi (meaning 'to heat'). The term exothermic was first coined by Marcellin Berthelot.

Helium

Helium is a chemical element with symbol He and atomic number 2. It is a colorless, odorless, tasteless, non-toxic, inert, monatomic gas that heads the noble gas group in the periodic table. Its boiling and melting points are the lowest among the elements and it exists only as a gas except in extreme conditions.

19. Nuclear Chemistry

CHAPTER HIGHLIGHTS & NOTES: KEY TERMS, PEOPLE, PLACES, CONCEPTS

Nucleosynthesis	Nucleosynthesis is the process that creates new atomic nuclei from pre-existing nucleons, primarily protons and neutrons. The first nuclei were formed about three minutes after the Big Bang, through the process called Big Bang nucleosynthesis. It was then that hydrogen and helium formed that became the content of the first stars, and is responsible for the present hydrogen/helium ratio of the cosmos.
Neutron diffraction	Neutron diffraction or elastic neutron scattering is the application of neutron scattering to the determination of the atomic and/or magnetic structure of a material. A sample to be examined is placed in a beam of thermal or cold neutrons to obtain a diffraction pattern that provides information of the structure of the material. The technique is similar to X-ray diffraction but due to their different scattering properties, neutrons and X-rays provide complementary information.

CHAPTER QUIZ: KEY TERMS, PEOPLE, PLACES, CONCEPTS

1. _________ or elastic neutron scattering is the application of neutron scattering to the determination of the atomic and/or magnetic structure of a material. A sample to be examined is placed in a beam of thermal or cold neutrons to obtain a diffraction pattern that provides information of the structure of the material. The technique is similar to X-ray diffraction but due to their different scattering properties, neutrons and X-rays provide complementary information.

   a. Neutron diffraction
   b. Diffraction
   c. Diffraction efficiency
   d. Diffraction grating

2. A _________ is an instrument for detecting and measuring ionizing radiation.

   It consists of a scintillator which generates photons of light in response to incident radiation, a sensitive photomultiplier tube which converts the light to an electrical signal, and the necessary electronics to process the photomultiplier tube output.

   _________s are widely used because they can be made inexpensively yet with good quantum efficiency and can measure both the intensity and the energy of incident radiation.

   a. Scintillation counter
   b. Clover
   c. Computed tomography imaging spectrometer
   d. CRISM

3. . In nuclear physics, _________ is a type of radioactive decay in which a beta particle (an electron or a positron) is emitted from an atomic nucleus. _________ is a process which allows the atom to obtain the optimal ratio of protons and neutrons.

_________ is mediated by the weak force.

a. Baryon number
b. Beta decay
c. Compton scattering
d. Bohr model

4. The _________, symbol N, is the number of neutrons in a nuclide.

   Atomic number plus _________ equals mass number: Z+N=A. The difference between the _________ and the atomic number is known as the neutron excess: D = N - Z = A - 2Z.

   _________ is rarely written explicitly in nuclide symbol notation, but appears as a subscript to the right of the element symbol. In order of increasing explicitness and decreasing frequency of usage:

   Nuclides that have the same _________ but a different proton number are called isotones.

   a. Neutron number
   b. Beta decay
   c. Binary collision approximation
   d. Binding energy

5. A _________ is an elementary particle and a fundamental constituent of matter. _________s combine to form composite particles called hadrons, the most stable of which are protons and neutrons, the components of atomic nuclei. Due to a phenomenon known as color confinement, _________s are never directly observed or found in isolation; they can be found only within hadrons, such as baryons, named up, down, strange, charm, bottom, and top .

   a. Bottom quark
   b. Quark
   c. Charm quark
   d. Constituent quark

ANSWER KEY
19. Nuclear Chemistry

1. a
2. a
3. b
4. a
5. b

---

20. Molecular Spectroscopy and Photochemistry

CHAPTER OUTLINE: KEY TERMS, PEOPLE, PLACES, CONCEPTS

Raman scattering

Atom

Light scattering

Scattering

Intensity

Diatomic molecule

Molecule

Rotational spectroscopy

Selection rule

Polarizability

Electromagnetic radiation

Electron

Radiation

Morse potential

Nuclear magnetic resonance spectroscopy

Chemical kinetics

Chemical reaction

Proton

Functional group

Presence

Spectroscopy

20. Molecular Spectroscopy and Photochemistry

CHAPTER OUTLINE: KEY TERMS, PEOPLE, PLACES, CONCEPTS

- Heteroatom
- Carbon
- Hydrogen
- Molecular orbital
- Photochemistry
- Coefficient
- Concentration
- Path length
- Absorption
- Fine structure
- Excited state
- Quantum state
- Fluorescence
- Internal conversion
- Intersystem crossing
- Phosphorescence
- Crossing
- Quantum yield
- Atmospheric chemistry
- Chlorofluorocarbon
- Atmosphere

20. Molecular Spectroscopy and Photochemistry

CHAPTER OUTLINE: KEY TERMS, PEOPLE, PLACES, CONCEPTS

	Mesosphere
	Stratosphere
	Thermosphere
	Troposphere
	Steady state
	Greenhouse effect
	Laser

CHAPTER HIGHLIGHTS & NOTES: KEY TERMS, PEOPLE, PLACES, CONCEPTS

Raman scattering	Raman scattering or the Raman effect is the inelastic scattering of a photon. It was discovered by C. V Raman and K. S. Krishnan in liquids, and by G. Landsberg and L. I. Mandelstam in crystals. The effect had been predicted theoretically by A. Smekal in 1923.
Atom	The atom is a basic unit of matter that consists of a dense central nucleus surrounded by a cloud of negatively charged electrons. The atomic nucleus contains a mix of positively charged protons and electrically neutral neutrons, which means 'uncuttable' or 'the smallest indivisible particle of matter'. Although the Indian and Greek concepts of the atom were based purely on philosophy, modern science has retained the name coined by Democritus.
Light scattering	Light scattering is a form of scattering in which light is the form of propagating energy which is scattered. Light scattering can be thought of as the deflection of a ray from a straight path, for example by irregularities in the propagation medium, particles, or in the interface between two media. Deviations from the law of reflection due to irregularities on a surface are also usually considered to be a form of scattering.
Scattering	Scattering is a general physical process where some forms of radiation, such as light, sound, or moving particles, are forced to deviate from a straight trajectory by one or more localized non-uniformities in the medium through which they pass. In conventional use, this also includes deviation of reflected radiation from the angle predicted by the law of reflection.

20. Molecular Spectroscopy and Photochemistry

CHAPTER HIGHLIGHTS & NOTES: KEY TERMS, PEOPLE, PLACES, CONCEPTS

Intensity	In physics, intensity is the power transferred per unit area. In the SI system, it has units watts per metre squared (W/m^2). It is used most frequently with waves (e.g. sound or light), in which case the average power transfer over one period of the wave is used.
Diatomic molecule	Diatomic molecules are molecules composed only of two atoms, of either the same or different chemical elements. The prefix di- is of Greek origin, meaning two.
Molecule	A molecule is an electrically neutral group of two or more atoms held together by chemical bonds. Molecules are distinguished from ions by their lack of electrical charge. However, in quantum physics, organic chemistry, and biochemistry, the term molecule is often used less strictly, also being applied to polyatomic ions.
Rotational spectroscopy	Rotational spectroscopy is concerned with the measurement of the energies of transitions between quantized rotational states of molecules in the gas phase. The spectra of polar molecules can be measured in absorption or emission by microwave spectroscopy or by far infrared spectroscopy. The rotational spectra of non-polar molecules cannot be observed by those methods, but can be observed and measured by Raman spectroscopy.
Selection rule	In physics and chemistry a selection rule, or transition rule, formally constrains the possible transitions of a system from one state to another. Selection rules have been derived for electronic, vibrational, and rotational transitions. The selection rules may differ according to the technique used to observe the transition.
Polarizability	Polarizability is the ability for a molecule to be polarized. It is a property of matter. Polarizabilities determine the dynamical response of a bound system to external fields, and provide insight into a molecule's internal structure.
Electromagnetic radiation	Electromagnetic radiation is one of the fundamental phenomena of electromagnetism, behaving as waves propagating through space, and also as photon particles traveling through space, carrying radiant energy. In a vacuum, it propagates at a characteristic speed, the speed of light, normally in straight lines. EMR is emitted and absorbed by charged particles.
Electron	The electron is a subatomic particle with a negative elementary electric charge. Electrons belong to the first generation of the lepton particle family, and are generally thought to be elementary particles because they have no known components or substructure. The electron has a mass that is approximately 1/1836 that of the proton.
Radiation	In physics, radiation is a process in which energetic particles or energetic waves travel through a vacuum, or through matter-containing media that are not required for their propagation. Waves of a mass filled medium itself, such as water waves or sound waves, are usually not considered to be forms of 'radiation' in this sense.

Morse potential	The Morse potential is a convenient model for the potential energy of a diatomic molecule. It is a better approximation for the vibrational structure of the molecule than the quantum harmonic oscillator because it explicitly includes the effects of bond breaking, such as the existence of unbound states. It also accounts for the anharmonicity of real bonds and the non-zero transition probability for overtone and combination bands.
Nuclear magnetic resonance spectroscopy	Nuclear magnetic resonance spectroscopy, most commonly known as NMR spectroscopy, is a research technique that exploits the magnetic properties of certain atomic nuclei. It determines the physical and chemical properties of atoms or the molecules in which they are contained. It relies on the phenomenon of nuclear magnetic resonance and can provide detailed information about the structure, dynamics, reaction state, and chemical environment of molecules.
Chemical kinetics	Chemical kinetics, also known as reaction kinetics, is the study of rates of chemical processes. Chemical kinetics includes investigations of how different experimental conditions can influence the speed of a chemical reaction and yield information about the reaction's mechanism and transition states, as well as the construction of mathematical models that can describe the characteristics of a chemical reaction. In 1864, Peter Waage and Cato Guldberg pioneered the development of chemical kinetics by formulating the law of mass action, which states that the speed of a chemical reaction is proportional to the quantity of the reacting substances.
Chemical reaction	A chemical reaction is a process that leads to the transformation of one set of chemical substances to another. Classically, chemical reactions encompass changes that only involve the positions of electrons in the forming and breaking of chemical bonds between atoms, with no change to the nuclei (no change to the elements present), and can often be described by a chemical equation. Nuclear chemistry is a sub-discipline of chemistry that involves the chemical reactions of unstable and radioactive elements where both electronic and nuclear changes may both occur.
Proton	The proton is a subatomic particle with the symbol p or p+ and a positive electric charge of 1 elementary charge. One or more protons are present in the nucleus of each atom. The number of protons in each atom is its atomic number.
Functional group	In organic chemistry, functional groups are lexicon-specific groups of atoms or bonds within molecules that are responsible for the characteristic chemical reactions of those molecules. The same functional group will undergo the same or similar chemical reaction(s) regardless of the size of the molecule it is a part of. However, its relative reactivity can be modified by nearby functional groups.
Presence	In filmmaking and television production presence is the 'silence' recorded at a location or space when no dialogue is spoken. This term is often confused with ambience.

20. Molecular Spectroscopy and Photochemistry

CHAPTER HIGHLIGHTS & NOTES: KEY TERMS, PEOPLE, PLACES, CONCEPTS

Spectroscopy	Spectroscopy is the study of the interaction between matter and radiated energy. Historically, spectroscopy originated through the study of visible light dispersed according to its wavelength, e.g., by a prism. Later the concept was expanded greatly to comprise any interaction with radiative energy as a function of its wavelength or frequency.
Heteroatom	In organic chemistry, a heteroatom is any atom that is not carbon or hydrogen. Usually, the term is used to indicate that non-carbon atoms have replaced carbon in the backbone of the molecular structure. Typical heteroatoms are nitrogen, oxygen, sulfur, phosphorus, chlorine, bromine, and iodine.
Carbon	Carbon fiber, alternatively graphite fiber, carbon graphite or CF, is a material consisting of fibers about 5-10 µm in diameter and composed mostly of carbon atoms. The carbon atoms are bonded together in crystals that are more or less aligned parallel to the long axis of the fiber. The crystal alignment gives the fiber high strength-to-volume ratio (making it strong for its size).
Hydrogen	Hydrogen is a chemical element with chemical symbol H and atomic number 1. With an atomic weight of 1.00794 u, hydrogen is the lightest element and its monatomic form (H) is the most abundant chemical substance, constituting roughly 75% of the Universe's baryonic mass. Non-remnant stars are mainly composed of hydrogen in its plasma state. At standard temperature and pressure, hydrogen is a colorless, odorless, tasteless, non-toxic, nonmetallic, highly combustible diatomic gas with the molecular formula H_2.
Molecular orbital	In chemistry, a molecular orbital is a mathematical function describing the wave-like behavior of an electron in a molecule. This function can be used to calculate chemical and physical properties such as the probability of finding an electron in any specific region. The term orbital was introduced by Robert S. Mulliken in 1932 as an abbreviation for one-electron orbital wave function.
Photochemistry	Photochemistry, a sub-discipline of chemistry, is the study of chemical reactions that proceed with the absorption of light by atoms or molecules. Everyday examples include photosynthesis, the degradation of plastics and the formation of vitamin D with sunlight.
Coefficient	In mathematics, a coefficient is a multiplicative factor in some term of an expression ; it is usually a number, but in any case does not involve any variables of the expression. For instance in $7x^2 - 3xy + 1.5 + y$ the first two terms respectively have the coefficients 7 and -3. The third term 1.5 is a constant. The final term does not have any explicitly written coefficient, but is considered to have coefficient 1, since multiplying by that factor would not change the term.
Concentration	In chemistry, concentration is the abundance of a constituent divided by the total volume of a mixture.

Several types of mathematical description can be distinguished: mass concentration, molar concentration, number concentration, and volume concentration. The term concentration can be applied to any kind of chemical mixture, but most frequently it refers to solutes and solvents in solutions.

Path length

Path length can mean one of several related concepts:

Absorption

In chemistry, absorption is a physical or chemical phenomenon or a process in which atoms, molecules, or ions enter some bulk phase - gas, liquid, or solid material. This is a different process from adsorption, since molecules undergoing absorption are taken up by the volume, not by the surface (as in the case for adsorption). A more general term is sorption, which covers absorption, adsorption, and ion exchange.

Fine structure

In atomic physics, the fine structure describes the splitting of the spectral lines of atoms due to quantum mechanical and relativistic corrections.

The gross structure of line spectra is the line spectra predicted by the quantum mechanics of non-relativistic electrons with no spin. For a hydrogenic atom, the gross structure energy levels only depend on the principal quantum number n.

Excited state

Excitation is an elevation in energy level above an arbitrary baseline energy state. In physics there is a specific technical definition for energy level which is often associated with an atom being excited to an excited state.

In quantum mechanics an excited state of a system (such as an atom, molecule or nucleus) is any quantum state of the system that has a higher energy than the ground state (that is, more energy than the absolute minimum).

Quantum state

In quantum physics, quantum state refers to the state of a quantum system. A quantum state is given as a vector in a Hilbert space, called the state vector. The state vector theoretically contains statistical information about the quantum system.

Fluorescence

Fluorescence is the emission of light by a substance that has absorbed light or other electromagnetic radiation. It is a form of luminescence. In most cases, the emitted light has a longer wavelength, and therefore lower energy, than the absorbed radiation.

Internal conversion

Internal conversion is a radioactive decay process where an excited nucleus interacts electromagnetically with an electron in one of the lower atomic orbitals, causing the electron to be emitted from the atom. Thus, in an internal conversion process, a high-energy electron is emitted from the radioactive atom, but not from a nucleon in the nucleus. Instead, the electron is ejected as a result of an interaction between the entire nucleus and an outside electron that interacts with it.

20. Molecular Spectroscopy and Photochemistry

CHAPTER HIGHLIGHTS & NOTES: KEY TERMS, PEOPLE, PLACES, CONCEPTS

Phosphorescence	Phosphorescence is a specific type of photoluminescence related to fluorescence. Unlike fluorescence, a phosphorescent material does not immediately re-emit the radiation it absorbs. The slower time scales of the re-emission are associated with 'forbidden' energy state transitions in quantum mechanics.
Crossing	In quantum field theory, a branch of theoretical physics, crossing is the property of scattering amplitudes that allows antiparticles to be interpreted as particles going backwards in time. Crossing states that the same formula that determines the S-matrix elements and scattering amplitudes for particle A to scatter with X and produce particle B and Y will also give the scattering amplitude for $A+\bar{B}+X$ to go into Y, or for $\bar{B}$ to scatter with X to produce $Y+\bar{A}$. The only difference is that the value of the energy is negative for the antiparticle.
Quantum yield	The quantum yield of a radiation-induced process is the number of times a specific event occurs per photon absorbed by the system. The 'event' is typically a kind of chemical reaction.
Atmospheric chemistry	Atmospheric chemistry is a branch of atmospheric science in which the chemistry of the Earth's atmosphere and that of other planets is studied. It is a multidisciplinary field of research and draws on environmental chemistry, physics, meteorology, computer modeling, oceanography, geology and volcanology and other disciplines. Research is increasingly connected with other areas of study such as climatology.
Chlorofluorocarbon	A chlorofluorocarbon is an organic compound that contains only carbon, chlorine, and fluorine, produced as a volatile derivative of methane and ethane. They are also commonly known by the DuPont brand name Freon. The most common representative is dichlorodifluoromethane (R-12 or Freon-12).
Atmosphere	The standard atmosphere is an international reference pressure defined as 101325 Pa and used as a unit of pressure.
Mesosphere	The mesosphere is the layer of the Earth's atmosphere that is directly above the stratopause and directly below the mesopause. In the mesosphere temperature decreases with increasing height. The upper boundary of the mesosphere is the mesopause, which can be the coldest naturally occurring place on Earth with temperatures below 130 K (-226 °F; -143 °C).
Stratosphere	The stratosphere is the second major layer of Earth's atmosphere, just above the troposphere, and below the mesosphere. It is stratified in temperature, with warmer layers higher up and cooler layers farther down. This is in contrast to the troposphere near the Earth's surface, which is cooler higher up and warmer farther down.
Thermosphere	The thermosphere is the layer of the Earth's atmosphere directly above the mesosphere and directly below the exosphere. Within this layer, ultraviolet radiation (UV) causes ionization.

20. Molecular Spectroscopy and Photochemistry

CHAPTER HIGHLIGHTS & NOTES: KEY TERMS, PEOPLE, PLACES, CONCEPTS

Troposphere	The troposphere is the lowest portion of Earth's atmosphere. It contains approximately 80% of the atmosphere's mass and 99% of its water vapour and aerosols. The average depth of the troposphere is approximately 17 km (11 mi) in the middle latitudes.
Steady state	In chemistry, a steady state is a situation in which all state variables are constant in spite of ongoing processes that strive to change them. For an entire system to be at steady state, i.e. for all state variables of a system to be constant, there must be a flow through the system (compare mass balance). One of the most simple examples of such a system is the case of a bathtub with the tap open but without the bottom plug: after a certain time the water flows in and out at the same rate, so the water level (the state variable being Volume) stabilizes and the system is at steady state.
Greenhouse effect	The greenhouse effect is a process by which thermal radiation from a planetary surface is absorbed by atmospheric greenhouse gases, and is re-radiated in all directions. Since part of this re-radiation is back towards the surface and the lower atmosphere, it results in an elevation of the average surface temperature above what it would be in the absence of the gases. Solar radiation at the frequencies of visible light largely passes through the atmosphere to warm the planetary surface, which then emits this energy at the lower frequencies of infrared thermal radiation.
Laser	A laser is a device that emits light through a process of optical amplification based on the stimulated emission of electromagnetic radiation. The term 'laser' originated as an acronym for Light Amplification by Stimulated Emission of Radiation. Lasers differ from other sources of light because they emit light coherently.

CHAPTER QUIZ: KEY TERMS, PEOPLE, PLACES, CONCEPTS

1. The _________ is a subatomic particle with a negative elementary electric charge. _________s belong to the first generation of the lepton particle family, and are generally thought to be elementary particles because they have no known components or substructure. The _________ has a mass that is approximately 1/1836 that of the proton.

   a. Electron
   b. Compton scattering
   c. Bohr model
   d. Bohr magneton

2. . _________ is concerned with the measurement of the energies of transitions between quantized rotational states of molecules in the gas phase. The spectra of polar molecules can be measured in absorption or emission by microwave spectroscopy or by far infrared spectroscopy.

The rotational spectra of non-polar molecules cannot be observed by those methods, but can be observed and measured by Raman spectroscopy.

a. Band emission
b. Breathalyzer
c. Cavity ring-down spectroscopy
d. Rotational spectroscopy

3. In physics, _________ is a process in which energetic particles or energetic waves travel through a vacuum, or through matter-containing media that are not required for their propagation. Waves of a mass filled medium itself, such as water waves or sound waves, are usually not considered to be forms of '_________' in this sense.

   _________ can be classified as either ionizing or non-ionizing according to whether it ionizes or does not ionize ordinary chemical matter.

a. CrystaSulf
b. Flue-gas desulfurization
c. Radiation
d. Scrubber

4. The _________ is a convenient model for the potential energy of a diatomic molecule. It is a better approximation for the vibrational structure of the molecule than the quantum harmonic oscillator because it explicitly includes the effects of bond breaking, such as the existence of unbound states. It also accounts for the anharmonicity of real bonds and the non-zero transition probability for overtone and combination bands.

a. Morse potential
b. Basis set superposition error
c. Bond hardening
d. Bond softening

5. The _________ is a basic unit of matter that consists of a dense central nucleus surrounded by a cloud of negatively charged electrons. The atomic nucleus contains a mix of positively charged protons and electrically neutral neutrons, which means 'uncuttable' or 'the smallest indivisible particle of matter'. Although the Indian and Greek concepts of the _________ were based purely on philosophy, modern science has retained the name coined by Democritus.

a. Atom
b. Chemistry
c. Calibration curve
d. Bulk material analyzer

ANSWER KEY
20. Molecular Spectroscopy and Photochemistry

1. a
2. d
3. c
4. a
5. a

---

21. Structure and Bonding in Solids

CHAPTER OUTLINE: KEY TERMS, PEOPLE, PLACES, CONCEPTS

- Crystallography
- Molecule
- Reflection
- Scattering
- Atom
- Ionic crystal
- Sodium chloride
- Cohesion
- Crystal structure
- Drude model
- Fluorite
- Amorphous solid
- Semiconductor
- Semimetal
- Insulator
- F-Center
- Frenkel defect
- Schottky defect
- Electron
- Alloy steel
- Lattice energy

21. Structure and Bonding in Solids

CHAPTER OUTLINE: KEY TERMS, PEOPLE, PLACES, CONCEPTS

______________	Absolute zero
______________	Kinetic energy
______________	Madelung constant
______________	Thermodynamics
______________	Thermodynamic cycle

CHAPTER HIGHLIGHTS & NOTES: KEY TERMS, PEOPLE, PLACES, CONCEPTS

Crystallography

Crystallography is the science that examines the arrangement of atoms in solids. The word 'crystallography' derives from the Greek words crystallon = cold drop / frozen drop, with its meaning extending to all solids with some degree of transparency, and grapho = write. A more comprehensive definition is: 'Crystallography is the science of condensed matter with emphasis on the atomic or molecular structure and its relation to physical and chemical properties.'

Before the development of X-ray diffraction crystallography, the study of crystals was based on their geometry.

Molecule

A molecule is an electrically neutral group of two or more atoms held together by chemical bonds. Molecules are distinguished from ions by their lack of electrical charge. However, in quantum physics, organic chemistry, and biochemistry, the term molecule is often used less strictly, also being applied to polyatomic ions.

Reflection

Reflection is the change in direction of a wavefront at an interface between two different media so that the wavefront returns into the medium from which it originated. Common examples include the reflection of light, sound and water waves. The law of reflection says that for specular reflection the angle at which the wave is incident on the surface equals the angle at which it is reflected.

Scattering

Scattering is a general physical process where some forms of radiation, such as light, sound, or moving particles, are forced to deviate from a straight trajectory by one or more localized non-uniformities in the medium through which they pass. In conventional use, this also includes deviation of reflected radiation from the angle predicted by the law of reflection.

Atom

The atom is a basic unit of matter that consists of a dense central nucleus surrounded by a cloud of negatively charged electrons. The atomic nucleus contains a mix of positively charged protons and electrically neutral neutrons, which means 'uncuttable' or 'the smallest indivisible particle of matter'. Although the Indian and Greek concepts of the atom were based purely on philosophy, modern science has retained the name coined by Democritus.

Ionic crystal

An ionic crystal is a crystal consisting of ions bound together by their electrostatic attraction. Examples of such crystals are the alkali halides, including potassium fluoride, potassium chloride, potassium bromide, potassium iodide, sodium fluoride, and other combinations of sodium, caesium, rubidium, or lithium ions with fluoride, bromide, chloride or iodide ions. NaCl has a 6:6 co-ordination.

Sodium chloride

Sodium chloride, also known as salt, common salt, table salt or halite, is an ionic compound with the formula NaCl, representing equal proportions of sodium and chlorine. Sodium chloride is the salt most responsible for the salinity of the ocean and of the extracellular fluid of many multicellular organisms. As the major ingredient in edible salt, it is commonly used as a condiment and food preservative.

Cohesion

Cohesion or Cohesive attraction or Cohesive force is the action or property of molecules sticking together, being mutually attractive.

Crystal structure

In mineralogy and crystallography, crystal structure is a unique arrangement of atoms or molecules in a crystalline liquid or solid. A crystal structure is composed of a pattern, a set of atoms arranged in a particular way, and a lattice exhibiting long-range order and symmetry. Patterns are located upon the points of a lattice, which is an array of points repeating periodically in three dimensions.

Drude model

The Drude model of electrical conduction was proposed in 1900 by Paul Drude to explain the transport properties of electrons in materials . The model, which is an application of kinetic theory, assumes that the microscopic behavior of electrons in a solid may be treated classically and looks much like a pinball machine, with a sea of constantly jittering electrons bouncing and re-bouncing off heavier, relatively immobile positive ions.

The two most significant results of the Drude model are an electronic equation of motion,

$$\frac{d}{dt}\mathbf{p}(t) = q\left(\mathbf{E} + \frac{\mathbf{p}\times\mathbf{B}}{m}\right) - \frac{\mathbf{p}(t)}{\tau},$$

and a linear relationship between current density J and electric field E

$$\mathbf{J} = \left(\frac{nq^2\tau}{m}\right)\mathbf{E}.$$

Here t is the time and p, q, n, m, and τ are respectively an electron's momentum, charge, number density, mass, and mean free time between ionic collisions.

Fluorite

Fluorite is a halide mineral composed of calcium fluoride, CaF_2. It is an isometric mineral with a cubic habit, though octahedral and more complex isometric forms are not uncommon.

Fluorite is a colorful mineral, both in visible and ultraviolet light, and the stone has ornamental and lapidary uses.

Amorphous solid

In condensed matter physics, an amorphous or non-crystalline solid is a solid that lacks the long-range order characteristic of a crystal.

In some older books, the term has been used synonymously with glass. Nowadays, 'amorphous solid' is considered to be the overarching concept, and glass the more special case: A glass is an amorphous solid that exhibits a glass transition.

Semiconductor

A semiconductor is a material which has electrical conductivity to a degree between that of a metal and that of an insulator (such as glass). Semiconductors are the foundation of modern electronics, including transistors, solar cells, light-emitting diodes (LEDs), quantum dots and digital and analog integrated circuits.

A semiconductor may have a number of unique properties, one of which is the ability to change conductivity by the addition of impurities ('doping') or by interaction with another phenomenon, such as an electric field or light; this ability makes a semiconductor very useful for constructing a device that can amplify, switch, or convert an energy input.

Semimetal

A Semimetal is a material with a very small overlap between the bottom of the conduction band and the top of the valence band. According to electronic band theory, solids can be classified as insulators, semiconductors, semimetals, or metals. In insulators and semiconductors the filled valence band is separated from an empty conduction band by a band gap.

Insulator

An electrical insulator is a material whose internal electric charges do not flow freely, and therefore does not conduct an electric current under the influence of an electric field. A perfect insulator does not exist, but some materials such as glass, paper and Teflon, which have high resistivity, are very good electrical insulators. A much larger class of materials, even though they may have lower bulk resistivity, are still good enough to insulate electrical wiring and cables.

F-Center

An F-Center or Farbe center is a type of crystallographic defect in which an anionic vacancy in a crystal is filled by one or more electrons, depending on the charge of the missing ion in the crystal or mainly due to the reason that when a compound is heated to a high temperature (mainly metallic oxides) the ions get excited and get displaced from their respective positions in their crystal structure but while doing so these ions leave behind some electrons in the vacated spaces. This leads to the phenomenon of colouring of compounds. This is used to identify many compounds, especially zinc oxide (yellow).

Frenkel defect

The Frenkel defect is a type of defect shown by crystalline solids. It consists in the displacement of an atom from its lattice position to an interstitial site, creating a vacancy at the original site and an interstitial defect at the new location.

Schottky defect

A Schottky defect is a type of point defect in a crystal lattice named after Walter H. Schottky. In non -ionic crystals it means a lattice vacancy defect.

In ionic crystals, the defect forms when oppositely charged ions leave their lattice sites, creating vacancies.

Electron

The electron is a subatomic particle with a negative elementary electric charge. Electrons belong to the first generation of the lepton particle family, and are generally thought to be elementary particles because they have no known components or substructure. The electron has a mass that is approximately 1/1836 that of the proton.

Alloy steel

Alloy steel is steel that is alloyed with a variety of elements in total amounts between 1.0% and 50% by weight to improve its mechanical properties. Alloy steels are broken down into two groups: low-alloy steels and high-alloy steels. The difference between the two is somewhat arbitrary: Smith and Hashemi define the difference at 4.0%, while Degarmo, et al., define it at 8.0%.

Lattice energy

The lattice energy of an ionic solid is a measure of the strength of bonds in that ionic compound. It is usually defined as the enthalpy of formation of the ionic compound from gaseous ions and as such is invariably exothermic. Lattice energy may also be defined as the energy required to completely separate one mole of a solid ionic compound into gaseous ionic constituents.

Absolute zero

Absolute zero is the lowest temperature possible. More formally, it is the temperature at which entropy reaches its minimum value. The laws of thermodynamics state that absolute zero cannot be reached using only thermodynamic means.

Kinetic energy

In physics, the kinetic energy of an object is the energy which it possesses due to its motion. It is defined as the work needed to accelerate a body of a given mass from rest to its stated velocity. Having gained this energy during its acceleration, the body maintains this kinetic energy unless its speed changes.

21. Structure and Bonding in Solids

CHAPTER HIGHLIGHTS & NOTES: KEY TERMS, PEOPLE, PLACES, CONCEPTS

Madelung constant	The Madelung constant is used in determining the electrostatic potential of a single ion in a crystal by approximating the ions by point charges. It is named after Erwin Madelung, a German physicist. Because the anions and cations in an ionic solid are attracting each other by virtue of their opposing charges, separating the ions requires a certain amount of energy.
Thermodynamics	Thermodynamics is a branch of natural science concerned with heat and its relation to energy and work. It defines macroscopic variables (such as temperature, internal energy, entropy, and pressure) that characterize materials and radiation, and explains how they are related and by what laws they change with time. Thermodynamics describes the average behavior of very large numbers of microscopic constituents, and its laws can be derived from statistical mechanics.
Thermodynamic cycle	A thermodynamic cycle consists of a collection of thermodynamic processes transferring heat and work, while varying pressure, temperature, and other state variables, eventually returning a system to its initial state. In the process of going through this cycle, the system may perform work on its surroundings, therefore acting as a heat engine. State quantities depend only on the thermodynamic state, and cumulative variation of such properties adds up to zero during a cycle.

CHAPTER QUIZ: KEY TERMS, PEOPLE, PLACES, CONCEPTS

1. _________ is the science that examines the arrangement of atoms in solids. The word '_________' derives from the Greek words crystallon = cold drop / frozen drop, with its meaning extending to all solids with some degree of transparency, and grapho = write. A more comprehensive definition is: '_________ is the science of condensed matter with emphasis on the atomic or molecular structure and its relation to physical and chemical properties.'

   Before the development of X-ray diffraction _________, the study of crystals was based on their geometry.

   a. Chemical test
   b. Chemical structure
   c. Crystallography
   d. Chemical clock

2. . The _________ is a type of defect shown by crystalline solids. It consists in the displacement of an atom from its lattice position to an interstitial site, creating a vacancy at the original site and an interstitial defect at the new location.

   a. Bjerrum defect

b. Cottrell atmosphere
c. Crystallographic defects in diamond
d. Frenkel defect

3. A _________ is an electrically neutral group of two or more atoms held together by chemical bonds. _________s are distinguished from ions by their lack of electrical charge. However, in quantum physics, organic chemistry, and biochemistry, the term _________ is often used less strictly, also being applied to polyatomic ions.

a. 3-Deazaneplanocin A
b. Bioconcentration
c. Molecule
d. Chemical biology

4. An _________ is a crystal consisting of ions bound together by their electrostatic attraction. Examples of such crystals are the alkali halides, including potassium fluoride, potassium chloride, potassium bromide, potassium iodide, sodium fluoride, and other combinations of sodium, caesium, rubidium, or lithium ions with fluoride, bromide, chloride or iodide ions. NaCl has a 6:6 co-ordination.

a. Barium fluoride
b. Ionic crystal
c. Boule
d. Caesium cadmium bromide

5. _________ is the change in direction of a wavefront at an interface between two different media so that the wavefront returns into the medium from which it originated. Common examples include the _________ of light, sound and water waves. The law of _________ says that for specular _________ the angle at which the wave is incident on the surface equals the angle at which it is reflected.

a. Cardinal point
b. Reflection
c. Chromatic aberration
d. Circle of confusion

ANSWER KEY
21. Structure and Bonding in Solids

1. c

2. d

3. c

4. b

5. b

---

22. Inorganic Materials

CHAPTER OUTLINE: KEY TERMS, PEOPLE, PLACES, CONCEPTS

- Conductivity
- Silicate
- Oxygen
- Silicon
- Olivine
- Magnesium
- Aluminosilicate
- Asbestos
- Mineral
- Thermal insulation
- Feldspar
- Weathering
- Zeolite
- Ceramic
- Thermal shock
- Thermal expansion
- Microstructure
- Atomic orbital
- Homogeneous
- Length scale
- Presence

22. Inorganic Materials

CHAPTER OUTLINE: KEY TERMS, PEOPLE, PLACES, CONCEPTS

- Pottery
- Diffusion
- Annealing
- Soda-lime glass
- Portland cement
- Calcium
- Chemical reaction
- Perovskite
- Refractory
- Ceramic materials
- Oxide
- Resistance
- Silicon nitride
- Boron nitride
- Sialon
- Nitrogen
- Silicon carbide
- Deposition
- Molar conductivity
- Conduction band
- Fermi level

22. Inorganic Materials

CHAPTER OUTLINE: KEY TERMS, PEOPLE, PLACES, CONCEPTS

______ Valence band

______ Absolute zero

______ Electron

______ Energy level

______ Molecule

______ Band gap

______ Insulator

______ Semiconductor

______ Doping

______ Charged particle

______ Dopant

______ Transistor

______ Current

______ Phosphor

Conductivity

The conductivity of an electrolyte solution is a measure of its ability to conduct electricity. The SI unit of conductivity is siemens per meter (S/m).

Conductivity measurements are used routinely in many industrial and environmental applications as a fast, inexpensive and reliable way of measuring the ionic content in a solution.

Silicate

Silicate compounds, including the minerals, consist of silicate anions whose charge is balanced by various cations. Myriad silicate anions can exist, and each can form compounds with many different cations. Hence this class of compounds is very large.

Oxygen

Oxygen is a chemical element with symbol O and atomic number 8. It is a member of the chalcogen group on the periodic table and is a highly reactive nonmetallic element and oxidizing agent that readily forms compounds (notably oxides) with most elements. By mass, oxygen is the third-most abundant element in the universe, after hydrogen and helium At STP, two atoms of the element bind to form dioxygen, a diatomic gas that is colorless, odorless, and tasteless; with the formula O2.

Many major classes of organic molecules in living organisms, such as proteins, nucleic acids, carbohydrates, and fats, contain oxygen, as do the major inorganic compounds that are constituents of animal shells, teeth, and bone.

Silicon

Silicon, a tetravalent metalloid, is a chemical element with the symbol Si and atomic number 14. It is less reactive than its chemical analog carbon, the nonmetal directly above it in the periodic table, but more reactive than germanium, the metalloid directly below it in the table. Controversy about silicon's character dates to its discovery; it was first prepared and characterized in pure form in 1823. In 1808, it was given the name silicium (from Latin: silex, hard stone or flint), with an -ium word-ending to suggest a metal, a name which the element retains in several non-English languages. However, its final English name, first suggested in 1817, reflects the more physically similar elements carbon and boron.

Olivine

The mineral olivine is a magnesium iron silicate with the formula $(Mg^{+2}, Fe^{+2})_2SiO_4$. It is a common mineral in the Earth's subsurface but weathers quickly on the surface.

The ratio of magnesium and iron varies between the two endmembers of the solid solution series: forsterite (Mg-endmember: Mg_2SiO_4) and fayalite (Fe-endmember: Fe_2SiO_4).

Magnesium

Magnesium is a chemical element with the symbol Mg and atomic number 12. Its common oxidation number is +2. It is an alkaline earth metal and the eighth most abundant element in the Earth's crust and ninth in the known universe as a whole. Magnesium is the fourth most common element in the Earth as a whole (behind iron, oxygen and silicon), making up 13% of the planet's mass and a large fraction of the planet's mantle.

22. Inorganic Materials

CHAPTER HIGHLIGHTS & NOTES: KEY TERMS, PEOPLE, PLACES, CONCEPTS

Aluminosilicate

Aluminosilicate minerals are minerals composed of aluminium, silicon, and oxygen, plus countercations. They are a major component of kaolin and other clay minerals.

Andalusite, kyanite, and sillimanite are naturally occurring aluminosilicate minerals that have the composition Al_2SiO_5.

Asbestos

Asbestos is a set of six naturally occurring silicate minerals used commercially for their desirable physical properties. They all have in common their eponymous asbestiform habit: long (roughly 1:20 aspect ratio), thin fibrous crystals. The prolonged inhalation of asbestos fibers can cause serious illnesses including malignant lung cancer, mesothelioma, and asbestosis (a type of pneumoconiosis).

Mineral

A mineral is a naturally occurring substance that is solid and stable at room temperature, representable by a chemical formula, usually abiogenic, and has an ordered atomic structure. It is different from a rock, which can be an aggregate of minerals or non-minerals and does not have a specific chemical composition. The exact definition of a mineral is under debate, especially with respect to the requirement a valid species be abiogenic, and to a lesser extent with regards to it having an ordered atomic structure.

Thermal insulation

Thermal insulation is the reduction of heat transfer between objects in thermal contact or in range of radiative influence. Thermal insulation can be achieved with specially engineered methods or processes, as well as with suitable object shapes and materials.

Heat flow is an inevitable consequence of contact between objects of differing temperature.

Feldspar

Feldspars are a group of rock-forming tectosilicate minerals that make up as much as 60% of the Earth's crust.

Feldspars crystallize from magma as veins in both intrusive and extrusive igneous rocks and are also present in many types of metamorphic rock. Rock formed almost entirely of calcic plagioclase feldspar is known as anorthosite.

Weathering

Weathering is the breaking down of rocks, soils and minerals as well as artificial materials through contact with the Earth's atmosphere, biota and waters. Weathering occurs in situ, or 'with no movement', and thus should not be confused with erosion, which involves the movement of rocks and minerals by agents such as water, ice, snow, wind, waves and gravity.

Two important classifications of weathering processes exist - physical and chemical weathering; each sometimes involves a biological component.

Zeolite

Zeolites are microporous, aluminosilicate minerals commonly used as commercial adsorbents.

The term zeolite was originally coined in 1756 by Swedish mineralogist Axel Fredrik Cronstedt, who observed that upon rapidly heating the material stilbite, it produced large amounts of steam from water that had been adsorbed by the material. Based on this, he called the material zeolite, from the Greek ??? (zéo), meaning 'to boil' and ????? (líthos), meaning 'stone'.

Ceramic

A ceramic is an inorganic, nonmetallic solid prepared by the action of heat and subsequent cooling. Ceramic materials may have a crystalline or partly crystalline structure, or may be amorphous (e.g., a glass). Because most common ceramics are crystalline, the definition of ceramic is often restricted to inorganic crystalline materials, as opposed to the noncrystalline glasses, a distinction followed here.

Thermal shock

Thermal shock occurs when a thermal gradient causes different parts of an object to expand by different amounts. This differential expansion can be understood in terms of stress or of strain, equivalently. At some point, this stress can exceed the strength of the material, causing a crack to form.

Thermal expansion

Thermal expansion is the tendency of matter to change in volume in response to a change in temperature.

When a substance is heated, its particles begin moving more and thus usually maintain a greater average separation. Materials which contract with increasing temperature are unusual; this effect is limited in size, and only occurs within limited temperature ranges .

Microstructure

Microstructure is defined as the structure of a prepared surface or thin foil of material as revealed by a microscope above 25× magnification. The microstructure of a material (which can be broadly classified into metallic, polymeric, ceramic and composite) can strongly influence physical properties such as strength, toughness, ductility, hardness, corrosion resistance, high/low temperature behavior, wear resistance, and so on, which in turn govern the application of these materials in industrial practice.

Atomic orbital

An atomic orbital is a mathematical function that describes the wave-like behavior of either one electron or a pair of electrons in an atom. This function can be used to calculate the probability of finding any electron of an atom in any specific region around the atom's nucleus. The term may also refer to the physical region or space where the electron can be calculated to be present, as defined by the particular mathematical form of the orbital.

Homogeneous

Homogeneous as a term in physical chemistry and material science refers to substances and mixtures which are in a single phase. This is in contrast to a substance that is heterogeneous. The definition of homogeneous strongly depends on the context used.

Length scale

In physics, length scale is a particular length or distance determined with the precision of one order of magnitude.

The concept of length scale is particularly important because physical phenomena of different length scales cannot affect each other and are said to decouple. The decoupling of different length scales makes it possible to have a self-consistent theory that only describes the relevant length scales for a given problem.

Presence

In filmmaking and television production presence is the 'silence' recorded at a location or space when no dialogue is spoken. This term is often confused with ambience.

Every location has a distinct presence created by the position of the microphone in relation to the space boundaries.

Pottery

'Pottery is the ceramic material which makes up potterywares, of which major types include earthenware, stoneware and porcelain. The place where such wares are made is also called a pottery. Pottery also refers to the art or craft of a potter or the manufacture of pottery.

Diffusion

Diffusion, in acoustics and architectural engineering, is the efficacy by which sound energy is spread evenly in a given environment. A perfectly diffusive sound space is one that has certain key acoustic properties which are the same anywhere in the space. A non-diffuse sound space would have considerably different reverberation time as the listener moved around the room.

Annealing

Annealing is a process of slowly cooling glass to relieve internal stresses after it was formed. The process may be carried out in a temperature-controlled kiln known as a lehr. Glass which has not been annealed is liable to crack or shatter when subjected to a relatively small temperature change or mechanical shock.

Soda-lime glass

Soda-lime glass, also called soda-lime-silica glass, is the most prevalent type of glass, used for windowpanes, and glass containers for beverages, food, and some commodity items. Glass bakeware is often made of tempered soda-lime glass.

Soda-lime glass is relatively inexpensive, chemically stable, reasonably hard, and extremely workable, because it is capable of being re-softened and re-melted numerous times, is ideal for recycling.

Portland cement

Portland cement is the most common type of cement in general use around the world, used as a basic ingredient of concrete, mortar, stucco, and most non-specialty grout. It usually originates from limestone. It is a fine powder produced by grinding Portland cement clinker (more than 90%), a limited amount of calcium sulfate (which controls the set time) and up to 5% minor constituents as allowed by various standards such as the European Standard EN 197-1:'

Calcium

Calcium is the chemical element with symbol Ca and atomic number 20. Calcium is a soft gray alkaline earth metal, and is the fifth-most-abundant element by mass in the Earth's crust. Calcium is also the fifth-most-abundant dissolved ion in seawater by both molarity and mass, after sodium, chloride, magnesium, and sulfate.

Calcium is essential for living organisms, in particular in cell physiology, where movement of the calcium ion Ca^{2+} into and out of the cytoplasm functions as a signal for many cellular processes.

Chemical reaction

A chemical reaction is a process that leads to the transformation of one set of chemical substances to another. Classically, chemical reactions encompass changes that only involve the positions of electrons in the forming and breaking of chemical bonds between atoms, with no change to the nuclei (no change to the elements present), and can often be described by a chemical equation. Nuclear chemistry is a sub-discipline of chemistry that involves the chemical reactions of unstable and radioactive elements where both electronic and nuclear changes may both occur.

Perovskite

Perovskite is a calcium titanium oxide mineral species composed of calcium titanate, with the chemical formula $CaTiO_3$.

The mineral was discovered in the Ural Mountains of Russia by Gustav Rose in 1839 and is named after Russian mineralogist Lev Perovski .

It lends its name to the class of compounds which have the same type of crystal structure as $CaTiO_3$ ($^{XII}A^{2+VI}B^{4+}X^{2-}{}_3$) known as the perovskite structure.

Refractory

A refractory material is one that retains its strength at high temperatures. ASTM C71 defines refractories as 'non-metallic materials having those chemical and physical properties that make them applicable for structures, or as components of systems, that are exposed to environments above 1,000 °F (811 K; 538 °C)'.

Refractory materials are used in linings for furnaces, kilns, incinerators and reactors.

Ceramic materials

Ceramic materials are inorganic, non-metallic materials made from compounds of a metal and a non metal. Ceramic materials may be crystalline or partly crystalline. They are formed by the action of heat and subsequent cooling.

Oxide

An oxide is a chemical compound that contains at least one oxygen atom and one other element in its chemical formula. Metal oxides typically contain an anion of oxygen in the oxidation state of -2. Most of the Earth's crust consists of solid oxides, the result of elements being oxidized by the oxygen in air or in water. Hydrocarbon combustion affords the two principal carbon oxides: carbon monoxide and carbon dioxide.

22. Inorganic Materials

CHAPTER HIGHLIGHTS & NOTES: KEY TERMS, PEOPLE, PLACES, CONCEPTS

Resistance

In the context of ecological stability, resistance is the property of communities or populations to remain 'essentially unchanged' when subject to disturbance. The inverse of resistance is sensitivity.

Silicon nitride

Silicon nitride is a chemical compound of the elements silicon and nitrogen, with the formula Si3N4. It is a white, high-melting-point solid that is relatively chemically inert, being attacked by dilute HF and hot H2SO4. It is the most thermodynamically stable of the silicon nitrides.

Boron nitride

Boron nitride is a chemical compound with chemical formula BN, consisting of equal numbers of boron and nitrogen atoms. BN is isoelectronic to a similarly structured carbon lattice and thus exists in various crystalline forms. The hexagonal form corresponding to graphite is the most stable and softest among BN polymorphs, and is therefore used as a lubricant and an additive to cosmetic products.

Sialon

Sialon ceramics are a specialist class of high-temperature refractory materials, with high strength, good thermal shock resistance and exceptional resistance to wetting or corrosion by molten non-ferrous metals, compared to other refractory materials such as, for example, alumina. A typical use is with handling of molten aluminium. They also are exceptionally corrosion resistant and hence are also used in the chemical industry.

Nitrogen

Nitrogen, symbol N, is the chemical element of atomic number 7. At room temperature, it is a gas of diatomic molecules and is colorless and odorless. Nitrogen is a common element in the universe, estimated at about seventh in total abundance in our galaxy and the Solar System. On Earth, the element is primarily found as the free element; it forms about 80% of the Earth's atmosphere.

Silicon carbide

Silicon carbide, also known as carborundum, is a compound of silicon and carbon with chemical formula SiC. It occurs in nature as the extremely rare mineral moissanite. Silicon carbide powder has been mass-produced since 1893 for use as an abrasive. Grains of silicon carbide can be bonded together by sintering to form very hard ceramics that are widely used in applications requiring high endurance, such as car brakes, car clutches and ceramic plates in bulletproof vests.

Deposition

Deposition, also known as desublimation, is a thermodynamic process, a phase transition in which gas transforms into solid. The reverse of deposition is sublimation.

One example of deposition is the process by which, in sub-freezing air, water vapor changes directly to ice without first becoming a liquid.

Molar conductivity

Molar conductivity is defined as the conductivity of an electrolyte solution divided by the molar concentration of the electrolyte, and so measures the efficiency with which a given electrolyte conducts electricity in solution. Its units are siemens per meter per molarity, or siemens meter-squared per mole. The usual symbol is a capital lambda, ?, or ?$_{m}$.

22. Inorganic Materials

Conduction band	The conduction band is the range of electron energies enough to free an electron from binding with its atom to move freely within the atomic lattice of the material as a 'delocalized electron'. Various materials may be classified by their band gap: this is defined as the difference between the valence and conduction bands. •In non-conductors, commonly known as insulators, the conduction band is higher than that of the valence band, so it takes infeasibly high energies to delocalize their valence electrons.
Fermi level	The Fermi level is the total chemical potential for electrons and is usually denoted by µ or E_F. The Fermi level of a body is a thermodynamic quantity, and its significance is the thermodynamic work required to add one electron to the body (not counting the work required to remove the electron from wherever it came from). A precise understanding of the Fermi level--how it relates to electronic band structure in determining electronic properties, how it relates to the voltage and flow of charge in an electronic circuit--is essential to an understanding of solid-state physics.
Valence band	In solids, the valence band is the highest range of electron energies in which electrons are normally present at absolute zero temperature. The valence electrons are bound to individual atoms, as opposed to conduction electrons, which can move freely within the atomic lattice of the material. On a graph of the electronic band structure of a material, the valence band is located below the conduction band, separated from it in insulators and semiconductors by a band gap.
Absolute zero	Absolute zero is the lowest temperature possible. More formally, it is the temperature at which entropy reaches its minimum value. The laws of thermodynamics state that absolute zero cannot be reached using only thermodynamic means.
Electron	The electron is a subatomic particle with a negative elementary electric charge. Electrons belong to the first generation of the lepton particle family, and are generally thought to be elementary particles because they have no known components or substructure. The electron has a mass that is approximately 1/1836 that of the proton.
Energy level	A quantum mechanical system or particle that is bound--that is, confined spatially--can only take on certain discrete values of energy. This contrasts with classical particles, which can have any energy. These discrete values are called energy levels.
Molecule	A molecule is an electrically neutral group of two or more atoms held together by chemical bonds. Molecules are distinguished from ions by their lack of electrical charge. However, in quantum physics, organic chemistry, and biochemistry, the term molecule is often used less strictly, also being applied to polyatomic ions.
Band gap	In solid-state physics, a band gap, also called an energy gap or bandgap, is an energy range in a solid where no electron states can exist.

22. Inorganic Materials

CHAPTER HIGHLIGHTS & NOTES: KEY TERMS, PEOPLE, PLACES, CONCEPTS

In graphs of the electronic band structure of solids, the band gap generally refers to the energy difference (in electron volts) between the top of the valence band and the bottom of the conduction band in insulators and semiconductors. This is equivalent to the energy required to free an outer shell electron from its orbit about the nucleus to become a mobile charge carrier, able to move freely within the solid material, so the band gap is a major factor determining the electrical conductivity of a solid.

Insulator

An electrical insulator is a material whose internal electric charges do not flow freely, and therefore does not conduct an electric current under the influence of an electric field. A perfect insulator does not exist, but some materials such as glass, paper and Teflon, which have high resistivity, are very good electrical insulators. A much larger class of materials, even though they may have lower bulk resistivity, are still good enough to insulate electrical wiring and cables.

Semiconductor

A semiconductor is a material which has electrical conductivity to a degree between that of a metal and that of an insulator (such as glass). Semiconductors are the foundation of modern electronics, including transistors, solar cells, light-emitting diodes (LEDs), quantum dots and digital and analog integrated circuits.

A semiconductor may have a number of unique properties, one of which is the ability to change conductivity by the addition of impurities ('doping') or by interaction with another phenomenon, such as an electric field or light; this ability makes a semiconductor very useful for constructing a device that can amplify, switch, or convert an energy input.

Doping

In semiconductor production, doping intentionally introduces impurities into an extremely pure semiconductor for the purpose of modulating its electrical properties. The impurities are dependent upon the type of semiconductor. Lightly and moderately doped semiconductors are referred to as extrinsic.

Charged particle

In physics, a charged particle is a particle with an electric charge. It may be either a subatomic particle or an ion. A collection of charged particles, or even a gas containing a proportion of charged particles, is called a plasma, which is called the fourth state of matter because its properties are quite different from solids, liquids and gases (plasma is the most common state of matter in the universe).

Dopant

A dopant, also called a doping agent, is a trace impurity element that is inserted into a substance in order to alter the electrical properties or the optical properties of the substance. In the case of crystalline substances, the atoms of the dopant very commonly take the place of elements that were in the crystal lattice of the material. These materials are very commonly either crystals of a semiconductor (silicon, germanium, etc)., for use in solid-state electronics; or else transparent crystals that are used to make lasers of various types.

CHAPTER HIGHLIGHTS & NOTES: KEY TERMS, PEOPLE, PLACES, CONCEPTS

Transistor

A transistor is a semiconductor device used to amplify and switch electronic signals and electrical power. It is composed of semiconductor material with at least three terminals for connection to an external circuit. A voltage or current applied to one pair of the transistor's terminals changes the current through another pair of terminals.

Current

A current in a fluid is the magnitude and direction of flow within that fluid. An air current presents the same properties specifically for a gaseous medium.

Types of fluid currents include•Boundary current•Current a current in a river or stream•Ocean current•Rip current•Subsurface currents•Turbidity current.

Phosphor

A phosphor, most generally, is a substance that exhibits the phenomenon of luminescence. Somewhat confusingly, this includes both phosphorescent materials, which show a slow decay in brightness (> 1 ms), and fluorescent materials, where the emission decay takes place over tens of nanoseconds. Phosphorescent materials are known for their use in radar screens and glow-in-the-dark toys, whereas fluorescent materials are common in cathode ray tube (CRT) and plasma video display screens, sensors, and white LEDs.

CHAPTER QUIZ: KEY TERMS, PEOPLE, PLACES, CONCEPTS

1. In physics, _________ is a particular length or distance determined with the precision of one order of magnitude. The concept of _________ is particularly important because physical phenomena of different _________s cannot affect each other and are said to decouple. The decoupling of different _________s makes it possible to have a self-consistent theory that only describes the relevant _________s for a given problem.

a. Conformal anomaly
b. Critical phenomena
c. Length scale
d. Condensation particle counter

2. The mineral _________ is a magnesium iron silicate with the formula $(Mg^{+2}, Fe^{+2})_2SiO_4$. It is a common mineral in the Earth's subsurface but weathers quickly on the surface.

The ratio of magnesium and iron varies between the two endmembers of the solid solution series: forsterite (Mg-endmember: Mg_2SiO_4) and fayalite (Fe-endmember: Fe_2SiO_4).

a. Baryte
b. Berthierite

c. Bertrandite
d. Olivine

3. A _________ in a fluid is the magnitude and direction of flow within that fluid. An air _________ presents the same properties specifically for a gaseous medium.

Types of fluid _________s include•Boundary _________•_________ a _________ in a river or stream•Ocean _________•Rip _________•Subsurface _________s•Turbidity _________.

a. Current
b. Barotropic fluid
c. Basset force
d. Batchelor scale

4. _________ is a calcium titanium oxide mineral species composed of calcium titanate, with the chemical formula $CaTiO_3$.

The mineral was discovered in the Ural Mountains of Russia by Gustav Rose in 1839 and is named after Russian mineralogist Lev Perovski .

It lends its name to the class of compounds which have the same type of crystal structure as $CaTiO_3$ ($^{XII}A^{2+VI}B^{4+}X^{2-}{}_3$) known as the _________ structure.

a. Perovskite
b. Berthierite
c. Bertrandite
d. Bismuthinite

5. _________ is the most common type of cement in general use around the world, used as a basic ingredient of concrete, mortar, stucco, and most non-specialty grout. It usually originates from limestone. It is a fine powder produced by grinding _________ clinker (more than 90%), a limited amount of calcium sulfate (which controls the set time) and up to 5% minor constituents as allowed by various standards such as the European Standard EN 197-1:'

_________ clinker is a hydraulic material which shall consist of at least two-thirds by mass of calcium silicates (3 $CaO \cdot SiO_2$ and 2 $CaO \cdot SiO_2$), the remainder consisting of aluminium- and iron-containing clinker phases and other compounds.'

a. Badab-e Surt
b. Bath Stone
c. Beachrock
d. Portland cement

ANSWER KEY
22. Inorganic Materials

1. c
2. d
3. a
4. a
5. d

23. Polymeric Materials and Soft Condensed Matter

CHAPTER OUTLINE: KEY TERMS, PEOPLE, PLACES, CONCEPTS

- Polymer
- Ideal solution
- Polymerization
- Copolymer
- Monomer
- Fiber
- High-density polyethylene
- Linear low-density polyethylene
- Low-density polyethylene
- Elastomer
- Vulcanization
- Degree
- Synthetic rubber
- Synthetic Metals
- Liquid crystal
- Molecule
- Membrane
- Micelle
- Detergent
- Concentration
- Monosaccharide

23. Polymeric Materials and Soft Condensed Matter

CHAPTER OUTLINE: KEY TERMS, PEOPLE, PLACES, CONCEPTS

Polysaccharide

Carbohydrate

Simple Sugars

Disaccharide

Condensation

Amino acid

Enzyme

Nucleic acid

Nucleotide

Component

Phosphate

Pyrimidine

Aldehyde

Ketone

Mole

Diffraction

Elementary particle

Organic compound

Polymer	A polymer is a large molecule composed of many repeated subunits, known as monomers. Because of their broad range of properties, both synthetic and natural polymers play an essential and ubiquitous role in everyday life. Polymers range from familiar synthetic plastics such as polystyrene (or styrofoam) to natural biopolymers such as DNA and proteins that are fundamental to biological structure and function.
Ideal solution	In chemistry, an ideal solution or ideal mixture is a solution with thermodynamic properties analogous to those of a mixture of ideal gases. The enthalpy of solution (or 'enthalpy of mixing') is zero as is the volume change on mixing; the closer to zero the enthalpy of solution is, the more 'ideal' the behavior of the solution becomes. The vapour pressure of the solution obeys Raoult's law, and the activity coefficients (which measure deviation from ideality) are equal to one.
Polymerization	In polymer chemistry, polymerization is a process of reacting monomer molecules together in a chemical reaction to form polymer chains or three-dimensional networks. There are many forms of polymerization and different systems exist to categorize them.
Copolymer	A heteropolymer or copolymer is a polymer derived from two monomeric species, as opposed to a homopolymer where only one monomer is used. Copolymerization refers to methods used to chemically synthesize a copolymer. Commercially relevant copolymers include ABS plastic, SBR, Nitrile rubber, styrene-acrylonitrile, styrene-isoprene-styrene (SIS) and ethylene-vinyl acetate.
Monomer	A monomer, pronounced mon'?-m?r, or MON-uh-mer, is a molecule that may bind chemically to other molecules to form a polymer. The term 'monomeric protein' may also be used to describe one of the proteins making up a multiprotein complex. The most common natural monomer is glucose, which is linked by glycosidic bonds into polymers such as cellulose and starch, and is over 77% of the mass of all plant matter.
Fiber	Fiber or fibre (from the French fibre) is a rope or string used as a component of composite materials, or matted into sheets to make products such as paper or felt. Fibers are often used in the manufacture of other materials. The strongest engineering materials are generally made as fibers, for example carbon fiber and Ultra-high-molecular-weight polyethylene.
High-density polyethylene	High-density polyethylene or polyethylene high-density (PEHD) is a polyethylene thermoplastic made from petroleum. Known for its large strength to density ratio, HDPE is commonly used in the production of plastic bottles, corrosion-resistant piping, geomembranes, and plastic lumber. HDPE is commonly recycled, and has the number '2' as its recycling symbol.
Linear low-density polyethylene	Linear low-density polyethylene is a substantially linear polymer (polyethylene), with significant numbers of short branches, commonly made by copolymerization of ethylene with longer-chain olefins.

Linear low-density polyethylene differs structurally from conventional low-density polyethylene (LDPE) because of the absence of long chain branching. The linearity of LLDPE results from the different manufacturing processes of LLDPE and LDPE. In general, LLDPE is produced at lower temperatures and pressures by copolymerization of ethylene and such higher alpha-olefins as butene, hexene, or octene.

Low-density polyethylene — Low-density polyethylene is a thermoplastic made from the monomer ethylene. It was the first grade of polyethylene, produced in 1933 by Imperial Chemical Industries (ICI) using a high pressure process via free radical polymerization. Its manufacture employs the same method today.

Elastomer — An elastomer is a polymer with viscoelasticity, generally having low Young's modulus and high failure strain compared with other materials. The term, which is derived from elastic polymer, is often used interchangeably with the term rubber, although the latter is preferred when referring to vulcanisates. Each of the monomers which link to form the polymer is usually made of carbon, hydrogen, oxygen and/or silicon.

Vulcanization — Vulcanization or vulcanisation is a chemical process for converting rubber or related polymers into more durable materials via the addition of sulfur or other equivalent 'curatives' or 'accelerators'. These additives modify the polymer by forming crosslinks (bridges) between individual polymer chains. Vulcanized materials are less sticky and have superior mechanical properties.

Degree — The term degree is used in several scales of temperature. The symbol ° is usually used, followed by the initial letter of the unit, for example "°C" for degree(s) Celsius. A degree can be defined as a set change in temperature measured against a given scale, for example, one degree Celsius is one hundredth of the temperature change between the point at which water starts to change state from Solid to liquid state and the point at which it starts to change from its gaseous state to liquid.

Synthetic rubber — Synthetic rubber, invariably a polymer, is any type of artificial elastomer mainly synthesised from petroleum byproducts. An elastomer is a material with the mechanical was established (Russia) by Sergei Lebedev in Yaroslavl under Joseph Stalin's First Five-Year Plan on July 7, 1932.

In 1935, German chemists synthesized the first of a series of synthetic rubbers known as Buna rubbers.

Synthetic Metals — Synthetic Metals is a peer-reviewed scientific journal covering electronic polymers and electronic molecular materials.

Liquid crystal — Liquid crystals are matter in a state that has properties between those of conventional liquid and those of solid crystal. For instance, a liquid crystal may flow like a liquid, but its molecules may be oriented in a crystal-like way. There are many different types of liquid-crystal phases, which can be distinguished by their different optical properties (such as birefringence).

Molecule — A molecule is an electrically neutral group of two or more atoms held together by chemical bonds.

Molecules are distinguished from ions by their lack of electrical charge. However, in quantum physics, organic chemistry, and biochemistry, the term molecule is often used less strictly, also being applied to polyatomic ions.

Membrane

A membrane is a thin, film-like structure that separates two fluids. It acts as a selective barrier, allowing some particles or chemicals to pass through, but not others. In some cases, especially in anatomy, membrane may refer to a thin film that is primarily a separating structure rather than a selective barrier.

Micelle

A micelle is an aggregate of surfactant molecules dispersed in a liquid colloid. A typical micelle in aqueous solution forms an aggregate with the hydrophilic 'head' regions in contact with surrounding solvent, sequestering the hydrophobic single-tail regions in the micelle centre. This phase is caused by the packing behavior of single-tailed lipids in a bilayer.

Detergent

A detergent is a surfactant or a mixture of surfactants with 'cleaning properties in dilute solutions.' These substances are usually alkylbenzenesulfonates, a family of compounds that are similar to soap but are more soluble in hard water, because the polar sulfonate (of detergents) is less likely than the polar carboxyl to bind to calcium and other ions found in hard water. In most household contexts, the term detergent by itself refers specifically to laundry detergent or dish detergent, as opposed to hand soap or other types of cleaning agents. Detergents are commonly available as powders or concentrated solutions.

Concentration

In chemistry, concentration is the abundance of a constituent divided by the total volume of a mixture. Several types of mathematical description can be distinguished: mass concentration, molar concentration, number concentration, and volume concentration. The term concentration can be applied to any kind of chemical mixture, but most frequently it refers to solutes and solvents in solutions.

Monosaccharide

Monosaccharides are the most basic units of carbohydrates. They are the simplest form of sugar and are usually colorless, water-soluble, crystalline solids. Some monosaccharides have a sweet taste.

Polysaccharide

Polysaccharides are polymeric carbohydrate molecules composed of long chains of monosaccharide units bound together by glycosidic bonds. They range in structure from linear to highly branched. Examples include storage polysaccharides such as starch and glycogen, and structural polysaccharides such as cellulose and chitin.

Carbohydrate

A carbohydrate is a large biological molecule, or macromolecule, consisting only of carbon, hydrogen (H), and oxygen (O), usually with a hydrogen:oxygen atom ratio of 2:1 (as in water); in other words, with the empirical formula $C_m(H_2O)_n$ (where m could be different from n). Some exceptions exist; for example, deoxyribose, a sugar component of DNA, has the empirical formula $C_5H_{10}O_4$.

23. Polymeric Materials and Soft Condensed Matter

CHAPTER HIGHLIGHTS & NOTES: KEY TERMS, PEOPLE, PLACES, CONCEPTS

Simple Sugars	Simple Sugars is a Pittsburgh-based cosmetics company run by teen entrepreneur Lani Lazzari. In 2013, Lani Lazzari appeared in Season 4 of the American reality television series Shark Tank where the business received a $100,000 investment from Dallas Mavericks owner Mark Cuban.
Disaccharide	A disaccharide or biose is the carbohydrate formed when two monosaccharides undergo a condensation reaction which involves the elimination of a small molecule, such as water, from the functional groups only. Like monosaccharides, disaccharides form an aqueous solution when dissolved in water. Three common examples are sucrose, lactose, and maltose.
Condensation	Condensation is the change of the physical state of matter from gas phase into liquid phase, and is the reverse of vaporization. It can also be defined as the change in the state of water vapor to water/any liquid when in contact with any surface. When the transition happens from the gaseous phase into the solid phase directly, the change is called deposition.
Amino acid	Amino acids are biologically important organic compounds made from amine ($-NH_2$) and carboxylic acid (-COOH) functional groups, along with a side-chain specific to each amino acid. The key elements of an amino acid are carbon, hydrogen, oxygen, and nitrogen, though other elements are found in the side-chains of certain amino acids. About 500 amino acids are known and can be classified in many ways.
Enzyme	Enzymes are large biological molecules responsible for the thousands of metabolic processes that sustain life. They are highly selective catalysts, greatly accelerating both the rate and specificity of metabolic reactions, from the digestion of food to the synthesis of DNA. Most enzymes are proteins, although some catalytic RNA molecules have been identified. Enzymes adopt a specific three-dimensional structure, and may employ organic (e.g. biotin) and inorganic (e.g. magnesium ion) cofactors to assist in catalysis.
Nucleic acid	Nucleic acids are polymeric macromolecules, or large biological molecules, essential for all known forms of life. Nucleic acids, which include DNA (deoxyribonucleic acid) and RNA (ribonucleic acid), are made from monomers known as nucleotides. Each nucleotide has three components: a 5-carbon sugar, a phosphate group, and a nitrogenous base.
Nucleotide	Nucleotides are organic molecules that serve as the monomers, or subunits, of nucleic acids like DNA and RNA. The building blocks of nucleic acids, nucleotides are composed of a nitrogenous base, a five-carbon sugar (ribose or deoxyribose), and at least one phosphate group. Nucleotides serve to carry packets of energy within the cell (ATP). In the form of the nucleoside triphosphates (ATP, GTP, CTP and UTP), nucleotides play central roles in metabolism.
Component	In thermodynamics, a component is a chemically-independent constituent of a system. The number of components represents the minimum number of independent species necessary to define the composition of all phases of the system.

Phosphate

A phosphate, an inorganic chemical, is a salt of phosphoric acid. In organic chemistry, a phosphate, or organophosphate, is an ester of phosphoric acid. Organic phosphates are important in biochemistry and biogeochemistry or ecology.

Pyrimidine

Pyrimidine is an aromatic heterocyclic organic compound similar to pyridine. One of the three diazines (six-membered heterocyclics with two nitrogen atoms in the ring), it has the nitrogens at positions 1 and 3 in the ring. The other diazines are pyrazine (nitrogens 1 and 4) and pyridazine (nitrogens 1 and 2).

Aldehyde

An aldehyde is an organic compound containing a formyl group. This functional group, with the structure R-CHO, consists of a carbonyl center (a carbon double bonded to oxygen) bonded to hydrogen and an R group, which is any generic alkyl or side chain. The group without R is called the aldehyde group or formyl group.

Ketone

In chemistry, a ketone is an organic compound with the structure RC(=O)R', where R and R' can be a variety of carbon-containing substituents. Ketones feature a carbonyl group (C=O) bonded to two other carbon atoms. Many ketones are known and many are of great importance in industry and in biology.

Mole

Mole is a unit of measurement used in chemistry to express amounts of a chemical substance, defined as the amount of any substance that contains as many elementary entities (e.g., atoms, molecules, ions, electrons) as there are atoms in 12 grams of pure carbon-12, the isotope of carbon with relative atomic mass 12. This corresponds to the Avogadro constant, which has a value of $6.02214129(27)\times10^{23}$ elementary entities of the substance. It is one of the base units in the International System of Units, and has the unit symbol mol and corresponds with the dimension symbol N. In honour of the unit, chemists often celebrate October 23 (a reference to the 10^{23} part of Avogadro's number) as 'Mole Day'.

The mole is widely used in chemistry instead of units of mass or volume as a convenient way to express amounts of reactants or of products of chemical reactions.

Diffraction

Diffraction refers to various phenomena which occur when a wave encounters an obstacle. In classical physics, the diffraction phenomenon is described as the apparent bending of waves around small obstacles and the spreading out of waves past small openings. Similar effects occur when a light wave travels through a medium with a varying refractive index, or a sound wave travels through one with varying acoustic impedance.

Elementary particle

In particle physics, an elementary particle or fundamental particle is a particle whose substructure is unknown, thus it is not known to be composed of other particles. Known elementary particles include the fundamental fermions (quarks, leptons, antiquarks, and antileptons), which generally are 'matter particles' and 'antimatter particles', as well as the fundamental bosons (gauge bosons and Higgs boson), which generally are 'force particles' that mediate interactions among fermions.

23. Polymeric Materials and Soft Condensed Matter

CHAPTER HIGHLIGHTS & NOTES: KEY TERMS, PEOPLE, PLACES, CONCEPTS

Organic compound	An organic compound is any member of a large class of gaseous, liquid, or solid chemical compounds whose molecules contain carbon. For historical reasons discussed below, a few types of carbon-containing compounds such as carbides, carbonates, simple oxides of carbon (such as CO and CO_2), and cyanides are considered inorganic. The distinction between 'organic' and 'inorganic' carbon compounds, while 'useful in organizing the vast subject of chemistry... is somewhat arbitrary'.

CHAPTER QUIZ: KEY TERMS, PEOPLE, PLACES, CONCEPTS

1. A _________ is a large molecule composed of many repeated subunits, known as monomers. Because of their broad range of properties, both synthetic and natural _________s play an essential and ubiquitous role in everyday life. _________s range from familiar synthetic plastics such as polystyrene (or styrofoam) to natural bio_________s such as DNA and proteins that are fundamental to biological structure and function.

   a. CrystaSulf
   b. Flue-gas desulfurization
   c. Polymer
   d. Scrubber

2. A _________ is an aggregate of surfactant molecules dispersed in a liquid colloid. A typical _________ in aqueous solution forms an aggregate with the hydrophilic 'head' regions in contact with surrounding solvent, sequestering the hydrophobic single-tail regions in the _________ centre. This phase is caused by the packing behavior of single-tailed lipids in a bilayer.

   a. Micelle
   b. Brownian motion
   c. Coacervate
   d. Colloid

3. In chemistry, a _________ is an organic compound with the structure RC(=O)R', where R and R' can be a variety of carbon-containing substituents. _________s feature a carbonyl group (C=O) bonded to two other carbon atoms. Many _________s are known and many are of great importance in industry and in biology.

   a. Bisthiosemicarbazone
   b. Biuret
   c. Ketone
   d. Carbamate

4. . In chemistry, an _________ or ideal mixture is a solution with thermodynamic properties analogous to those of a mixture of ideal gases.

The enthalpy of solution (or 'enthalpy of mixing') is zero as is the volume change on mixing; the closer to zero the enthalpy of solution is, the more 'ideal' the behavior of the solution becomes. The vapour pressure of the solution obeys Raoult's law, and the activity coefficients (which measure deviation from ideality) are equal to one.

a. Bunsen solubility coefficient
b. Concentrate
c. Ideal solution
d. Crenation

5. _________ refers to various phenomena which occur when a wave encounters an obstacle. In classical physics, the _________ phenomenon is described as the apparent bending of waves around small obstacles and the spreading out of waves past small openings. Similar effects occur when a light wave travels through a medium with a varying refractive index, or a sound wave travels through one with varying acoustic impedance.

a. Filtration
b. Filter paper
c. Differential mobility detector
d. Diffraction

ANSWER KEY
23. Polymeric Materials and Soft Condensed Matter

1. c
2. a
3. c
4. c
5. d

CPSIA information can be obtained at www.ICGtesting.com
Printed in the USA
LVOW09s2046050914

402714LV00001B/12/P

9 781497 000032